Growing Orchids
IN THE CARIBBEAN

Marilyn H.S. Light

CARIBBEAN

© Copyright text Marilyn Light 1995
© Copyright illustrations Marilyn Light 1995

All rights reserved. No reproduction, copy or transmission of this publication may be made without written permission.

No paragraph of this publication may be reproduced, copied or transmitted save with written permission or in accordance with the provisions of the Copyright, Designs and Patents Act 1988, or under the terms of any licence permitting limited copying issued by the Copyright Licensing Agency, 90 Tottenham Court Road, London W1P 9HE.

Any person who does any unauthorised act in relation to this publication may be liable to criminal prosecution and civil claims for damages.

First published 1995 by
MACMILLAN EDUCATION LTD
London and Oxford
Companies and representatives throughout the world

www.macmillan-caribbean.com

ISBN 0–333–63202–8

12 11 10   9   8   7   6   5   4
13 12 11 10 09 08 07 06 05

Printed in Thailand

A catalogue record for this book is available from the British Library.

This book is printed on paper suitable for recycling and made from fully managed and sustained forest sources.

Contents ✿

Acknowledgements		v
Introduction		vii
Growing Orchids	How orchids grow	1
	Potting materials, fertilizers, water, evaporative cooling	3
	Housing, shade and light	9
	Orchids in the landscape, in trees, as bedding plants, on fences and posts, in baskets, pots and on mounts	12
Propagating Orchids	By division and from seed, stem propagation, pollen and seed storage, de-flasking	20
	Registration of hybrids, awards	24
Challenges	Pests, diseases, pesticide toxicity, weeds and stress	26
	Import regulations and plant health: CITES	33
Orchid Selections	Orchid species and hybrids for every garden	34
Appendix I	Orchid Nurseries and Suppliers	51
Appendix II	Orchid Publications	53
Appendix III	Orchid Selections	54
Glossary		59
Bibliography		61
General Index		62
Plant Names Index		64

Acknowledgements ✺

I learned how to grow orchids from those with a wealth of experience. I read, questioned, listened, observed and experimented with the techniques I had learned. There are so many different kinds of orchids and garden situations that it is virtually impossible to grow all of the orchids well using one simple technique. I discovered that the secret to good orchid growing lies first with choosing plants best suited to one's garden environment. Hybrid orchids are often more vigorous and floriferous than species. Secondly, the orchid grower must be quick to observe when a plant fails to thrive and be willing to experiment with a different approach. These skills are best learned from experienced growers. I acknowledge the counsel of the late Francis A. Hunte who showed me how to choose orchids that would not only survive but thrive in my care.

Contemporary experience is extremely valuable, especially when evaluating the usefulness of orchid hybrids. I thank Caribbean orchid growers Michael Birkett, Stephen Collins, David Leach and Anthony Tangkai, who willingly shared their experience.

I thank Michael MacConaill for his photographic assistance and Dr. Carl L. Withner for his assistance in confirming the identity of *Schomburgkia humboldtii*.

June 1994

Introduction

To successfully raise orchid plants we must understand their cultural requirements. We should also know how to modify the garden environment to meet their needs. An orchid garden can be designed with both landscaping objectives and personal goals in mind. View the garden from different points such as the balcony, pool area or patio before building a shadehouse or planting orchids. Resolve to maintain and enhance the best views. If you wish to have flowers for year-round enjoyment, you must carefully consider what kinds of orchids can thrive in your situation and give you what you want. Consider day and night temperatures, seasonal fluctuations in temperature and rainfall, prevailing winds, available shade and variations in shade over time and season when choosing the kinds of orchids to grow. Ask neighbours and members of the local orchid society about which orchids are easy to grow and which fail to thrive or bloom in your locality, before investing in plants. Better still, join an orchid society. Lists of orchid nurseries and of periodicals dealing with orchid culture are found in the Appendix.

Discover as much as you can about the orchids you would like to grow including their cultural requirements, size at maturity, flowering frequency and fragrance. Pay particular attention to the day/night temperature differential in your garden as this is an important factor in successfully blooming orchids such as *Phalaenopsis*. If after planting, certain orchids fail to thrive, consider moving them to a different location. Occasionally a plant is inherently weak but more often the malaise is caused by inappropriate light, temperature or humidity. A pest or disease problem may be temporarily eased with the application of appropriate pesticides but will recur if the cultural problem is not dealt with. A simple adjustment of shading or location is sometimes all that is needed to help an orchid thrive. Understanding orchids and how they grow is the ultimate challenge to the grower. Knowing when to be vigilant and how to modify the tropical garden environment to meet orchid growth and blooming requirements will open the gateway to success.

Growing Orchids

How orchids grow

The way in which orchids grow decides their shape and how they may be vegetatively propagated. Monopodial orchids such as *Phalaenopsis* and *Vanda* grow continuously from one point: the orchid grows in height or length. The principal growing point (meristem) produces hormones that suppress development of other buds existing behind it. If the principal meristem is damaged or if it is mechanically removed, hormonal influence decreases and previously dormant buds begin to grow. Thus monopodial orchids will develop side branches (keikis) when the principal growing point is damaged by crown rot or when a top cutting is removed for propagation purposes. Keikis can be removed once they develop roots or they can be left attached to the parent plant.

Orchids such as *Cattleya, Dendrobium, Oncidium* and *Paphiopedilum* have sympodial growth. Sympodial orchids produce shoots from buds located along a prostrate stem (rhizome). As the growths mature, new shoots arise from buds at the base of the newly matured shoot: the orchid grows laterally. As with monopodial orchids, the growing point exerts hormonal influence, suppressing the development of buds further back along the rhizome. If the principal growing point is damaged or excised, dormant buds at the base of shoots further back along the rhizome may be activated. Severing the rhizome of sympodial orchids is another way to activate dormant buds since the hormonal influence of the growing point to other parts of the rhizome is interrupted. Large specimens can be encouraged to produce many new growing points by partially severing the rhizome between pseudobulbs. Retain a minimum of three pseudobulbs per division. This can be done while the plant is still in the pot or growing on a mount, ensuring that the orchid is minimally disturbed while initiating new growth.

Orchid roots are quite different to those of other garden plants. Orchids that grow on the surface of trees (epiphytes) have roots with a white spongy covering. Only the green root tip is uncovered. The

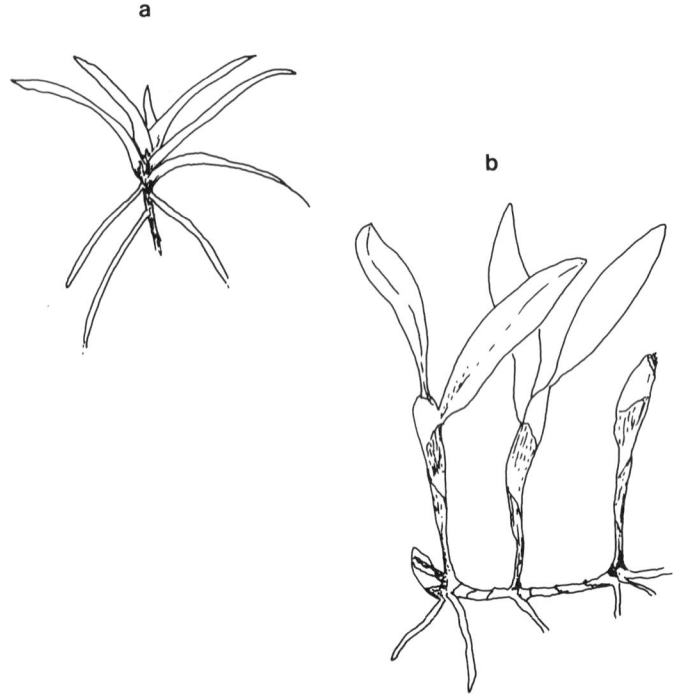

FIGURE 1. Orchid growth patterns
a) Monopodial growth e.g. *Vanda* b) Sympodial growth e.g. *Cattleya*.

spongy covering not only protects the root from desiccation but also absorbs moisture and dissolved mineral nutrients from the environment. Epiphyte roots ramble over the surface of the tree bark, holding the plant firmly in place. Roots are often infected with fungi (mycorrhizae) that further extend the absorptive root surface. Mycorrhizae are also important in harvesting phosphorus for plant use. Tree-dwelling orchids have either thick roots as in *Vanda* or thin roots as in *Oncidium*. Thick-rooted sorts grow best in coarse potting medium, when mounted on a slab of bark or grown in a basket. Grow thin-rooted orchids in finer potting mixtures.

Terrestrial orchids grow in soil or leaf mould. As their hairy roots are more susceptible to drying, such orchids should be grown in a porous, freely draining mixture that holds moisture while permitting air to reach the roots.

Orchid leaves are thick, succulent and covered with a protective waxy layer as in *Cattleya* or thin and delicate as in *Ludisia*. Thick-leaved orchids generally tolerate greater light and dryness. Many orchids have thickened stems (pseudobulbs). Pseudobulbs are upright as in *Ansellia* or pendant as in *Dendrobium anosmum*. Pseudobulbs store water and nutrients to carry an orchid through a dry season. Monopodial orchids as in *Phalaenopsis* lack pseudobulbs: the succulent leaves serve as the water store. Orchids are mostly long-lived but a few such as *Psygmorchis (Oncidium) pusilla* are short-lived, surviving only a few years on their natural twig or leaf habitat. Orchids produce flowers singly from the centre of a shoot as in *Paphiopedilum*, in pairs and trios all along a pseudobulb as in *Dendrobium anosmum*, in a raceme from the top of the shoot as in *Epidendrum schomburgkii*, or as a spray emerging from an axillary leaf at the base of a shoot as in *Oncidium sphacelatum*. The flower buds are often enclosed in a protective sheath that splits as the buds expand. Certain orchids such as *Oncidium papilio, Phalaenopsis violacea* and *Epidendrum ilense* rebloom from the same inflorescence.

Potting materials, fertilizers and water

> Growing orchids in containers presents the challenge of choosing the most appropriate potting medium and container type. The medium must be freely draining.

POTTING MATERIALS

Bark Chips – Various sized pieces of fir bark are a favoured potting medium in temperate greenhouses but are less useful in the humid tropics. Bark retains water and decays quickly. Try a mixture of one part bark chips with two parts Promix® to grow Paphiopedilums. Light weight.

Charcoal – Use small pieces or large chunks, alone or in combination with crock with Vandas, Ascocendas, Phalaenopsis and Cattleyas. Charcoal does not decay but can become coated with mineral deposits at which point it should be replaced. Moderate weight.

Crock (broken, unglazed clay tile) – Use small to medium-sized chunks, alone or in combination with other materials to pot large Cattleyas, Dendrobiums, Phalaenopsis and Vandas. Crock does not decay but can become covered with algae and minerals after time. Soak in rainwater to remove salts. Heavy weight.

New Zealand Sphagnum Moss – This natural product is available in bale and pellet form. Use this moss to start Phalaenopsis seedlings. Moss retains much water and absorbs moisture from humid air. Water with care. Do not leave seedlings in moss longer than six months. Light to moderate weight.

Perlite® – This white, inert porous mineral product is sold in various particle sizes. Use as a blend of one part Perlite®, two parts fir bark chips and one part charcoal to improve drainage and porosity when potting Oncidiums and smaller Cattleyas. Perlite® does not decay but can compact after time. Light weight.

Promix® – A formulation composed of milled sphagnum moss, vermiculite (expanded mica) and Perlite®. Blend Promix® with bark chips or charcoal to improve porosity. Use moistened Promix® experimentally to raise Paphiopedilums and other terrestrial orchids. Seedlings and young plants of *Oncidium papilio* thrive in Promix® over a gravel base. Light to moderate weight.

Red Lava Rock – A porous natural product produced during volcanic eruption. Red Lava Rock will retain moisture so is not recommended for potting phalaenopsis-type Dendrobiums. It can be used with Cattleyas, Oncidiums and Phalaenopsis. Heavy weight.

Rockwool – Rockwool is prepared from basalt, melted and spun into fine filaments. Both absorbent and non-absorbent forms are sold. Rockwool is used alone or in combination with other materials such as charcoal and Perlite®. Dry rockwool particles are irritant. Wet the product before using. Do not allow plants potted in rockwool to dry out between waterings. Light weight.

Styrofoam Packing Materials – Polystyrene foam packing material ('peanuts') is both inert and an amenable substrate for orchid roots. The main shortcoming is its weight, so light that it will blow out of pots unless held in place with a layer of a much heavier medium.

Tree Fern – This product is derived from a tall, tropical fern stem. The 15 cm (6 inch) diameter upper stem is used to support Vandas. The bottom part is thicker with a softer outer layer. Slabs are sometimes carved to form pots or baskets. Small slabs can be wired for use as hanging mounts. Vertical grain alignment allows quick drainage. Softer tree fern fibre is a useful medium for raising orchid seedlings, alone or in combination with New Zealand Sphagnum Moss. Chunks are suitable for potting Cattleyas, Tetramicras, Stanhopeas, etc. It resists decay but can retain salts as water evaporates. Periodically flush it with rainwater. This material lasts four to six years. Moderate weight.

The simplest potting material is none at all! Try raising Ascocendas, Dendrobiums and Vandas in empty clay pots or wooden baskets (rafts). Water and fertilize frequently.

FERTILIZERS

Growers using a balanced fertilizer recommended for orchid culture will be rewarded with vigorous plants and plentiful blooms. Fertilizer formulations such as 7-7-7 refer to the ratio of available N (Nitrogen) −P (Phosphorus)−K (Potassium), respectively. Nitrogen promotes growth while phosphorus boosts flower production. Formulations may contain additional nutrients (trace elements) such as Magnesium, Iron and Calcium. For best results use dilute liquid fertilizer containing trace elements with every watering. Suggested formulations and dilutions are given in Table 1. Follow the manufacturer's recommendations when using a different formulation.

Occasional heavy applications of fertilizer can damage plants. Soft and floppy shoots will develop if too much nitrogen or too strong a fertilizer is applied. Water with plain water once after five applications to avoid mineral salt accumulation around roots.

TABLE 1 Fertilizer application guidelines

Plant growth state	Apply/withhold fertilizer	Suggested formulation and dilution
SEEDLINGS (just out of flask)	apply once immediately upon de-flasking then every two weeks until new roots and shoots appear	7-7-7 + trace elements 0.5 ml/litre (⅛ tsp. per gallon)
SEEDLINGS (after new roots have formed)	apply with every watering	7-7-7 + trace elements 1 ml/litre (¼ tsp. per gallon)
SEEDLINGS (near blooming size)	apply with every watering	7-9-5 + trace elements 2 ml/litre (½ tsp. per gallon)
FLOWER PRODUCTION	apply with every watering	3-12-6 + trace elements 2 ml/litre (½ tsp. per gallon)
FLOWERING	apply weekly (avoid spraying flowers)	7-9-5 + trace elements 2 ml/litre (½ tsp. per gallon)
DORMANCY	Do not apply fertilizer	n/a

WATER

Water is used to irrigate, mist, cool and to apply soluble products such as fertilizers and pesticides. Small quantities of water applied at intervals during the day cool the plants. One heavy application is used to provide water and fertilizer. Time the last water application such that the plants dry before nightfall. Withhold water during rainy weather or if injurious rot develops in the collection.

Water a few orchids by hand using a watering pot and pump mister. Water large collections with a hose or with an automated delivery system. Automate the delivery frequency with a programmable device. Battery-powered, automated irrigation systems require battery replacement about every six months. A pump pressure of 30 psi (pounds per square inch) is sufficient to produce a fine mist from discharge nozzles. Do not use pesticide suspensions composed of insoluble particles in irrigation/misting equipment as particles may block nozzle openings. Local irrigation specialists can recommend equipment to discharge one to one hundred litres per minute.

Rainwater is the most abundant source of good quality water. The problem is how to store adequate quantities during the rainy season for use during drought. Estimate the quantity of water normally used during watering to calculate the quantity to be stored. Plan to store a minimum of 7 500 litres (1 500 gallons), much more for large collections. Construct reservoirs for ease of collection and delivery, with allowance for overflow. Construct an underground reservoir from concrete blocks or a poured concrete form, lining it with a rubber pool liner. Provide an opening for maintenance but keep this securely locked when not in use to avoid entry of a child or pet. A series of drums or a boiler can also be used as a reservoir. Screen unsightly drums with shrubbery or hide them under shadehouse benches. Use plastic drums or those lined with a substance that will not leach harmful mineral salts and other noxious substances into the stored water. Cover reservoirs to limit evaporation, mosquitoes and algal growth. Collect water from the roof of the dwelling or shadehouse and channel it into the reservoirs.

Ground water may be suitable for watering but it often contains dissolved minerals that are damaging to orchids. There may not be a problem with occasional use of hard water containing dissolved calcium and magnesium, although hard water will leave unsightly white deposits on plants after it evaporates. Avoid using brackish (salty) water. Measure the mineral content of water with a conductivity meter such as the pocket-sized Salt Pen® . The lower the mineral content, the better the water quality for orchids.

Reverse osmosis is a process that removes hardness components, microorganisms and chemical contaminants from water. Units process 50-1000 litres (10-200 gallons) per day. The units are expensive but should be considered where water quality is a concern.

Watering orchids in the landscape can be a challenge, especially when the orchids are placed high in trees. Black irrigation tubing can be run up trees. The same spray nozzles used so effectively in the shadehouse will provide a fine mist in the trees provided the system is adequately pressurized. Conceal tubing with orchids, philodendrons, ferns and other epiphytes. Deliver both water and fertilizer using this method.

Conserve water. It is a precious resource. If seasonal or prolonged droughts are frequent and water storage is a problem, the best advice is to grow drought-tolerant orchids such as *Dendrobium discolor*, *Schomburgkia humboldtii*, and *Tetramicra canaliculata*.

Create microclimates for orchid roots. Support orchids such as Vandas while providing both moisture and evaporative cooling to the roots. Mount the plants on posts made of drainage tile. Fired clay tile is unglazed to be strong yet porous. Asbestos tile can also be used. Plug the tile at the base. Bury it partly in the ground, fill with rain water and cover with a removable lid. Refill the tile with water as needed.

TABLE 2 Watering guidelines

By situation	Water more frequently	Water less frequently
CONTAINER TYPE	clay pot, slab, tree or post	plastic pot, basket, bed
POTTING MEDIUM	charcoal, crock, lava rock, no medium	bark, tree fern, moss, humus
SEASON	dry season	rainy season
AIR MOVEMENT	breezy, windy	little air movement
TEMPERATURE	hot	cool
PLANT TYPE	thin foliage, no pseudobulbs	thick succulent foliage, pseudobulbs
BRIGHTNESS	sunny	overcast, cloudy
PLANT GROWTH STATE	active growth	dormant, no growth

EVAPORATIVE COOLING

Evaporative cooling works on the principle that as water evaporates from a surface, energy and heat are dissipated and the surface cools. One essential requirement is that the surrounding air is not already saturated with moisture; water can only evaporate into unsaturated air. The lowest temperature that can be reached before evaporation ceases at a given Relative Humidity is the DEWPOINT. Orchids can be cooled directly by misting them with water. Using a fan to blow drier air over the leaves enhances the cooling effect, the speed of cooling depends upon the air flow. Table 3 gives the calculated maximum cooling that can be obtained at a given temperature and humidity.

A fan or even a breeze blowing through openings in a moist wall of cement or coralstone blocks will cool the shadehouse interior. Blowing a strong air current through a mat that is continually being moistened with water will produce a similar effect. Fans can be powered by solar power. A local contractor can advise on the equipment and how to operate it.

TABLE 3 Maximum possible cooling effect (in °C) due to evaporation, under varying temperature and humidity levels

Relative humidity	Temperature (°C)				
	15°	20°	25°	30°	35°
100%	0	0	0	0	0
90%	1.8	1.8	1.8	1.8	1.8
80%	3.4	3.5	3.5	3.9	3.9
70%	5.3	5.5	5.6	6.0	6.3
60%	7.8	7.9	8.1	8.4	8.8
50%	10.2	10.6	11.1	11.6	12.1
40%	13.7	14.1	14.5	15.1	15.5
30%	17.7	18.3	18.9	19.5	20.3

Housing, shade and light

HOUSING AND SHADE

Grow valuable orchids in shadehouses for security and to shelter the plants from excessive light, wind and rain. Build housing from local materials such as cement, coralstone or cinder blocks, decay-resistant wood and corrosion-resistant metal. A shadehouse should be a minimum of 3 m (10 ft) high to provide adequate ventilation. Cover the roof and sides with polypropylene shadecloth appropriate to the type of orchid being grown. Shadecloth is purchased in standard widths of 6 and 12 feet. Specify the shade rating required (30, 51, 63, 73, 80, 92 or 95%). Two or more layers of shadecloth can be used but will provide slightly less shade than their combined shade ratings. While 80% is needed for Phalaenopsis and seedling orchids, 30-50% shade may be ample for Cattleyas and strap-leaf Vandas. It is not necessary to take the shadecloth to the ground although it should be taken low enough to provide shade to the lowest shelves. If wanted, place translucent fibreglass sheeting on top of the shade cloth to control rain entry. Align housing and shelving to take advantage of cooling breezes. A north-south alignment is preferred but other alignments can be considered to take advantage of the location. For additional security and support, cover the walls with sturdy mesh wire.

Tip! To calculate the effect of using two or more layers of shadecloth, remember that the shade provided by the lower layer is a percentage of the light transmitted by the layer above. You cannot simply add the two ratings together. Multiply the percent transmission of each layer, divide by one hundred, then subtract the result from 100 to obtain the new shade rating.

Example: Two layers of shadecloth are each rated at 30% shade. Seventy per cent (70%) of the light passes through the first layer. A further 70% of that light passes through the second cloth layer to the orchids.
Multiply the percentage transmissions of the two layers, i.e. $70 \times 70 = 4\,900$.
Divide by 100.
49% of sunlight passes through two layers of 30% shadecloth.
Subtract 49 from 100: the new rating is 51% shade.

The shadehouse floor can be covered with cement, gravel, grass or a heavy duty, commercial landscape fabric may be used. While cement is slippery when wet and grass must be cut, landscape fabric provides long lasting, durable easy-to-clean flooring. Fabric lets water in while blocking light to weeds beneath.

The placement of orchids within the shadehouse is largely decided by their size, growth habit and the grower's preference. Good air movement is essential: plants should not be crowded. Pots and baskets can be suspended with wire from overhead supports although moving among suspended plants can be difficult. Bench trays made from wire mesh allow free air circulation and hold pots firmly in place. A-frame supports optimize growing space. Construct them from pairs of rectangular, wire mesh panels angled approximately 75° from the horizontal. Run the panels the length of the shadehouse if wanted, leaving ample space for passage at either end.

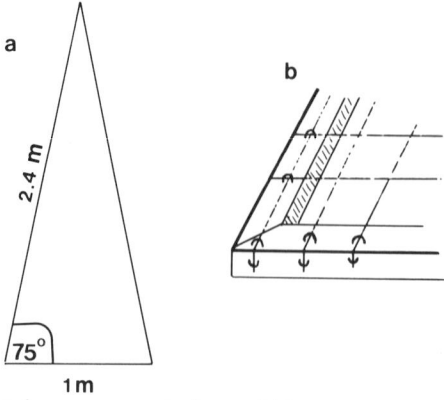

FIGURE 2. A-frame supports for orchids
a) Position two wire mesh panels at 75° from the horizontal
b) Fasten wire mesh to the wooden frame with heavy staples

No orchid house would be complete without a potting bench. Provide a place for potting materials, tools, and a container for waste.

LIGHT

Plants need light to grow. Too much sunlight will overheat leaves, slow growth and even kill sensitive plants. Less than optimum light will result in poor flower production and susceptibility to disease.

Orchids adapted to full sun exposure often have a reduced surface area as in terete-leaved Vandas. The leaves of *Dendrobium discolor* shade themselves by growing one over the other in layers. Orchids that thrive in full sun do so because there is ample humidity and air movement, however what thrives in full sun in one garden may not do so in another. Some experimentation is always required.

Seedlings of even sun-tolerant orchids should always be grown with some shade first, then gradually adapted to a sunny location. Adult plants should be provided the most light appropriate to the type, given the garden conditions. Semi-terete Vandas may do better with 30% shade in a drier garden, especially where weeks go by without cloud cover or rain. These same plants may flourish without shade where showers and cloud cover are a daily occurrence.

Some orchids grow best with shade. Leaf shape is a clue as to the amount of shade needed by a plant. Paphiopedilums and many other terrestrial orchids grow best in the shade. Temperature may be more consequential to their vigour than the amount of light they receive. The best way to keep plants and their roots cool is to provide shade. To learn the most appropriate light regime for a particular plant under your conditions, start a new plant under 50-80% shade or in dappled sunlight then move it into a brighter or shadier location according to how it behaves. If a plant requires more light, it will bend towards a brighter light source. With too little light, plants produce soft, floppy shoots and thinner leaves. Flower production will be reduced. Provide progressively more light to such orchids until growth is stabilized.

Plants receiving too much light will react in a variety of ways including stunted growth and reddened foliage. Sometimes the orchid is reacting more to overheating than to too much light. Improve air circulation and increase misting frequency to enhance evaporative cooling.

Blind sheaths on Cattleyas may be caused by an inappropriate duration of exposure to light (photoperiod). The difference between day and night varies little in the Caribbean but is still sufficient to signal photoperiod-sensitive plants to bloom in a particular season. Such orchids depend upon a series of uninterrupted long nights for several weeks or months. Any interruption of the induction process will arrest flower development. A street light, landscape lighting and artificial illumination of the shadehouse, even for a few minutes every night during the induction period is sufficient a disruption. Occasional slug hunts by night, using a flashlight, are not too disruptive.

TABLE 4 Comparative daylengths in the Caribbean and main orchid-growing regions

Place	Latitude (to nearest degree)	Minimum daylength (approx)	Maximum daylength (approx)
Nassau, Bahamas	25°N	10 h 25 min	13 h 35 min
Bridgetown, Barbados	13°N	11 h 15 min	12 h 45 min
St. Georges, Grenada	12°N	11 h 15 min	12 h 45 min
Kingston, Jamaica	18°N	10 h 55 min	13 h 5 min
San Juan, Puerto Rico	18°N	10 h 55 min	13 h 5 min
Port-of-Spain, Trinidad	11°N	11 h 20 min	12 h 40 min
St. Croix, Virgin Islands	17°N	11 h	13 h
Cairns, Australia	17°S	11 h	13 h
Manila, Philippines	15°N	11 h 5 min	12 h 55 min
Singapore	1°N	11 h 55 min	12 h 5 min
Bangkok, Thailand	14°N	11 h 10 min	12 h 50 min
Miami, Florida, U.S.A.	26°N	10 h 20 min	13 h 40 min
Honolulu, Hawaii, U.S.A.	21°N	10 h 45 min	13 h 15 min

ORCHIDS AS LANDSCAPE SPECIMENS

Think size, colour and total impact when choosing orchids as landscape specimens. For drier gardens, choose among showy *Cyrtopodium punctatum*, floriferous and fragrant *Ansellia africana*, golden-flowered *Dendrobium discolor* and elegant *Den. stratiotes*. All will flourish if planted in a sunny spot between boulders and stumps to support them. The plants should preferably be vigorous flowering-size seedlings. Start the orchids in clay pots containing tree fern chunks and broken crock. Use hollowed tree fern stumps or even hollowed sections of log to hold the orchids. Vandas particularly appreciate the cool humid interior of the log as a rooting surface. Drainage is important, take care that the containers drain freely. Prepare the ground beneath the site by removing about 25 cm (1 ft) of soil and filling the hole with broken crock and coarse sand or pebbles. Arrange the tree stump(s) and boulders, leaving space for the plants. Habituate the orchids to their new location, providing light shade until new roots become established. Pay particular attention to fertilizer and watering until the orchid roots scramble over the surrounding structure. Well-rooted orchids will be less dependent upon regular watering. Employ bromeliads, cycads and even clumping palms as foliage accents or to provide light shade.

Sobralias should be considered for wetter gardens. These orchids will thrive in light gaps along paths or streams where overhead trees provide some protection from the sun although the site should not be densely shaded. Sobralias are dual-purpose plants, giving both blooms and attractive foliage. *Sobralia* blooms last only one day but they bloom sequentially over long periods. The flowers can be rose to mauve, white or yellow. Clumps of *Sobralia* can be established on a gentle slope above a stream with a ground cover such as *Episcia* beneath. Water seeping down the slope will offer almost ideal conditions for the roots. Alternatively, plant some smaller Sobralias as a backdrop to a pool. *Sobralia macrantha* will thrive in cooler upland gardens while warm-growing *Sob. violacea* is recommended for sea level properties.

Prepare the chosen site by removing unsuitable mineral soil and filling the hole with a layer of drainage materials such as broken crock or rocks followed by tree fern chunks and chopped coconut husk. Leave a space for the orchid. Prepare a space at least four square metres (6 square feet) for more heavily rooted Sobralias. Plant vigorous flowering-size seedlings or divisions of mature plants. Remove Sobralias from their pot and plant them directly in the prepared site keeping the plants at the same depth as they were in the pot. A top dressing of well-rotted compost and regular watering and fertilizer applications are beneficial.

NATURALIZING IN TREES

Orchids grow in trees don't they, so why not in your garden? All you need are suitable trees and some orchids. If conditions are right, you may even have orchid seedlings establish themselves nearby.

Some of the best trees for establishing orchids are deciduous. The Frangipani (*Plumeria*) or Flamboyant (*Delonix regia*) in full bloom would compete with the most colourful orchids flowering simultaneously. Choose orchids that bloom when the trees are deciduous and not in flower. Choices include pink and white-flowered forms of *Schomburgkia humboldtii*, golden yellow and red *Schomburgkia thomsoniana* and white *Caularthron bicornutum*. These orchids will also grow on palm trunks and walls. Plant vigorous blooming-size seedlings or divisions when the trees are beginning to leaf out. New tree foliage provides shade for the establishing orchid plants. Be certain to mount the plants where they will receive enough light: mature plants should be plump and yellowish-green. Place the orchid plants in the crotch between major limbs or elsewhere. Tie in place using nylon fishing line, raffia or Monel® wire. Nailing an orchid onto a tree can damage the tree. Place a pad of coarse coconut fibre beneath the orchid roots if the tree surface is uneven. Encourage rapid root development by spraying the orchids daily with water and weekly with dilute liquid fertilizer. Remove the fishing line or wire after the orchids are firmly established. Well situated orchids will eventually form large clumps.

Mount pendulous Cymbidiums in trees that can support their eventual weight. Compact, blue-flowered Lignum Vitae (*Guaicum officinale*) is a good choice, a large Frangipani tree is another. Warm-growing Cymbidiums such as *Cym. finlaysonianum* (olive green flowers/white lip with red markings) and *Cym. canaliculatum* var. *sparkesii* (burgundy-red waxy blooms) will provide years of enjoyment. Position these orchids in the lower crotch of limbs such that the long pendant inflorescence will be displayed at eye level. Plant seedlings in a ball of coconut fibre and moss. Mature plants need less pampering. Tie smaller plants in place with nylon fishing line, larger specimens with Monel® wire. Tree leaves will eventually collect about the roots, forming compost. The fishing line and wire should be removed when the orchids are well established.

Many other trees can be used to advantage in the orchid garden environment. The corrugated spongy bark of trees such as Calabash (*Crescentia cujete*), Cordia (*Cordia sebestena*) and the Tulip Tree (*Spathodea campanulata*) makes an ideal substrate for rooting epiphytes. Similarly, the scaly bark of *Citrus* and Guava (*Psidium guajava*) seems to favour orchid establishment. Growers will discover that a carefully placed orchid will grow towards its most appropriate position on the tree. Sometimes this position will be away from the viewer, much to their chagrin, but the orchid will flourish. Whether attempting to establish the Pigeon Orchid (*Dendrobium crumenatum*), clumps of ever-blooming *Mormolyca ringens*, night-fragrant Lady-of-the-Night, *Brassavola nodosa* or the striking mule-ear *Oncidium lanceanum*, remember to place these orchids at an appropriate height for viewing. Attach the plant at or just above shoulder height to the east side of the main trunk or to the upper surface of limbs where the plants will receive morning sun. The orchid roots will give a clue as to the most appropriate mount. Thinner rooted sorts may prefer the protection of a pad of moss or coconut husk fibre to start them off. Tie all in place with fishing line. Water and fertilize regularly when the orchids are in active growth.

ORCHIDS AS BEDDING PLANTS

Need a splash of colour in a sunny spot? Try reed-stem Epidendrums such as *Epi. schomburgkii, Epi. cinnabarinum* and hybrid *Epi.* Joseph Lii (Orange Glow × *cinnabarinum*). These plants are tall, even taller when in bloom, so site the bed where there is protection from wind. Raise these plants from offsets (keikis) or from seed. Prepare a bed of humus, sand, chunks of coconut husk and well-rotted manure or aged bagasse. The mix should be both water-retentive and porous. Plant keikis or seedlings, water and fertilize then stand back and watch them grow. They make great cut flower arrangements in combination with decorative foliage and tropical fruit. For the mass effect, plant many orchids with space between for each individual to grow. Spacing will depend upon the rate of growth and plant habit.

A novel orchid bedding plant for the sunny garden is mauve-flowered *Tetramicra canaliculata*. Establish this orchid among vertical chunks of tree fern or coconut husk held firmly in place with rocks or coral stone. The plants are mostly vertical so many will be needed to produce a show. Water and fertilize regularly until roots are established then periodically according to the growing conditions. For added interest, interplant with miniature Aloes.

Shaded gardens can have orchid beds too. The Jewel Orchids, often overlooked because of their insignificant flowers, will thrive in beds of coarse sand and compost. A mature leafy rosette will be 15-20 cm (6-8 in) in diameter. This orchid spreads by creeping stems (stolons). It will rapidly cover the bed surface if conditions are ideal.

Aranda (Arachnis × Vanda) and *Mokara (Arachnis × Ascocentrum × Vanda)* are vandaceous intergeneric hybrids that can be grown in beds for year round cut flower production. Establish beds of bagasse, wood shavings, sawdust, or coconut husk fibre. Make the beds approximately 60 cm (24 inches) above the ground. Shadecloth or lath shading can be installed. Place support poles for shadecloth at approximately 1 m (40 in) intervals. Place laths north to south. Shading should be at least 3 m (10 ft) high for the tall plants and allow efficient air circulation. Plant rooted cuttings or keikis at 25 cm (10 in) intervals. Cuttings should be a minimum 40 cm (15 in) long and have two or three well-developed roots. Provide support posts of Wallaba or other wood. Plan to refurbish the bedding material annually before the rainy season. Develop a preventive maintenance programme to avoid major pest and disease problems.

FENCES AND POSTS

A fence or wall can be a bit boring without some living cover. If the fence is substantial enough to support the weight of vining plants, you might grow *Arachnis flos-aeris, Vandopsis gigantea, Vandopsis lissochiloides* or an intergeneric hybrid such as *Vandachnis* Premier (*Arach. flos-aeris × Vdps. lissochiloides*). The flowers range in colour from golden brown through pale yellow with red bars. These plants can be massive and are fast growing provided it is always warm. Fasten them to posts of tree fern, Wallaba (*Eperua falcata*) or other suitable wood positioned on the sunny side of the fence. Pile coconut husks around the base of the plants to conserve moisture and to shelter the roots. Water and fertilize regularly.

Many vandaceous orchids can be grown attached to wooden or tree fern posts. Arrange the posts in tiers down a slope or in groups for mass effect. Terete and semi-terete Vandas thrive in sunny locations while strap-leaf Vandas and Renantheras do best with some shade. Air movement is critical to ensure freedom from injurious rots and to cool the plants during the heat of the day. *Vanda teres* and many of its hybrids are well suited to posts of tree fern. Fasten mature seedlings or cuttings firmly to the posts using raffia or fishing line. Mist the plants frequently until roots begin to grow. The roots meander through the coarse fern while flowering shoots and even more roots sway above. Alternatives to tree fern are wooden posts and clay pipes. *V.* Miss Joaquim (*teres × hookeriana*) and *V.* Andres Segovia (Miss Joaquim × *tricuspidata*) are two old favourites. *V.* Poepoe 'Diana' is a free-flowering white Vanda similar to *V.* Miss Joaquim. It is sometimes referred to locally as *V.* "Diane". Terete Vandas can be purchased as seedlings or as top cuttings of proven clones.

Compact *Vanda tesselata* and some of its popular hybrids, proportionately suited to smaller gardens, can be grown similarly in full sun or under 40% shade. Renantheras such as *Ren. storiei* and its hybrids are best raised under light shade provided by cloth or tall trees. The large red flowers are so brilliant and produced in such numbers that the shadecloth is hardly noticed. Fertilize these orchids by spraying the roots.

ORCHIDS IN BASKETS, POTS AND ON MOUNTS

Orchids with a rampant growth habit are highly suited to basket culture as are those orchids with pendant stems and flowers. Raise these orchids to flowering then move them to the living area to be enjoyed in bloom. Grow strap-leaf Vandas and Ascocendas in baskets or rafts made of teak or similar rot-resistant wood. Simply tie the plant in place and let the roots ramble. It is perfectly normal for roots to hang freely below the basket. Suspend the basket by wire or polypropylene cord from overhead supports. Use at least three evenly spaced attachments to stabilize the basket. Do not crowd the plants. Provide appropriate shade, water and fertilizer to promote vigorous growth and frequent blooming.

Brazilian Miltonias, golden yellow Oncidiums such as *Onc. ampliatum* and *Onc. sphacelatum*, black and green-flowered *Coelogyne pandurata*, and magenta or white *Cattleya skinneri* are excellent subjects for basket culture. These orchids make such substantial specimens that they may become too heavy to move. Grow them in a sturdy wire or wooden basket lined with moss or 'cloth' obtained from coconut palms. Fill the container with a coarse mixture of tree fern, charcoal and crock. Overpotting within reason is appropriate here as these orchids will soon outgrow a modest container. Larger specimens can be permanently suspended from a tree limb where they will be the centres of attraction when in bloom.

> *Labels are important:* use aluminium plant labels to identify your orchids. Attach labels to orchid plants or to their containers/mounts. Use an ordinary pencil to record the name and potting date.

Orchids such as Cattleyas, Paphiopedilums, and Phalaenopsis are often grown in pots. Plastic pots are lightweight and easy to clean but the walls are impermeable to water. Enlarge drainage holes to ensure root aeration. Roots do not cling to plastic so suffer less damage during repotting. Clay pots are fragile, heavy and porous. Sometimes they are constructed with side openings or slots to improve drainage and aeration. Heavier clay pots are useful when using lightweight potting materials.

Choose a pot diameter and depth to accommodate the orchid for two years. Shallow pots are preferable to deep ones. Never overpot! You might wish to cover drainage openings with pieces of nylon netting to prevent the entry of slugs. When using plastic pots and light material, place a few piece of crock in the bottom for stability. Examine the plant to be potted. Remove dead or damaged roots and foliage using a sterile blade. Position the plant in the pot such that there is plenty of space for new growth to develop. Fill the pot with fresh, moist potting material. The plant should remain at the same depth as before. Use a wire clip to ensure that newly planted orchids do not tip out of their containers. Clips fit over the pot edge and extend across the pot.

> *Tip!* Phalaenopsis orchids produce many roots that grow out of the container. It is not necessary to contain all these roots when repotting.

Potted orchids are usually set on benches, tables or in trays. They may also be suspended by hooks from an overhead or an A-frame support to increase the effective growing area and to improve ventilation. Prepare S-shaped hooks from strong wire. Make holes in the plastic pot edge where required using a hot nail. One hole will be enough for the A-frame: three holes will be needed for an overhead support. Insert one end of the hook in the hole, the other end is hooked onto the support. S-hooks can be custom-made to fit all pot sizes.

> *To control the spread of viruses* use 30 cm (12 in) lengths of 2 cm (¾ in) diameter bamboo as disposable potting tools. Use a fresh tool for each plant.

Growing orchids on mounts whether it is sawed timber, slabs of cork bark or sections of trees and tree ferns, requires attention first to the kind of material, its relative longevity under local conditions, then to the orchid size and growth habit. Plan for at least five years growth: do not undermount. If using a branch with intact bark such as a piece of Calabash (*Crescentia*), *Bauhinia*, Shack-shack (*Albizia*) or *Cordia*, cut a section about 7-10 cm (2½-4 in) diameter and 30 cm (12 in) long. If larger diameter branches are not available and you need greater breadth, cut several sections and wire them together. Use sections of cork bark for those recalcitrant species needing extra speedy drainage. Heavily fissured cork bark has many crevices for rambling roots yet sheds water rapidly and resists decay. *Cattleya walkeriana* and *Broughtonia sanguinea* are particularly well suited to cork slab culture. They may succumb to injurious rot if grown in a pot or on slabs of damp bark.

Secure a hanging support to the upper part of the mount. Screw-eyes and hooks work well at first but will eventually pull out of decaying wood. A better strategy is to tightly wrap several turns of Monel® or plastic-covered bell wire around the mount, making a loop over the top and using the last bit to form a handle. Twist the handle to form a loop.

Mount orchids when they are just starting their growth cycle. This is particularly important with those orchids that resent disturbance. Examine the orchid, noting the likely direction of the new growth. If the orchid has previously been growing in a pot, remove any dead roots. Position the plant towards the base of the mount so that there will be plenty of space for it to grow. Tie the plant firmly in place using several turns of raffia or nylon fishing line. Hang the mount in a lightly shaded spot and mist frequently until the roots have become firmly attached to the surface. When an orchid outgrows its support, prepare it for the stress of division by first cutting the rhizome to induce the development of new growing points. Divide the plant, mount and all, only after new shoots and roots form on each portion. Attach each piece to a fresh mounting surface. Alternatively, the overgrown mount can be attached to a new and larger support, perhaps even to a tree! Assess each situation separately.

Propagating Orchids 🌸

> Sterilize propagation tools between use to prevent the spread of orchid viruses.

Vegetative propagation

Orchids may be propagated by division as in *Cattleya* and *Oncidium*, by top cutting as in *Vanda* and *Renanthera*, and through the removal of offsets (keikis) as in *Epidendrum*. *Phalaenopsis* and *Doritaenopsis* sometimes produce keikis on the inflorescence. They can also be vegetatively propagated by stem propagation. This procedure stimulates dormant buds located on an inflorescence to develop into rooted plantlets. Orchids may also be propagated artificially in a process called mericloning. Here the growing point (meristem) is removed under sterile conditions and cultured in a special liquid nutrient solution with shaking. The tissue grows, is chopped, placed in fresh solution with shaking, and so on until the desired number of pieces has been acquired. These pieces of undifferentiated plant tissue are cultured on solid medium where, no longer disorientated by shaking, each forms a shoot and roots. Once the newly formed plants are large enough, they are removed to pots. Commercial laboratories specialize in raising large numbers of identical propagules (mericlones) of orchids selected for their floriferousness and other attributes. If too many propagules are derived from the same tissue, variations can arise. Variations could be different colour and/or flower form, deformed flowers and/or foliage, and lack of vigour.

All vegetatively propagated orchids bear the same name as the parent plant. They will also be virused if the mother plant is infected at the time of propagation. Before submitting a plant for mericloning, have it tested for virus.

PROPAGATION BY DIVISION

Divide sympodial orchids such as *Cattleya* and *Oncidium* into two or more parts by simply severing the rhizome with a sterile knife. Division is best done at the time of repotting. Examine the orchid. The plant should just be starting to develop new shoots and roots. Look for the growing points. Allow at least three growths or pseudobulbs per division. The larger each division is, the more likely it is that the plant will resume growth quickly. Trim each division of damaged and dead roots. Shake off old potting materials and repot.

> *Tip!* Some orchids such as *Cattleya dowiana* and their hybrids, develop roots only after the new growth has developed. Divide such orchids with care when new roots are just beginning to develop. Avoid damaging the existing roots.

PROPAGATION BY TOP CUTTING

Monopodial orchids such as Vandas, Ascocendas, Arandas and Mokaras are easily propagated by top cutting. The plant must be large enough that the top bears two or three well-developed roots. Sever the stem below the roots using a sterile blade. Dip the cut end in fungicidal powder, fine charcoal or powdered sulphur to avoid decay. Mount the cutting as required. Provide shade and mist frequently until the roots become attached to the mount. The remainder will grow one or more offsets (keikis). These can be removed once two or three roots have formed.

STEM PROPAGATION

Phalaenopsis and *Doritaenopsis* are not suited to propagation by top cutting or division. They are more quickly propagated by a method called stem propagation. The inflorescence bears one or more dormant buds that will start forming plantlets when removed from the plant and cultured separately in bottles of sterile nutrient medium. Stem propagation of Phalaenopsis-type orchids is preferred to meristem propagation. While stem-propagated plants are more expensive, they are more likely to be true to type.

The method is simple. Someone may do the procedure locally or you can try it yourself. You will need containers of sterilized stem propagation medium, one for each section bearing a dormant bud.

A fresh stem bearing flowers and buds is severed from the plant using a sharp, sterile blade. Clean the stem by wiping it with a paper towel dampened with alcohol. Remove the tiny leaf-like bract that covers each dormant bud along the inflorescence. Suitable buds are below the flowers. Remove any flowers and flower buds. Divide the inflorescence into sections, each bearing an exposed dormant bud. Sterilize the pieces by immersing them in a solution of one part liquid bleach to nine parts water for ten minutes. Using a sterilized tool, remove the sections and place them in a covered container of sterile water. Under sterile conditions, remove each section and plant it in the medium. Be certain not to plant the section upside-down. Seal the containers and place in subdued light. A plantlet should develop from the bud and after several months will develop roots. A well-rooted plantlet can be removed to its own pot.

Propagating orchids from seeds

If we are going to pollinate orchid flowers in the hope of producing seed of a species or of a new hybrid, we must know where to find the pollen and where it must be placed to achieve pollination. A major distinguishing feature of orchid flowers is the column, a structure uniting the pistil and stamens. There is usually only one fertile stamen although slipper orchids have two. The ovary that will later form the seed-bearing capsule is located below the point of attachment of the petals and sepals. The pollen is found in masses (pollinia) located towards the end of the column beneath the anther cap. Pollinia are usually attached by a filament to a sticky disk. It is the disk that sticks to part of a visiting insect as it investigates the orchid bloom. The pollen receiving structure (stigma) is located just behind the anther cap and pollinia, generally on the undersurface of the column. With artificial pollination the grower, using a simple tool such as a toothpick, removes the pollen from a suitable flower and deposits it onto the stigma of another flower.

Pollination is no guarantee of the production of viable seed. Some orchid flowers are self-incompatible. Many attempts to make an artificial hybrid can meet with failure and the reasons for this are complex. Outcross species whenever possible, pollinating flowers of one plant with pollen from a different clone. Also, the flowers should be pollinated when still fresh although not necessarily when they have just opened. Flowers may be most receptive when at their fragrance peak.

Pollination initiates the development of ovules in the ovary. The process can take anything from a few days to several months depending on the species. Developing ovules cause the ovary to swell, often leading the grower to believe that seed is already being produced, however, only after fertilization has happened can seeds begin to develop. If fertilization is not possible because of genetic or other reasons, seed will not form and the capsule will abort development. Phalaenopsis require about two months after pollination to begin developing seed. Further growth of the ovary/capsule after this time means that seed is being matured within. Orchids require varying periods of time to mature their seed. Cattleyas need about 150 days, Paphiopedilums and Oncidiums require 200 days, but reed-stem Epidendrums need only 60 to 90 days. Consult the bibliography (page 61) for more information.

POLLEN AND SEED STORAGE

When an orchid blooms but another potential recipient is not yet in flower, you must harvest the pollen and store it safely for future use. Pollen stores well for several months if wrapped in paper and stored in the refrigerator. For longer periods, store packets of pollen in the refrigerator in a sealed glass container with saturated calcium choride solution. Always label the pollen packets with the name and date of collection.

Orchid seed germinates best when sown directly from an opened capsule. There are thousands of seeds in a capsule: you may not wish to sow them all at once. Place air dried seed in paper packets. Label the packets and store as for pollen.

The seeds of orchids lack a food store and thus are unable to germinate without assistance. In nature, they are helped by an appropriate fungus (mycorrhizae). We can germinate orchid seeds without the fungus. Seeds are sown on a sterilized mixture of sugars, minerals and other growth agents. These mixtures are called flasking media. Commercial sources are listed in the Appendix (page 51). Ask locally if someone will be willing to sow the seeds for you. If you want to learn how to do this yourself, consult references given in the bibliography (page 61). Some orchids grow quickly and can be removed to pots within a year.

REMOVING ORCHID SEEDLINGS FROM FLASK

Often it is expedient and economical to purchase orchid seedlings when they are still in their sterile flask or bottle. Not only are the plants free from pests and diseases but they are very much less expensive than the same number of older seedlings. Removing the seedlings 'from flask' does require some planning and expertise. Many species and hybrids such as Phalaenopsis and Cattleyas grow all year round. These can be removed from flask and potted up at any time other than during the height of the rainy season, when there is a higher than average risk of injurious rots. Orchids such as Catasetums having defined growth and rest periods must be de-flasked only when the plants are growing and never when they are just entering their dormant period. Seedlings exhibit seasonal dormancy even in flask.

De-flask all orchids when they have a vigorous root system and are 5-10 cm (2-4 in) tall. Open the bottle and pour in some fresh tap water. Swirl gently to loosen the plantlets. Try to shake out the seedlings but if they are too large to pass through the bottle opening, you must break the container. Wrap the bottle in newspaper then strike it sharply with a hammer. Try not to crush the contents. Take each seedling in turn, flushing excess medium from the roots with a gentle stream of water. Avoid breaking roots or crushing leaves. Grade the seedlings by size and number of roots. Plant similar-sized seedlings in a community pot or tray of fresh, moist potting medium. Spray the seedlings with an all-purpose fungicide to control rot. Shade and good air movement are important. Apply dilute fertilizer regularly once new roots have begun to emerge. Remove seedlings from community pots after one year or when they become crowded, whichever happens first.

REGISTRATION OF HYBRID ORCHIDS

If you successfully raise a new hybrid orchid and its flowers and performance merit recognition, you may wish to register the cross. The name you give the cross must be unique. Consult Sander's List of Orchid Hybrids and The Handbook on Orchid Nomenclature and Registration. You must provide a colour photograph or 35 mm slide of the flower(s), a brief description of the first blooms, also the date of making the cross and the date of first flowering. This information must be submitted on a standard form available from the Registrar. See the Appendix (page 53) for details. There is a fee for registration.

AWARDS

Orchid species and hybrids are considered by judges of internationally recognized bodies such as the American Orchid Society (AOS) and the Royal Horticultural Society (RHS). Judges meet regularly. American Orchid Society judges participate in a regional

1.1

1.2

1.3

1.4

PLATE 1

1-1 Spotted and striped Phalaenopsis bloom well in the lowland tropics. Here is a fine example. *Phal.* Florida Stripe (Georges Seurat × Hawaiian Charmer). Photo by M. Light.

1-2 *Phal. venosa* contributes the yellow colour to *Phal.* Marquesas (*venosa* × Zuma Red Eye). Fading is considered a fault. Photo by M. MacConaill.

1-3 To obtain a good flower presentation, do not move a plant until the flower buds open. Photo by M. Light.

1-4 *Phal. violacea* hybrids often have fragrant blooms. *Phal.* Penang Violacea (*micholitzii* × *violacea*). Photo by M. Light.

2.1

2.2

2.3

2.4

PLATE 2

2-1 Dendrobiums such as *Den.* Kalagas (Lili Marlene × *stratiotes*) are floriferous. Photo by M. Light.

2-2 *Dendrobium discolor* and its many hybrids thrive in full sun. Photo by M. Light.

2-3 Expect yellow-green flower colour to vary with light exposure and flower age. *Dendrobium* Karie Wakida 'Karia' AM/AOS (Shigaki Neal × May Neal). Photo by M. Light.

2-4 Selected clones of *Den.* Ekapol can be purchased as mericlones. Photo by M. Light.

3.1

3.2

3.3

3.4

PLATE 3

3-1 Mount *Den. anosmum* in a tree to have a shower of blooms from March until May. Photo by M. MacConaill.

3-2 *Dendrobium phalaenopsis* and *Den. bigibbum* hybrids require perfect drainage so they have been potted in broken pieces of crock. Photo by M. Light.

3-3 Tall antelope-type Dendrobiums bloom well in a sunny location. Photo by M. Light.

3-4 Sympodial orchids such as *Cattleya* and *Dendrobium* may be mounted on thick disks of tree fern. Photo by M. Light.

4.1

4.2

4.3

4.4

PLATE 4

4-1 Some of the easiest orchids to grow on trees are Schomburgkias such as *Schmb. humboldtii*. Photo by M. Light.

4-2 Schomburgkias are bred with Cattleyas to reduce inflorescence length and to increase flower size. *Schombocattleya (C. guttata* × Harry Dunn) carries nine 12 cm (5 in) wide flowers on a 45 cm (15 in) inflorescence. Photo by M. MacConaill.

4-3 *Cattleya* Pearl Harbor (Bow Bells × Celia) blooms in November/December. Photo by M. MacConaill.

4-4 The Nun Orchid (*Caularthron (Diacrium) bicornutum*) blooms in March. Photo by M. Light.

5.1

5.2

5.3

PLATE 5
5-1 Superior clones of *Cattleya walkeriana* in both the 'alba' and lavender forms are used to produce floriferous yet modest-sized hybrids. Photo by M. Light.
5-2 *Cattleya* guatemalensis (*skinneri* × *aurantiaca*) 'Lakeview'. Flowers change colour as they mature. Photo by M. Light.
5-3 The influence of the *Broughtonia* parent is very evident in *Cattleytonia* Jet Set (Maui Maid × *Bro. sanguinia alba*). The flowers are 6.6 cm (2½ in) wide on a 50 cm (20 in) inflorescence. Photo by M. MacConaill.
5-4 *Cattleya skinneri* makes a stunning basket specimen. Photo by M. Light. (overleaf)

5.4

6.1

6.2

6.3

6.4

PLATE 6
6-1 *Spathoglottis unguiculata* is wonderfully fragrant of grapes. Photo by M. Light.
6-2 Establish a bed of reed-stemmed Epidendrums in a sheltered but sunny garden bed. *Epidendrum* Joseph Lii (Orange Glow × *cinnabarinum*) is prized as a cut flower. Photo by M. Light.
6-3 Understand floral structure before attempting hybridization. The toothpick points to the pollinia. The indentation immediately below the pollinia is the pollen-receptive stigma. Photo by M. MacConaill.
6-4 Label orchids and developing capsules. Photo by M. MacConaill.

PLATE 7

7-1 Raise *Renanthera storiei* under 30% shade. Photo by M. Light.
7-2 *Ascocenda* Bicentennial (Bonanza × Yip Sum Wah). Photo by M. Light.
7-3 *Ascda.* Su-Fun Beauty (*V.* Bankapi × Pralor). Photo by M. Light.
7-4 Mokaras such as *Mkra.* Chark Kuan (*Aranda* Christine × *Ascda.* Cholburi) provide year round bloom and make excellent cut flowers. Photo by M. Light.

8.1

8.2

8.3

8.4

PLATE 8

8-1 The spidery flower shape of *Arachnis* is a dominant trait. *Arachnis* Maggie Oei (*hookerana* × *flos-aeris*). Photo by M. Light.

8-2 Mount large trailing orchids such as *Arachnis* on a post or a fence. Photo by M. Light.

8-3 Orchids such as *V*. Ruby Prince (Ruby × Cooperi) can be grown on upright tiles filled with water to keep the roots cool. Photo by M. Light.

8-4 Terete Vandas flourish when mounted on treefern posts. Photo by M. Light.

PLATE 9

9-1 *Vanda* Seethong (Thananchai × Seeprai). *V.* Thananchai is a proven parent and grandparent in the production of fine yellow Vandas. Photo by M. Light.

9-2 The shape, colour and markings of *Ascda*. Surin (*V.* Thanantess × Guo Chia Long) are reminiscent of two ancestors, *V. dearii* and *V. tesselata*. The *Ascocentrum* parent (*Asctm. curvifolium*) has influenced the spike habit. Photo by M. Light.

9-3 Compact *V. tesselata* in its typical colour form. Photo by M. MacConaill.

9-4 An alba form of *V. tesselata* was used to make this pale clone of *V.* Thanantess (Thananchai × *tesselata*). Photo by M. Light.

10.1

10.2

10.3

10.4

PLATE 10

10-1 Flowers of *Ansellia africana* range from pale yellow to rich chocolate brown. Photo by M. MacConaill.

10-2 *Cyrtopodium punctatum* thrives in a drier garden. Photo by M. MacConaill.

10-3 Strongly fragrant flowers of *Zygopetalum intermedium* are well presented on 60 cm (2 ft) spikes. Photo by M. MacConaill.

10-4 *Coelogyne* (*pandurata* × Burfordiense) presents eight or more, 7.5 cm (3 in) wide flowers per inflorescence. Photo by M. MacConaill.

11.1

11.2

11.3

11.4

PLATE 11

11-1 *Paphiopedilum* Miss Faith Hanbury (*niveum* × *glaucophyllum*) has delicate yet long lasting blooms. Photo by M. MacConaill.

11-2 *Paphiopedilum* F.C. Puddle (Acteus × Astarte) is an old favourite that blooms freely in Caribbean collections. Photo by M. MacConaill.

11-3 *Phragmipedium* Eric Young (*besseae* × *longifolium*) blooms in shades of red through apricot and peach. Photo by M. MacConaill.

11-4 Jewel Orchids such as *Ludisia discolor* are so-called because of their exquisite foliage. Photo by M. Light.

12.1

12.2

12.3

12.4

PLATE 12

12-1 The secret of raising the Butterfly Orchid, *Psychopsis (Onc.) papilio*, is careful attention to watering and to the freshness of the potting medium. Photo by M. MacConaill.

12-2 Brazilian Miltonias such as *Milt.* Anne Warne may produce fewer flowers per inforescence when grown at too high a night temperature. Photo by M. Light.

12-3 *Oncidium ampliatum* is a favourite orchid for hanging baskets. Photo by M. Light.

12-4 *Oncidium* Florida Gold 'Merkel' AM/AOS (*splendidum × bicallosum*). Photo by M. MacConaill.

13.1   **13.2**

13.3   **13.4**

PLATE 13

13-1 Crown rot of Phalaenopsis does not necessarily end the life of a valuable orchid. The two keikis that have formed may be removed when they develop two or more roots. Photo by M. Light.

13-2 Twisty Top Disease of *Dendrobium*. Photo by M. Light.

13-3 Fungal lesions on Vanda leaves are rough to the touch. Photo by M. Light.

13-4 Spider mite-infested Phalaenopsis leaves are silvery, pitted and appear scorched. Photo by M. Light.

14.1

14.2

14.3

14.4

PLATE 14
14-1 This shadehouse is situated at the top of a slope to take advantage of cooling breezes. Photo by M. Light.
14-2 Shadecloth is mounted high above the orchids to improve ventilation. Photo by M. Light.
14-3 Eavestroughing fastened inside a carport makes a comfortable home for Phalaenopsis. Photo by M. Light.
14-4 Check the spray nozzles of an automated mister system periodically for blockage. Photo by M. Light.

15.1

15.2

15.3

15.4

PLATE 15
15-1 To remount an orchid such as *Broughtonia sanguinea*, simply fasten a fresh mount to the old one. Photo by M. Light.
15-2 *Cymbidium finlaysonianum* grows exceptionally well in a tree crotch. Photo by M. Light.
15-3 Pot *Oncidium splendidum* in a blend of tree fern fibre and charcoal. Photo by M. Light.
15-4 Keikis forming at the base of a Vanda or Ascocenda may be removed or left to form a larger specimen. Photo by M. Light.

monthly judging covering a specific area, e.g. Florida – Caribbean Region. They also are present at orchid shows such as those held in Jamaica, Trinidad, San Juan (Puerto Rico), St. Thomas (U.S. Virgin Islands) and Miami (Florida). Cultivars that have been judged superior to others or to have horticultural merit are granted a particular award. Nurseries will list awarded cultivars by name with the award abbreviated after the clonal name.

Awards for Flower Quality
FCC = First Class Certificate (90-100 points)
AM = Award of Merit (80-89 points)
HCC = Highly Commended Certificate (75-79 points)
JC = Judges Commendation (An award for hybrids showing promise)

Award for Cultural Perfection (an award for the grower's skill)
CCM = Certificate of Cultural Merit

Award for a new species or hybrid showing horticultural promise
CHM = Certificate of Horticultural Merit

Challenges ❀

Pests

There are multitudes of pests that attack orchids. Aphids suck juices from tender shoots and flower buds. Sucking insects can transmit virus diseases. Thrips damage flower buds rendering flowers useless for exhibition or sale. Snails and slugs feed at night, leaving a slimy trail through their path of destruction. Birds are sometimes troublesome in the dry season, feasting on juicy orchid flowers for the moisture they contain.

Some pests are more easily controlled than others. Screening separates orchids from birds. Metaldehyde bait and spray, judiciously and regularly applied, will control most slugs. However, it is almost impossible to stop thrips blowing into an orchid collection. They will carry out their destructive rasping before you even know they are present. There is no better control than grower vigilance. Stop the problem before it becomes a big one.

THRIPS

A heavy thrips attack will devastate orchid blooms. All orchids can be attacked but damage is often restricted to certain kinds in a mixed collection. Adult thrips can fly. They feed and lay eggs in orchid buds and blooms. Pale yellow nymphs attack flowers and buds close to where they hatched, damaging blooms even before they are fully opened. The flowers appear scorched but on close examination, characteristic silvery marks and tiny black droppings can be seen. Contact pesticides will kill thrips. Spray with products recommended for thrips control, using the manufacturer's instructions. Nymphs hidden in buds will escape the pesticide. Monitor the thrips population by hanging bright yellow sticky cards at flower level throughout the growing area. Place one card per 100 square metres (1 000 square feet). The cards should be checked weekly and be replaced monthly during the dry season. Flying thrips are strongly attracted to the yellow colour. Not only will adults be trapped before they cause damage but the grower will be forewarned of an impending invasion.

MEALY BUGS AND SCALE INSECTS

These sucking insects can be especially difficult to control as they are resistant to many insecticides. Mealy bugs are white, cottony insects that hide in leaf sheaths and among roots. Scale insects are shield-shaped brownish insects that feed on the undersurface of leaves and in flowers. Ants are attracted to the 'honeydew' excreted by them. Honeydew is a sugary solution which sticks to leaves and supports the growth of black sooty mould. The source of pests is often infested shrubbery or palms growing upwind of the orchids. Vines permitted to grow over the lath house frequently harbour pests.

Insect Growth Regulators such as Applaud® and Enstar® are innovative insecticides that interfere with larval development and the egg laying ability of sucking insects such as mealy bugs, white fly, aphids, scale insects and leaf hoppers. Read the product instructions carefully to decide rates of application and appropriate precautions.

SPIDER MITES

Mites are tiny relatives of spiders. They damage leaves of Phalaenopsis, Dendrobium and many other orchids, especially during the dry season when the grower should be especially vigilant. Damaged leaves will appear scorched, the surface silvery and pitted. Treat infested orchids by spraying them with a miticide such as Pentac® (dienochlor) or Kelthane® (dicofol). Thoroughly wet the foliage and use a wetter/sticker to improve the adherence of the pesticide. Mites, like insects, can become resistant to pesticides. Alternate between pesticides to avoid resistance to any one. The Agriculture Department probably can recommend an effective product for local use.

Diseases

VIRUS

Viral diseases are the most dreaded diseases of orchids. There is no cure. A virus can cripple, disfigure and weaken plants as in 'Twisty Top' of Dendrobium. Some orchids exhibit no outward signs of infection but remain as reservoirs of infection for other plants in the collection. Two viruses are transmitted solely by the grower.

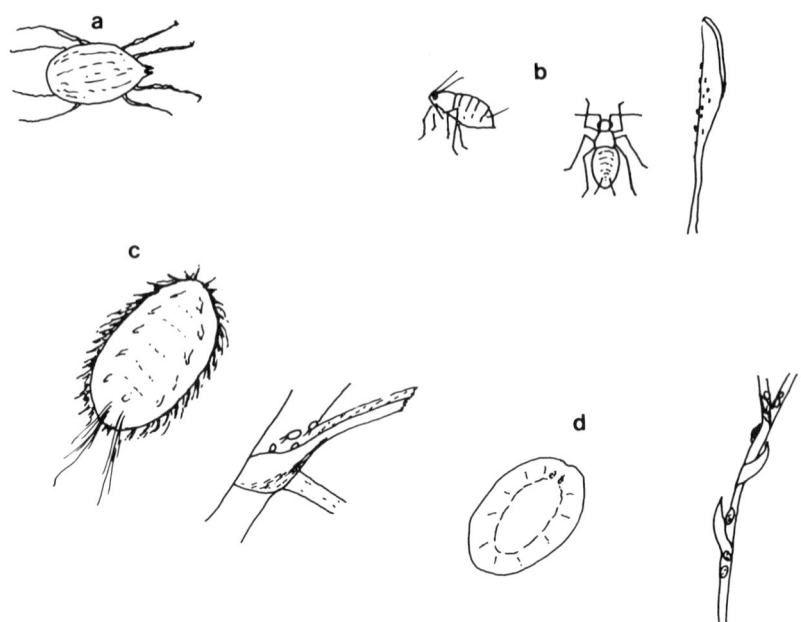

FIGURE 3. Pests
a) Spider mite b) Aphids c) Mealy bugs d) Scale insects

These common viruses are the Cymbidium Mosaic Virus (CMV) and the Odontoglossum Ringspot Virus (ORSV). They are most commonly spread by a cutting tool contaminated with infected sap. Other less commonly encountered viruses are spread by insects. Bean Yellow Mosaic Virus is spread by aphids from infected bean plants to orchids. The presence of these and certain other viruses can be determined by laboratory testing procedures for a small fee. Those wishing to learn more about orchid viruses and testing procedures are advised to consult the bibliography (page 61).

VIRUS DISEASE (all orchids)
SYMPTOMS: Deformed or disfigured foliage and flowers; streaked blooms (colour break). Some infected plants exhibit no symptoms at all.
CONSEQUENCES: Failure to thrive; reduced flower production. Infected plants are reservoirs of infection.
CONTROL: There is no known cure! Destroy by burning, all confirmed infected plants. Isolate suspected plants. Always use sterile cutting tools when dividing or potting plants and when cutting flowers.

Steps to keep viral infections out of a collection
1) Assemble a collection of virus-free plants. Seedlings in flask are less likely to be infected than divisions of plants long in cultivation.
2) Use sterile cutting and potting tools. Sterilize cutting tools after each use by soaking for 10 minutes in a solution of either 10% liquid bleach or saturated tri sodium phosphate solution.
3) Test plants for the presence of virus.
4) Destroy by burning or at least isolate proven infected plants.

> **Saturated tri sodium phosphate (TSP)** Add half a cup of TSP to two gallons of hot water. CAUTION The solution is very corrosive. Mix well using a wooden paddle. Add more TSP until some crystals remain undissolved. A saturated solution is necessary to inactivate viruses.

LEAF SPOTS AND BLOTCHES

Leaf-spotting fungi such as *Cercospora*, *Septoria* and *Phyllosticta* produce unsightly speckles and blotches on the leaves of orchids such as Dendrobium, Cattleya and Vanda. The spots are rough to the touch, microscopic examination will reveal the presence of fungal tissue and distinctive spores. Premature leaf fall reduces plant vigour and flowering potential. Severely infected plants may die prematurely.

> **LEAF SPOTS and BLOTCHES** *(Cercospora, Septoria, Phyllosticta)*
> SYMPTOMS: Speckles and blotches, rough to the touch, on leaves, particularly Dendrobium, Cattleya, Oncidium, Vanda.
> CONSEQUENCES: Premature leaf fall, plant death.
> CONTROL: Burn diseased material. Improve air circulation. Spray with appropriate fungicide.

BLACK ROT

Black Rot is a particularly aggressive infection of Cattleyas caused by *Phytophthora*. A new shoot suddenly turns black: the rot moves rapidly, killing the rest of the plant. A whitish 'bloom' of fungus spores may be seen on the diseased tissue. Heat-stressed orchids are most susceptible. This disease is more prevalent during the rainy season as it is spread primarily by splashing water.

> **BLACK ROT** *(Phytophthora)*
> SYMPTOMS: New growth turns black. White 'bloom' of spores on surface.
> CONSEQUENCES: Rot moves rapidly through rest of plant. Plant dies. Highly contagious during rainy season.
> CONTROL: Disease spread primarily by splashing water. Shelter plants from rain. Isolate infected plants. Burn diseased material. Spray or dust with appropriate fungicide.

BLACK LEG/DRY ROT

Dendrobiums and Vandas growing in waterlogged potting or bedding materials are susceptible to a slow but inexorable rot of the roots and stem from below. The causative fungi are *Fusarium* and *Rhizoctonia*. Pseudobulbs becomes spongy and discoloured. The leaves, especially in Vanda, will yellow and drop off one by one until none are left and the plant dies. Plants can be salvaged. Uninfected pseudobulbs of Dendrobiums can be removed to form keikis. If a Vanda has many aerial roots, sever the stem above the line of infection. Since the disease is caused primarily by poor culture, fungicides are not recommended for control.

> **BLACK LEG/DRY ROT** *(Fusarium, Rhizoctonia)*
> SYMPTOMS: Pseudobulb of Dendrobium becomes spongy and discoloured at the base. The leaves of Vanda turn yellow then drop off from the base up to the growing point.
> CONSEQUENCES: Infected plants eventually die. Uninfected portions of stem can be salvaged.
> CONTROL: This disease is caused primarily by poor culture. Fungicides are not recommended. Use potting/bedding materials appropriate to the plant type. Replace potting materials before they become stale and waterlogged. Burn infected material.

BACTERIAL SOFT ROT

Soft rots are difficult to diagnose but whatever the causative agent, they can be devastating to an orchid collection. Orchids will be more vulnerable to infection if they are overfertilized, given insufficient light and ventilation and if they are permitted to remain wet especially in the crown. Rots are a problem during the wet season, also after storms when plants are bruised and torn by high winds. Shelter susceptible plants from rain. Be vigilant for rot during the wet season.

BACTERIAL SPOT/ROT *(Pseudomonas, Erwinia)*
SYMPTOMS: Soft, brown, smelly, fluid-filled blisters on leaves and in the crown of Phalaenopsis, Paphiopedilum, Catasetum.
CONSEQUENCES: Highly contagious. Crown rot will quickly kill a plant. Leaf spots can be excised and the plant saved.
CONTROL: Withhold water. Improve ventilation. Remove and burn infected tissue. Be careful not to break the blisters. Consider the fertilizer being used: reduce the nitrogen and increase the potassium component. Pot Phalaenopsis so that the crown drains freely. Use Physan-20®, 7.5 ml in 5 litres (½ tbsp. per gallon) as a preventive spray.

Reduce the impact of diseases in an orchid collection through garden sanitation and cultural practice.
1) Keep the growing area free of dead leaves and spent flowers.
2) Remove and burn diseased foliage and flowers.
3) Use sterile cutting tools.
4) Treat cut surfaces with powdered charcoal or a fungicidal powder.
5) Maintain good air movement within the growing area.
6) Provide a light regime appropriate to the plant type.
7) Do not crowd the plants.
8) Cull plants that become easily reinfected despite good cultural practice.

Pesticide toxicity
Many pesticides are harmful to humans, pets, fish and beneficial insects. Certain products will damage orchids, especially the flowers. Read the product label and follow all instructions carefully. Always test a new product on a few plants representative of the collection before applying it to all the orchids. Some orchids such as *Oncidium papilio* are more sensitive than others. Never apply pesticides when the orchids are heat- or drought-stressed. Follow all safety precautions recommended by the manufacturer including safe disposal of spray, unused pesticide and containers.

WEEDS

Various plants will grow in containers with orchids, competing with them for fertilizer and water. Weeds include Oxalis, Shine Bush (*Peperomia*), Lace Plant (*Pilea*) and ferns. The grower should be alert to the invasion of weeds. Not only do they compete with the orchids for space but they will also harbour pests. Remove the weeds by hand before they become firmly established and reproduce. Repotting may be necessary.

Stress

When an orchid does not bloom the cause may be insufficient light, inappropriate daylength or high night temperature. Some orchids are habitually shy bloomers.

HIGH NIGHT TEMPERATURE

The warmth of the lowland tropics is often the greatest impediment to successfully raising and flowering orchids. Some orchids require a substantial temperature differential (as much as 10°C) between night and day. Not all individuals in a population can be expected to act the same way. The best way to get warmth-tolerant orchids is to purchase a division or mericlone of a proven clone or take a chance with a flask of hybrid seedlings bred for warmth tolerance. Those individuals best adapted to your growing conditions will be more vigorous, disease-resistant, and will bloom easily at maturity. If the opportunity exists, take less tolerant plants from your collection to a garden at a higher altitude. Even a hundred metres (330 feet) difference in elevation can make a difference. Cool night temperatures and decreasing day length initiate flower spikes on Phalaenopsis.

BUD BLASTING

Buds that yellow and drop before opening are said to 'blast'. This frustrating problem can happen if the orchid and buds are subjected to stress such as too high or too low a temperature, drought or air pollution such as smoke and exhaust. Cane fires and automobile exhaust can both produce ethylene in concentrations that lead to premature aging of flower buds. Buds may also blast after a plant is moved, ostensibly to protect the buds from rain, sun or pests. Some cultivars of Dendrobium and Phalaenopsis are definitely more prone to bud drop. As the problem is primarily one of culture, control lies in keeping orchids stress-free during the blooming season.

Import regulations and plant health

CITES The Convention on International Trade in Endangered Species is a treaty established to control and monitor the trade in endangered species. A permit system regulates and monitors trade in endangered species including orchids. Orchids are all considered vulnerable but to varying degrees. Trade in Appendix I species including *Cattleya trianae, Peristeria elata, Renanthera imshootiana, Vanda coerulea,* and all Paphiopedilum species is restricted. Trade in all other orchids (Appendix II) is permitted. Artificially propagated Appendix I species are considered Appendix II provided a certificate of artificial propagation is issued by the appropriate authority of the exporting country. Orchids growing in flask are considered artificially propagated: both Appendix I and II orchids growing in flask are exempt from further control but it is best to check locally before placing an order to find out whether this is the local interpretation. Do not assume that a foreign nursery will be aware of the regulations. Formally request the required documentation.

PLANT HEALTH CERTIFICATE Each country protects the health of local crops by requiring that a certificate of plant health accompany imported plants. Orchids from tropical countries can harbour insect pests and diseases that could affect the local economy. Request that a certificate accompany a foreign shipment.

IMPORT PERMITS Each country has a government department that manages the issue of import permits. When applying for an import permit you will need to know the species to be imported including their appropriate scientific names, the number of plants, the exporter and importer name and address. The authority may require specific declarations as to the health of the plants.

Orchid Selections

SYMBOLS

∥ posts
∪ baskets or mounted (upright habit)
∩ baskets or mounted (pendant habit)
X orchids for garden beds
∀ pot plants

ANGRAECUM *(Angcm.)* ∀ ∥

Most warm-growing Angraecums will thrive in sea level Caribbean gardens while those species requiring a cool rest period after blooming or a marked day/night temperature differential to flower are best grown in gardens at higher altitudes. The fragrant showy ivory-white blooms of warm-growing *Angcm. sesquipedale* are a garden delight. This monopodial orchid adapts readily to a brightly lit, humid growing area with a sturdy wooden post as support for the many thick rambling roots. Like many Angraecums, this orchid prefers not to be disturbed once it reaches maturity and begins flowering. Another large-growing species is *Angcm. eburneum*. It bears long, showy racemes of green and white flowers. Select seedlings derived from lowland stock for warm tropical gardens. Popular hybrid, *Angcm.* Veitchii, combining traits of both the parent species, is highly recommended. The culture of all of the above is similar. Miniature *Angcm. distichum* displays charming dark green, distichous foliage and citrus-scented, sparkling-white short-stemmed flowers produced at regular intervals. Grow this species at higher elevations where there is a marked cool season. A day/night temperature differential of 10°C is required. Mount the plant on a piece of tree fern to ramble and eventually form a ball of foliage and flowers. This plant grows and flowers all year. [30-50% shade]

AERIDES *(Aer.)* ∀ ∥ ∩

The species name of *Aerides odorata* says it all – fragrance! This beautiful, spicy-scented orchid can be grown in a basket with chunks of coconut husk and charcoal. Try growing it on a tree trunk or on a post in bright filtered sunlight. The plant can get quite massive with age so be certain to choose a substantial support. Feed and water regularly. The waxy spurred blooms are mostly white with blotches or staining of magenta pink and are well displayed on a pendant cylindrical inflorescence. The larger the plant, the more side shoots, flowers and fragrance so it is well worthwhile raising this species to specimen size. [40% shade]

ANSELLIA *(Aslla.)* U

Known also as the Leopard Orchid, *Aslla. africana* (Africa) produces long, branched sprays of bright yellow and brown-spotted flowers at the top of sturdy pseudobulbs. Situate this drought-tolerate plant in seasonally deciduous trees or grow it in a large clay pot or in a basket. The Leopard Orchid needs bright light to flower well. [30% shade]

ARACHNIS *(Arach.)* ∀ ||

These orchids provide a beautiful garden showpiece and cut flowers as well. The spidery flower shape of *Arachnis* is seen in *Arach.* Maggie Oei (*hookerana × flos-aeris*). Obtain species and hybrids as top cuttings, as divisions (keikis) or as mericlones of selected cultivars. [Full sun]

ARANDA *(Arachnis × Vanda)* ||

Older hybrid *Aranda* Christine (*Arach. hookeriana × V.* Hilo Blue) produces many stems of starry, densely spotted magenta pink flowers. Selected cultivars of *Aranda* Noorah Alsagoff (*Arach. hookerana × V.* Dawn Nishimura) have stunning blue-violet blooms with a darker contrasting lip. [30% shade to full sun]

ASCOCENDA *(Ascda.) = (Ascocentrum × Vanda)* U

The ideal Ascocenda has compact growth, well shaped and presented, flat flowers of brilliant colour. Second or third generation Ascocendas such as *Ascda.* Princess Mikasa 'Sapphire' (Royal Sapphire × *V. coerulea*) have larger flowers but modest plant size. Avoid hybrids with too much *Vanda* influence. The plants can be large and carry disproportionately small flowers. *Ascda.* Su-Fun Beauty 'Orange Belle' AM/AOS (*V.* Bangkapi × Pralor) is indeed a beauty. The 5 cm (2½ in) diameter flowers are fluorescent orange with light red stippling. Cultivars of *Ascda.* John De Biase (*V.* Kasem's Delight × Yip Sum Wah) are quite variable; some have cherry red blooms, others blue-purple flowers with darker markings. [30-50% shade]

BLETIA

Bletia purpurea is commonly cultivated in garden beds. It will even flourish in pockets of humus on exposed, weathered coralstone. Provide some shade and extra water until the root system is well established. This orchid may seed into the surrounding area. The long, pleated leaves resemble those of *Spathoglottis* and seedling palms; take care not to weed out seedlings! Rosy pink to purple flowers are borne sequentially over many weeks during the dry season, usually in early spring. [Full sun]

BRASSAVOLA *(B.)* ∩

Lady-of-the-night, *B. nodosa*, is so-called because of its exceptional evening fragrance. Like many night-fragrant orchids, the flowers are white. Plant habit is semi-pendant making this an ideal subject for baskets, mounts and for establishment on overhanging branches. This species has been extensively hybridized with other genera of the Cattleya alliance giving rise to a veritable palette of flower colour from mauve through red and yellow. Many of these hybrids can be used in trees to create bowers of orchids in bloom. *Brassocattleya (Bc.)* Maikai *(B. nodosa* × *C. bowringiana)* bears clusters of ten or more lavender flowers. *Brassolaelia (Bl.)* Richard Mueller *(B. nododa* × *L. milleri)* has yellow flowers, lightly to heavily spotted red. The flower shape and compact plant habit of *B. nodosa* often carries through several generations. [30-50% shade]

BRASSIDIUM *(Brsdm.)* = *(Brassia* × *Oncidium)* ∪

Several lines of breeding have been used to produce superior warmth-tolerant intergeneric hybrids within the Oncidium alliance. Hybrids made with warmth-tolerant *Onc. sphacelatum, Onc. maculatum,* and *Milt. spectabilis* dominate the scene. An older hybrid, *Brsdm.* Betty N. Shiraki *(Onc. sphacelatum* × *Brs. verrucosa)* is vigorous and floriferous, an ideal plant for mounting on a post or on a tree limb. It is also suited to planting in large baskets with chunks of tree fern and charcoal. The arching sprays of 20 or more yellow, lemon-scented, spotted blooms present quite a show. [30-50% shade]

BROUGHTONIA *(Bro.)* ∪

Bro. sanguinea is a small orchid with long inflorescences. The most common flower colour is red, white (alba) forms are also cultivated. When making hybrids with it use the *Broughtonia* flower as the pollen recipient. Capsules take about 60 days to mature. *Broughtonia* has been hybridized with other members of the Cattleya alliance to give hybrids such as *Laeliocatonia (Lctna.)* Lillian Melendez *(Lc.* Caribbean Clown × *Ctna.* Keith Roth). *Broughtonia* contributes the long inflorescence habit to the hybrid. Each inflorescence will carry four or more 6 cm (2½ in) wide, sparkling pink flowers, splashed wine rose. *Cattleytonia (Ctna.)* Jet Set (Maui Maid × *Bro. sanguinea* alba) displays eight or more 5 cm (2 in) wide white flowers on long, strong inflorescences. [30-50% shade]

CATTLEYA *(C.)* ∀ ∪

Some Cattleya species and hybrids form great specimens with ease because of their branching, sympodial habit. *Cattleya skinneri* presents lovely clusters of rose purple or white flowers in spring. *Cattleya guatemalensis*, the natural hybrid of *C. skinneri* with *C. aurantiaca*, is another spring bloomer. Cultivars give a rainbow of colour ranging from white through yellow, orange, salmon and mauve. Both orchids are superb in baskets.

Not all Cattleya hybrids flower well in hot climates. Intergeneric hybrids with cool-growing *Sophronitis* are sometimes susceptible to disease. Also, flower colour may not be as bright as expected. Miniature *C. walkeriana* and hybrids such as rose-lavender-flowered *Laeliocattleya (Lc.)* Love Knot *(L. sincorana* × *C. walkeriana)* flourish and bloom well. [50-80% shade]

CAULARTHRON (syn. *Diacrium [Diacm.]*) ∪

The Nun Orchid, *Caularthron bicornutum*, is a splendid spring bloomer for mounts, trees, pots or baskets. Plants grown with sufficient light will have stout, yellow green pseudobulbs and strong inflorescences. Many floriferous and colourful hybrids such as lavender pink *Dialaeliocattleya (Dialc.)* Amethyst Snowflake *(Dial.* Snowflake × *C. amethystoglossa)*, can be effectively used in the landscape. [30-50% shade]

CYRTOPODIUM *(Cyrt.)* ☒

The Cowhorn Orchid, *Cyrt. punctatum*, flowers from April through May. This species and its relatives, *C. andersonii* and *C. paniculatum* are large plants having characteristic cylindrical pseudobulbs and terminal branched inflorescences. Large, pale inflorescence bracts are heavily barred brown, adding to the visual display. Hollowed stumps are particularly useful holders for these massive plants. Cyrtopodiums can be grouped for a mass effect. Inter-plant with succulent plants such as Aloes or smaller Agaves. Water and feed heavily during growth. Withhold water for a short time once growths mature. [30% shade – full sun]

DENDROBIUM *(Den.)*
Dendrobium anosmum ∩

This garden treasure, once known as *Den. superbum*, is a large, pendant, deciduous orchid. Water and feed heavily when it is in active growth. Stop watering once canes cease growth; buds and flowers follow. Grow it in sturdy hanging baskets or fasten it to the trunk or crotch of a rough-barked tree. Canes can grow to 2 m (6 ft). A well-grown plant will reward the owner with a sheet of fruit-scented blossoms beginning in March. The usual flower colour is mauve although bicolour and pure white forms are also cultivated. One clever way to grow this orchid is to carefully wrap three or more thin, flexible canes around a thick disk of tree fern. Fasten the canes in place with wire. Hang the mount in a brightly lit spot. When keikis form and begin to root, water and fertilize heavily to encourage quick and abundant growth. While only a few blooms can be expected from the first crop of pendant canes, the second growth and flowering will be much more substantial. [30-50% shade]

Antelope-type Dendrobiums X

Antelope Dendrobiums are so named because of their twisted horn-like petals. The sizes of these orchids and their floriferousness lend them to planting in beds around the patio. *Den. antennatum* flowers virtually year round. *Den. stratiotes* is similar having larger chartreuse-horned flowers on 1 m (3 ft) long pseudobulbs. Some handsome hybrids have been made such as *Den.* Kalagas (*stratiotes* × Lili Marlene). *Den. strebloceras* has mostly pink flowers with caramel 'horns'. These orchids and their hybrids can be prone to stem rot so it is advisable to pot them in clay pots with crock. Large pots can be arranged in groups for mass effect. Pack coconut husks around the pots to stop the top heavy plants from blowing over. [30% shade to full sun]

The pseudobulbs of *Den. discolor* (syn. *Den. undulatum* and *Den. bromfieldii*) can grow to more than 2 m (6 ft). The golden brown to yellow-green flowers come in March, lasting for months. The natural hybrid *Den. superbiens*, is the result of out-crossing with *Den. bigibbum*. This hybrid fortunately inherits the colour and plant size of the latter parent resulting in a modest-sized plant with rose purple, twisted blooms. It makes a fine cut flower. [30% shade to full sun]

The Pigeon Orchid, *Den. crumenatum*, has the curious ability to flower all at once about ten days after a substantial rain shower. (You can fool the orchid with a cooling drench of water to get the same effect.) Mount this orchid on a thick branch or tree trunk. [30-50% shade].

Phalaenanthe Dendrobiums

Den. phalaenopsis and *Den. bigibbum* are two similar and easily confused Australasian Dendrobiums. Inflorescences resemble those of Phalaenopsis therefore the name. New growths develop at the base of or from nodes on mature pseudobulbs. Leaves are leathery, sometimes deciduous, especially if the orchids are abruptly moved to too bright a location. Mature plants carry sprays of up to 20 or more flowers, often with several inflorescences per new pseudobulb. Old ones also produce sprays adding to the display. Flowers last six to eight weeks, keeping well when cut. What they lack in scent, they make up for in colour and form. Flower colours range from the purest white to the darkest red-purple. For novelty, there are striped and two-tone blooms. Hybrids of these species are some of the most rewarding orchids for tropical settings. They can, however, be frustrating in their intolerance of poor culture.

The species and their hybrids can be more difficult to grow in the humid tropics as they require a dryish rest after blooming. If conditions are not right for flowering or if the plant becomes infected with stem or root rot, keikis will form from the upper nodes of the pseudobulbs. Keiki production is sometimes the first sign that something is amiss. Be especially vigilant during the rainy season when plants are most susceptible to rot.

These orchids grow best under cover where one can control watering. Good air movement is essential; plants should not be crowded. Pots can be suspended with wire from overhead supports or hung from vertical or A-frame wire mesh panels. Bright filtered light encourages flowering whilst sparing plants from excessive heat. Heat-stressed Dendrobiums are prone to spider mite attack. Provide a minimum 50% shade. Cover the shadecloth with fibreglass sheeting to stop the rain. Pot these Dendrobiums in crock or charcoal or mount them on a treefern slab. Do not overpot. The growing season is short, about five months, so take care that the plants are watered and fertilized adequately during this time to obtain maximum growth. The frequency of fertilizing should gradually be increased from twice a month at the beginning of the growing season to once a week later on. Once the pseudobulb has ceased growing in length (the blunt top of the cane will be visible), switch from a balanced fertilizer such as 7-9-5 or 20-20-20 to a high phosphorus, blossom booster formula such as 3-12-6 or 15-30-15. Gradually reduce the frequency of watering and fertilizer application as the pseudobulbs increase in diameter. Swelling nodes mark the emergence of flower spikes. Cease fertilization and limit watering during the dry season or about ten months after the commencement of growth.

Plants may be misted during this time. Resume regular watering when a new shoot begins to grow, after about a three-month rest. If wanted, repot plants when root growth is just apparent at the base of a new shoot. Do not wait until the new growth is well on its way. Choose Dendrobiums suited to your unique growing conditions. Remove from your collection any plants which are especially prone to rot, bud drop, or keiki production in place of blossoms. There are many excellent clones that are not so fussy. To obtain as effective a selection as possible, purchase plants bred in different geographical regions such as Australia, Hawaii and Thailand. Customizing your collection will save you disappointment, save the environment by reducing use of fungicidal sprays, and will secure your financial investment. You will also have more flowers to enjoy. Especially vigorous clones can be established in trees. [50% shade]

DIACRIUM (See Caularthron)

DORITIS *(Dor.)* ∀

Dor. pulcherrima is a Phalaenopsis-like orchid with upright spikes of small flowers. Magenta, mauve, white and blue colour forms are grown. The plant quickly forms offsets at the base which should be left in place. *Doritis* blooms in summer, passing this trait on to some of its hybrids with Phalaenopsis. Grow *Doritis* in a pot or basket using a coarse potting medium. Water and fertilize all year round as these orchids have no dormant period. [50-70% shade]

DORITAENOPSIS *(Dtps.)* = *(Doritis × Phalaenopsis)* ∀

Dtps. Purple Gem *(Dor. pulcherrima × Phal. equestris)* are compact, floriferous plants. Mature plants bear many upright spikes of small colourful flowers. Flower colour ranges from white through pink and magenta depending upon the colour forms used to make the cross. Hybrids many generations removed from *Doritis* such as *Dtps.* Zuma White Puff (White Chiffon × Orglade's Puff), have very full white flowers on an arching spray. The flowers can measure over 12 cm (4¾ in) in diameter. Modern *Doritaenopsis* resemble *Phalaenopsis* and can be raised under similar growing conditions. [50-80% shade]

EPIDENDRUM *(Epi.)*

Reed-stem Epidendrums

The group includes *Epi. cinnabarinum*, *Epi. ibaguense*, *Epi. schomburgkii*, *Epi. secundum* and *Epi. radicans*. Flowers are produced sequentially in clusters at the end of a long inflorescence, each flower lasting about one week. Colours range from a rich orange-red to yellow, mauve, magenta and white.

Reed-stem Epidendrums make splendid cut flowers. *Epi. radicans* grows best in cooler upland gardens in full sun. It is a very untidy plant, its sprawling stems root freely at each node. *Epi. schomburgkii* favours the warmer gardens of the lowland tropics. It is a robust though tidy grower, producing tall erect stems without roots. This species can be grown in humus-filled garden beds or in tubs of coconut husk chunks mixed with compost. Most reed-stem Epidendrums grow easily from seed. Harvest the capsules when they begin to split and scatter the seed on shaded beds of moist compost or well-matured bagasse. Keep the bed damp. A few months later the seedlings will be large enough to handle. Select the most vigorous ones for trial. Choose the ones you prefer for patio and garden beds.

Hybrid *Epi.* Joseph Lii grows to 1 m (3 ft) tall and carries an average of 40 flowers and buds per inflorescence. Flower colour is redorange. *Epicattleya (Epc.)* Orange Star (Fireball × *Epi. cinnabarinum*) bears fewer blooms per inflorescence but they are larger, measuring about 7.5 cm (3 in) in diameter. The flowers are 'old gold' with a rusty red lip. [30% shade – full sun]

GONGORA *(Gga.)* ∩

This orchid may have short-lived flowers but vigorous specimens can produce spectacular displays of pendant racemes in succession year round. Each inflorescence measures 60 cm (24 in) or more in length. Gongoras such as brown-spotted *Gga. powellii* (sometimes confused with *Gga. maculata* or *Gga. quinquenervis*) and more richlycoloured *Gga. tricolor* are warm-growers, readily adapting to a partly shaded garden location. Because of their pendant racemes, Gongoras must be grown in open mesh baskets or be mounted on a large, vertical slab of tree fern. They can also be grown in a tree crotch. These orchids grow rapidly and appreciate regular applications of fertilizer and water. If rainfall is lacking, be certain to flush fertilized plants frequently to avoid salt buildup. [30-50% shade]

GRAMMATOPHYLLUM *(Gram.)* X

Grammatophyllums are potentially massive epiphytes that can be grown in large pots or hollowed stumps. *Gram. scriptum* bears multiple spikes of many 5 cm (2½ in) wide olive green flowers, variously stippled brown. Plants stand up to 1 m (3 ft) tall, blooming in summer after the dry season. *Gram. speciosum* is perhaps the largest, standing several metres tall at maturity. The large, 8-10 cm (3-4 in) wide flowers are attractively marked yellow and reddish brown. Grammatophyllums require high light and copious quantities of water and fertilizer when in active growth. Above all, they need space to grow. Site these magnificent orchids in a sunny location, leaving plenty of space for growth all round. [Full sun]

JEWEL ORCHIDS ∀ X

Anoectochilus formosana (Anct.)
This species presents round-leaved rosettes of reticulate-netted foliage. Cream leaf veins and midrib contrast with a reddish-green leaf colour. The whole is set off by pink leaf edging.
Ludisia (Lud.) (syn. *Haemaria (Haem.)*)
Lud. discolor forms handsome rosettes of velvety red leaves veined a golden cream. White flowers are produced on an upright spike in spring.

Both orchids are recommended for pot culture in a shadehouse or for establishment in shady garden beds, especially at higher elevations where the nights are cool. Control slugs and snails that will damage the beautiful foliage. [70-80% shade]

MILTONIA *(Milt.)* U ∀

Brazilian Miltonias such as *Milt. spectabilis, clowesii, regnellii* and their hybrids grow and flower easily in warm climates. They may, however, have fewer flowers if the night temperatures are consistently above 20°C. Grow Brazilian Miltonias on slabs of tree fern, in large, shallow baskets or in pots. Species and hybrids that have a spreading habit are unsuitable for pots. Flower colours range from ivory white through shades of yellow, orange, rich purple, pink and brown, often with attractive and contrasting patterns of spots and blotches on the petals and sepals. A cascade of similarly coloured lines or spots may decorate the lip. Plants become yellowish green when about to bloom.

N.B. Do not confuse *Miltonia* with Columbian *Miltoniopsis* which is not recommended for Caribbean gardens.

Milt. spectabilis var. *moreliana* has very dark purple flowers but only one or two blooms per inflorescence. It has a sprawling habit.
Milt. Belle Glade 'Everglades' JC/AOS (Castanea × Lanikai) is clear lemon yellow on the petals and sepals. A yellow waterfall pattern decorates the white lip. This flower has a fine shape and good substance. Expect six or more well-spaced flowers per inflorescence.
Milt. Anne Warne (*bluntii* × *spectabilis*) is prone to sprawl like its

Milt. spectabilis parent. Velvety purple *Milt.* Honolulu 'Warne's Best' HCC/AOS (Gayety × Anne Warne) grows much more compact. [40-70% shade]

MOKARA *(Mkra.)* = *(Arachnis × Ascocentrum × Vanda)* ||
Popular Mokaras combine the best traits of their parents. *Ascocentrum* reduces plant size and brightens the colour. *Vanda* contributes to flower size and flatness while the *Arachnis* contributes to flower shape and floriferousness. *Mkra.* Princess Mikasa (*Aranda* Christine × *Ascda.* Hilo Rose) is a strap-leaved orchid bearing multiple stems of five to eight flat, deep rose pink blooms. *Mkra.* Chark Kuan 'Ruby' (*Aranda* Christine × *Ascda.* Cholburi) has rounder, rich pink flowers stippled all over with ruby red spots. Typically, this cultivar carries 12 or more flowers on a plant 60 cm (2 ft) tall. Other Mokaras bear white, yellow, rich orange or red flowers. [30% shade]

ONCIDIUM *(Onc.)* U
Mule-ear type
Many *Oncidium* species and hybrids find a place in Caribbean gardens. Mule ear-types with their small pseudobulbs but very large, thick and succulent leaves resembling 'mule's ears', are recommended for growing in baskets and on mounts. Whilst they can survive in full sun they are best raised with some light shade. The Cedros Bee, *Onc. lanceanum*, has spotted foliage and many colourful flowers borne on short, branched, 40 cm (16 in) long inflorescences. The petals and sepals are spotted brown on gold, the lip is rosy pink. This species is believed to have formed a natural hybrid with *Onc. luridum, Onc. haematochilum. Onc. luridum* has a long 2.5 m (8 ft) inflorescence and small brown-spotted flowers. *Onc. haematochilum* has a modest 1 m (3 ft) long inflorescence and larger, reddish spotted flowers. *Onc.* Noel Schoenrock (Pepita de Restrepo × *lanceanum*) carries 2-3 m (6-10 ft) long, branched sprays of flowers, each with 40 or more 4-5 cm (1½-2 in) wide, heavy-substanced, solid mahogany-coloured blooms with bright yellow lips. Some cultivars have lips spotted red. *Onc. splendidum* is an attractive plant even out of bloom. The flowers have a large, bright yellow lip and reddish brown, blotched petals and sepals that may be reflexed. Hybrids such as *Onc.* Florida Gold (*splendidum × bicallosum*) are highly recommended. [30% shade]
Other types
Onc. ampliatum is a favourite orchid for mounting in trees or for growing to specimen size in baskets. Flattened and wrinkled pseudobulbs are topped with several dark green, leathery leaves. Bright

yellow flowers with reddish brown markings are produced in profusion from 1 m (3 ft) long, branched inflorescences. *Onc. sphacelatum* is a yellow-flowered species suited to large baskets or pots. It has large, ridged pseudobulbs and long, thin leaves. The 2 m (6 ft) long branched inflorescences carry as many as 100 yellow flowers barred with chestnut brown. Selected forms have compact, well-flowered inflorescences, not long, straggly ones. [30-50% shade]

Known as the Butterfly Orchid, *Onc. papilio* (syn. *Psychopsis papilio*) is treasured for its characteristic flowers and re-blooming habit. The dorsal petals and sepal are dark golden brown variously banded yellow and are held upright like antennae. Flowers last several weeks. Fallen blooms are soon replaced by others developing from the same inflorescence. The plants have leathery, spotted foliage atop squat pseudobulbs. These orchids can be a challenge to grow. Just as everything is going well, they can succumb to rot. The secret lies in keeping the growing medium fresh and freely-draining. These plants require a surprising quantity of water but detest stagnant potting material. Try growing the species on vertical slabs of tree fern. Use liquid pesticides with caution as the species is susceptible to solvent-carrier damage. [50% shade]

Equitant Oncidiums (*Tolumnia* (syn. *Oncidium*))
These are truly dainty orchids. They have fans of flattened, succulent leaves, fine roots and upright sprays of flowers ranging in colour from white through yellow, pink and purple. They require daily watering and perfect drainage. Air movement about the plants is essential to their continued good health. The best way to grow them is mounted on a ball of tree fern. Prepare the mount so that the tree fern grain is vertical. Fasten rooted seedlings or divisions to the mount with raffia or thread. Hang the plant in a bright location, gradually giving it more light until the foliage becomes slightly bronzed. *Onc. variegatum* is one of the easiest to grow. It can be grown as above or mounted on Citrus branches. [30% shade]

PAPHIOPEDILUM ∀

Paphiopedilums can be a challenge to grow if the appropriate species and hybrids are not chosen. Choose warm-growing species such as *Paph. philippinense*, a multi-floral species requiring more light than most. Three or more brownish purple flowers are carried on inflorescences, 50 cm (20 in) tall. Prized forms have much twisted petals coloured a rich mahogany brown. The potting medium should never be allowed to dry out. Pot large plants in clay pots filled with coarse compost. Provide 30-50% shade.

Paph. niveum is a charming white-flowered species from Thailand.

Normally two or more pristine white blooms are open at once. Grow this species in coarse compost with added bits of limestone, coralstone or marble. From the time buds are apparent, water it heavily for five months. It is easy to grow but needs a dry, six-week rest about six months after blooming. *Paph. niveum* is the parent and grandparent of many hybrids suited to tropical culture. The ivory white flowers of *Paph.* F.C. Puddle (Acteus × Astarte) are a joy to behold and long lasting too! [50% shade]

Paph. glaucophyllum is a lovely Javanese species which bears several flowers in succession over an extended period. The petals are white, spotted purple; the lip is deep pink. Pot this species and its hybrids in a rich, coarse compost with added limestone [15 ml (1 tbsp.) per pot]. Keep the potting medium moist except during a short rest after a new shoot has matured. Avoid getting water trapped in the crown. *Paph.* Utgard (*glaucophyllum × chamberlainianum*) is recommended as is *Paph.* Miss Faith Hanbury (*niveum × glaucophyllum*). [50% shade]

PHALAENOPSIS *(Phal.)* ∀ ∪

[see also Doritis (*Dor.*) and Doritaenopsis (*Dtps.*)]

Phalaenopsis species, hybrids and intergeneric hybrids are easy to grow but some can prove challenging to flower in the lowland tropics. Most often the problem with reluctant bloomers is high night temperature. Move them to a garden at a higher altitude or provide cooler night temperatures and these orchids will bloom. Modern hybrids have such complex parentage that it is difficult to predict behaviour. Most hybrids having flowers that are white, white with a red lip or striped on a pink or white base bloom well. Pinks such as *Phal.* Hawaiian Classic (Mahalo × Zauberrot) and *Phal.* Hakalau Spirit (Hakalau Prize × French Delight) bloom with ease. Yellow Phalaenopsis such as *Phal'.* Misty Green (Bamboo Baby × Barbara Moler) do well but other yellows such as *Phal.* Oberhausen Sun (Golden Amboin × *lueddemanniana*) may only form keikis. The only sure way to discover how a seedling will behave is to try blooming it in your garden. Before investing in expensive stem propagations, seek some assurance that the plant can flower under your growing conditions. Some growers suspect that temperature can also affect spike length and flower size. Bear this in mind when assessing flower quality. [80% shade]

Pink-flowered *Phal. schilleriana* will produce only keikis on an inflorescence if the night temperature during the bud initiation period is above 20°C. This species provides a shower of pale pink blooms if grown cooler. Raise this species in pots or baskets, mounted on a shady wall or in a tree. [70% shade]

Phal. venosa has proven useful in breeding yellows and sunset shades. When bred with white or striped flowers as in *Phal. Marquesas* (*venosa* × Zuma Red Eye), it gives yellow to greenish flowers with varying degrees of red or pink striping. Hybridized with deep pinks as in *Phal. Pago Pago* (*venosa* × Lippeglut), it can give rich sunset tones of apricot and coral pink. [80% shade].

Phalaenopsis orchids grow year-round. Water them more frequently during the dry season, less frequently during the wet season. Apply dilute fertilizer with every watering. Cool the plants by misting several times daily during hot weather. Heat-stressed orchids are prone to infestations of spider mite. Be vigilant. Also guard against crown rot which can occur when water remains in the crown of leaves. Seedlings can be potted in New Zealand sphagnum moss but larger plants should be grown in coarse material such as charcoal, crock and tree fern chunks. Position adult plants such that the crown is not vertical but slanted slightly to the horizontal, permitting any water caught in it to escape. As an experiment, try potting a few *Phalaenopsis* in mix of 40% bark, 40% charcoal and 20% Promix® in small pots. Make lots of holes in the pots for drainage and aeration. This alternative may prove worthwhile under your growing conditions.

Stake flower spikes when they are 15-25 cm (6-10 in) long. Use a thin bamboo cane or metal stake to support the inflorescence, as it grows, at approximately 15 cm (6 in) intervals, leaving the top to drape gracefully once buds become visible. Do not change the orchid position after it has been staked. [80% shade].

PHRAGMIPEDIUM *(Phrag.)* ∀

Phragmipediums need higher light than Paphiopedilums and they require abundant water all year round. Pot them in Promix®, in a blend of Promix® and bark or in coarse compost. Ensure that there is adequate drainage. There are over 20 species, most of which are found at moderate elevation in parts of Central and South America. Some such as *Phrag. longifolium* are large plants with tall, 1 m (3 ft) inflorescences. This species produces interesting, greenish yellow flowers sequentially over a long period. Others species such as *Phrag. besseae* are smaller with an inflorescence measuring about 50 cm (20 in). Flowers of this species are orange red. *Phrag.* Eric Young (*besseae* × *longifolium*) is a modest-sized plant with several brightly coloured flowers on an inflorescence 50 cm (20 in) tall. [30% shade].

PSYCHOPSIS (see *Oncidium*)

RENANTHERA *(Ren.)* ||

Renantheras are prized for their bright red flowers on tall plants. *Ren. storiei*, with its large reddish orange flowers on large branched sprays, is popular in gardens [30% shade]. *Ren. monachica* is a small plant with red-spotted, yellow flowers [50% shade]. Useful hybrids include easy to bloom *Ren.* Brookie Chandler (*storiei* × *monachica*) or *Renanopsis* Lena Rowold (*storiei* × *Vandopsis lissochiloides*) for mounting on posts and fences [30% shade]. *Renanstylis* Queen Emma (*Ren. storiei* × *Rhynchostylis gigantea*) produces dense, pendulous sprays of red purple flowers. This large plant is best suited to basket culture [50% shade]. When Renantheras are bred with Ascocendas as in *Kagawara (Kag.)*Firebird (*Ren. storiei* × *Ascda.* Red Gem), the flowers are still starry in shape but fuller and very red. *Kag.* Christie Low (*Ren.* Nancy Chandler × *Ascda* Mem. Choo Laikeun) favours the Ascocenda parent in shape; Vanda tesselation is apparent. The plant is more compact and floriferous. Pot these compact hybrids in baskets: mount taller growing specimens on posts. [30-50% shade].

SCHOMBURGKIA *(Schom.)* U

Schomburgkias are the perfect orchids to mount in trees. Hybrids with *Cattleya* and other allied genera are equally worthwhile. Choose pink or white-flowered forms of *Schom. humboldtii*, magenta pink *Schom. tibicinis*, yellow and red-flowered *Schom. thomsoniana*, or brownish red *Schom. undulata*. The flowers are at the ends of very long, sometimes branched inflorescences, some measuring over 2 m (6 ft). Flowering season is generally from March through May. Mount a blooming-size seedling or strong division on the trunk or major limbs of a suitable tree or on a palm at or below eye level. Plants will eventually form mats of pseudobulbs and grow up the tree. Alternatively, Schomburgkias can be raised in large baskets with chunks of tree fern or charcoal as potting material. Once established, Schomburgkias resent disturbance. [Full sun to 30% shade]

Cattleyas have been bred with Schomburgkias in an attempt to reduce inflorescence length while increasing flower size and improving the shape. Hybrids are not often listed for sale so it may be worthwhile raising some locally from seed. *Schombocattleya (Smbc.)* Trudy Fennell (*C. granulosa* × *Schom. thomsoniana*) has large yellow-green flowers of *Schomburgkia* form with a magenta lip. *Smbc.* Meringue (*Smbc.* Snow White × *C. walkeriana alba*) is a Cattleya-sized plant suited to pot culture and to baskets. Two to six large white flowers are borne on comparatively short inflorescences. The petals are wavy, reminiscent of the *Schomburgkia* ancestry while the lip has been broadened through the *Cattleya* influence. [30% shade].

SPATHOGLOTTIS *(Spa.)* ☒

Spathoglottis plicata is commonly grown in sunny garden beds, in drums and in large tubs. It has short, rounded pseudobulbs at or just below ground level and will thrive when planted in a mixture of compost, well-rotted manure, sand and soil. Apply additional compost yearly before the rains. Lift and divide clumps every three years, re-planting them in fresh material. Plants are variable in size and vigour, some cultivars are much taller than others. The tallest have 1 m (3 ft) inflorescences with a dozen or more flowers opening sequentially over a long period. Flower colours range from pink through magenta, yellow to white. Seed capsules are frequently formed. Collect seed from mature capsules of the most vigorous and best-flowered plants. Sow it just below the surface of a partly shaded bed of well-rotted bagasse or compost. Water well until shoots with their characteristic pleating appear. Apply dilute fertilizer and keep the bed weeded. About nine months later, select the most vigorous seedlings for planting elsewhere. The pleated foliage is quite attractive but can be damaged by liquid pesticides including those applied to control slugs. [Full sun].

Spa. unguiculata prefers a partly shaded situation where it will bloom virtually year round. It is not deciduous. Flowers are rich magenta purple, the scent resembling that of grape juice. All *Spathoglottis* are useful cut flowers; individual blooms can serve as boutonnieres. [30% shade].

TOLUMNIA (syn. *Oncidium*) see Oncidium

VANDA *(V.)* ‖ U ☒

Vandas are categorized by leaf shape. Terete leaves are the most sun-tolerant; the leaves are almost round in cross section. Well-known terete hybrid, *V.* Miss Joaquim (*hookeriana* × *teres*), is still widely grown in garden beds. Strap-leaf Vandas have open, flattened leaves. When a terete-leaved Vanda is crossed with a strap-leaved one, the result is a semi-terete Vanda. Crossing a semi-terete with a strap-leaf gives a quarter-terete. Observe the foliage of a Vanda. The shape in cross-section will decide the degree of shade needed. Round leaves and those V-shaped in cross section tolerate more light than strap-leaved types which should be provided with 40% shade.

A premier parent of many modern Vandas, *V. sanderiana*, has pairs of closely-packed, strap-like leaves and few roots. It grows best in the hot, humid tropics, blooming once a year in autumn in response to the shortening day. Large, flat flowers are well presented on erect, cylindrical inflorescences. The infrequent blooming and poor rooting system of *V. sanderiana* are considered faults by breeders. Hybrids with *V. coerulea, V. dearii,* and other species are not generally sensitive to day length and they are much more vigorously rooted. *V.* Seethong (Thananchai × Seeprai) is a vigorous, strap-leaf Vanda. It carries a cylindrical display of large, flat, sunset gold flowers measuring 10 cm (4 in) in diameter. [40% shade]. *V.* Udom Delight (Mevr. L. Velthuis alba × Rasri Gold) has semi-terete, V-shaped foliage. Eleven or more luminous, pale pink flowers measuring 10 cm (4 in) in width are borne on a 1 m (3 ft) tall plant. Markings of *V. sanderiana* are apparent on the lower sepals. *V.* Wisteria Velvet (Miss Joaquim × Thailand Beauty) has similar foliage. It bears many 9 cm (3½ in) wide, blue violet flowers with broad purple lips. Both hybrids bloom well in full sun and under 30-40% shade.

Compact Vandas can be raised in baskets. No potting material is necessary. Secure the plant in place and provide shade until the plant becomes established. *V. tesselata* and some of its hybrids are recommended for basket culture. The more vigorous, tall-growing Vandas, especially those to be grown in full sun, are best mounted on posts of wood, tree fern or clay tile. Tie the plant securely in place. Pay special attention to watering and feeding until the plants become established. Water and feed Vandas regularly for optimum flower production.

Various fungi afflict Vandas. Some cause unsightly leaf spots, others may kill a plant. Burn infected leaves and dead plants. When raising Vandas in beds, change the mulch yearly to avoid it becoming stale. Old, waterlogged mulch may provide an opportunity for fungi to enter the orchid from the lower stem and roots, eventually killing the plant.

VANDOPSIS *(Vdps.)* ‖ ∪

Vandopsis are large, vigorous plants with brightly coloured yellow flowers variously spotted brown and red. *Vandachnis (Vchns.)* Premier *(Arach. flos-aeris × Vdps. lissochiloides)* is an old favourite. They are best grown on posts and fences in full sun. *Vandopsis* has been crossed with *Vanda* to give *Opsisanda (Opsis.)* as in *Opsis.* Dusty Purple *(V. parishii × V.* Jennie Hashimoto). Flower size is increased while plant size is reduced. *Vandopsis* crossed with *Rhynchostylis (Rhy.)* as in *Opsistylis (Opst.)* Memoria Mary Natrass *(Vdps. gigantea × Rhy. gigantea)* grows easily in a large basket, even at maturity. The 10 to 15 waxy blooms are cream-coloured, boldly spotted with red markings and are borne on pendulous sprays. Some clones have flowers almost entirely red. Raise *Opsisanda* and *Opsistylis* under 40% shade, *Vandopsis* and *Vandachnis* in full sun.

ZYGOPETALUM *(Zygo.)* ∀

Zygopetalums are interesting South American orchids that are drought-resistant and tolerant of bright light. They will grow well in gardens where the nights are cool. The large, hyacinth-scented flowers of *Zygo. intermedium* sport a striking lip, lined blue-violet on white. These orchids grow very quickly and can be grown in pots with coarse compost. Provide copious water during growth and fertilize regularly. Flowering is mostly between November and February. [30% shade].

Appendix I 🌼
Orchid Nurseries and Suppliers

(Neither the author nor the publisher can assume responsibility for any transactions between the suppliers listed below and the reader.)

Coqui Nurseries Inc.
P.O. Box M
Bayamon, Puerto Rico 00620
Phalaenopsis

Critter Creek Laboratory
400 Critter Creek Road
Lincoln CA 95648
U.S.A.
Virus tests

Everglades Orchids Inc.
1101 Tabit Rd.
Belle Glade FL 33430
U.S.A.
Warmth-tolerant Cymbidiums and Oncidinae Intergenerics

Fennell Orchid Co. Inc. – The Orchid Jungle
2650 SW 27th Ave., Suite 100
Miami, FL 33133
U.S.A.
Vandaceous and miscellaneous

G & B Orchid Laboratory
2426 Cherimoya Drive
Vista
CA 92084
U.S.A.
Flasking media and supplies

H & R Nurseries Inc.
41-240 Hihimanu St.
Waimanalo
HI 96795
U.S.A.
Cattleya Alliance, Dendrobiums and miscellaneous

Hamlyn Orchids Ltd.
31 Kings House Ave.
Kingston 6
Jamaica
West Indies
Phalaenopsis, Dendrobium and Cattleya Alliance

JEM Orchids
6595 Morikami Park Rd.
Delray Beach, FL 33446
U.S.A.
Catasetum, Paphiopedilum and miscellaneous

Kultana Orchids
39/6 Nawong Pracha Patana Road
Donmaung, Bangkok 10210
Thailand
Vandaceous

Orchids by Eli
83 Dr. Cueto St.
Utuado, Puerto Rico 00761
Cattleya Alliance, Oncidiums and Dendrobiums

Orchids from Karen McFarlane
13 Howe St.
Gordonvale,
North Queensland 4865
Australia
Hard cane Dendrobiums, Phalaenopsis and Vandas

The Orchid Plantation
400 N. Fig Tree Lane
Plantation, FL 33317
U.S.A.
Phalaenopsis

R.F. Orchids, Inc.
28100 SW 182 Ave.
Homestead, FL 33030-1804
U.S.A.
Vandaceous

Udom Orchids
65 Ram Indra Road
Kannayao, Bangkapi
Bangkok 10230
Thailand
Vandaceous

Appendix II
Orchid Publications

The Orchid Review
Orchid Journal of the Royal Horticultural Society.
RHS awards and hybrid registrations appear in every issue.
Subscription price (1994): six issues per year £19.95, £10 extra for airmail.

Membership Dept.
The Royal Horticultural Society
P.O. Box 313
80, Vincent Square
London SW1P 2PE
United Kingdom

The American Orchid Society Bulletin
Monthly publication of the American Orchid Society.
Subscription price (1994): (outside the U.S.A.) twelve issues per year US$36.

A.O.S. Membership Department
6000 South Olive Avenue
West Palm Beach
Florida 33405
U.S.A.

Lindleyana
Quarterly scientific publication dedicated to technical orchidology.
Subscription price: US$24 per year.

A.O.S. Membership Department
6000 South Olive Avenue
West Palm Beach
Florida 33405
U.S.A.

Orchids Australia
Bi-monthly publication by the Australian Orchid Council Inc.
Subscription price: (outside Australia) surface mail $38.00 Australian dollars per year.

Publications Director: Don Gallagher
P.O. Box 11
Highbury, S.A. 5089
Australia

Appendix III Orchid Selections

Orchid	Plant size	Fragrance	Light	Watering	Temperature	Use
Aerides	large, vining	spicy, pleasant	40% shade	daily	warm-growing	landscape baskets
Angraecum sesquipedale	large, upright	intense, floral	dappled sunlight 30-50% shade	daily except during dormancy after blooming	intermediate to warm-growing	landscape large pots
Ansellia africana	large, upright	day fragrant	full sun 30% shade	daily, drought tolerant	warm-growing cold tolerant when dormant	landscape in trees
Arachnis species & inter-generic hybrids	large, vining	sometimes apparent	30% shade full sun	daily	warm-growing	fences, posts cut flower
Ascocenda (Vanda × Ascocentrum)	small to medium, upright	sometimes	30-50% shade	daily	intermediate to warm-growing	baskets pot plant
Bletia purpurea	medium, upright	none	full sun	weekly except when dormant	warm-growing	bedding plant cut flower

Appendix III 55

Orchid	Plant size	Fragrance	Light	Watering	Temperature	Use
Brassavola nodosa	upright	floral at night	30-50% shade	daily, drought tolerant	intermediate to warm-growing	in trees, baskets
Broughtonia sanguinea	small, compact	none	30-50% shade	weekly	warm-growing	in trees mounted, baskets
Cattleya species, hybrids and inter-generic hybrids	small to large upright	variable	50-80% shade	weekly	intermediate to warm-growing	pot plants baskets in trees cut flower
Caularthron bicornutum	medium upright	slight pineapple	30-50% shade	weekly, somewhat drought tolerant	intermediate to warm-growing	in trees baskets
Coelogyne pandurata	medium to large spreading	slight, sweet	50% shade	weekly	intermediate to warm-growing	baskets large pots
Cymbidium finlaysonianum	large pendant	none	30-50% shade	weekly	warm-growing	baskets in trees
Cyrtopodium andersonii	large upright	not noticeable	full sun 30% shade	weekly	warm-growing	landscape large pots
Dendrobium anosmum	large pendant	sweet raspberries	30% shade	daily except during dormancy	intermediate to warm-growing	in trees large baskets

Orchid	Plant size	Fragrance	Light	Watering	Temperature	Use
Dendrobium bigibbum & hybrids	small to large upright	none	50% shade	daily except during dormancy	intermediate to warm-growing	pots in trees cut flower
Dendrobium crumenatum	small upright	none	30-50% shade	daily	warm-growing	in trees
Dendrobium discolor	large upright	none	full sun	daily	warm-growing	landscape
Doritis pulcherrima	small upright	none	50-70% shade	daily	intermediate to warm-growing	pots baskets
Encyclia cordigera	medium upright	none	30-50% shade	weekly	intermediate to warm-growing	mounted in trees
Epidendrum ilense	large upright to semi-pendant	slight fishy	50-70% shade	daily	warm-growing	pot plant bedding plant landscape
Epidendrum nocturnum	medium, semi-pendant	fragrant at night	50% shade	daily	warm-growing	mounted in trees
Epidendrum schomburgkii	large upright	none	full sun	daily	warm-growing	landscape bedding plant

Appendix III 57

Orchid	Plant size	Fragrance	Light	Watering	Temperature	Use
Gongora tricolor	medium, upright, pendant inflorescence	strong	30-50% shade	daily	intermediate to warm-growing	baskets in trees
Grammatophyllum speciosum	very large upright	some	full sun 30% shade	daily	warm-growing	landscape
Lycaste cochleata	medium upright	oranges	50% shade	daily except during dormancy	intermediate to warm-growing	baskets
Miltonia spectabilis	medium upright	some	50-70% shade	daily	intermediate to warm-growing	baskets
Mormolyca ringens	small upright	some	50% shade	daily	intermediate to warm-growing	in trees mounted
Oncidium ampliatum	medium to large upright	none	30-50% shade	weekly	warm-growing	in trees baskets
Oncidium lanceanum	medium upright	none	30% shade	weekly	warm-growing	in trees mounted
Oncidium sphacelatum	medium to large upright	none	30-50% shade	weekly	intermediate to warm-growing	baskets in trees

Orchid	Plant size	Fragrance	Light	Watering	Temperature	Use
Paphiopedilum philippinense	medium upright	none	30-50% shade	weekly	warm-growing	pot plant
Phalaenopsis species & hybrids	small to medium, upright to semi-pendant	some	70-80% shade	daily	intermediate to warm-growing	pot plant in trees mounted
Renanthera species & hybrids	medium to large, upright	some	30-50% shade	daily	warm-growing	posts in trees
Rhynchostylis species & hybrids	medium to large	spicy, intense	30-50% shade	daily	warm-growing	baskets
Schomburgkia thomsoniana	medium to large, upright	some	30% shade to full sun	weekly	warm-growing	landscape in trees
Sobralia xantholeuca	large, upright	none	30-50% shade	daily	intermediate to warm-growing	landscape
Spathoglottis unguiculata	medium upright	of grapes	30-50% shade	weekly	warm-growing	bedding plant
Vanda species & inter-generic hybrids	medium to large, upright	spicy, intense	full sun to 40% shade	daily	intermediate to warm-growing	posts in baskets landscape

Glossary 🌸

Alliance – A horticultural term referring to allied genera. E.g., the Cattleya Alliance of genera such as *Cattleya, Laelia, Brassavola, Schomburgkia,* etc.

Bagasse – The fibrous remains of sugar cane after it has been crushed and the sugary sap extracted.

Bract – A modified leaf.

Clone – A plant unique from others in that it arose from one seed. All vegetative propagations of a clone carry the same name.

Community Pot – A group of seedlings raised together in the same container.

Cultivar – A plant in cultivation. All vegetative propagations of a cultivar carry the same name. Clones in cultivation can also be called cultivars.

Distichous – Leaves tightly arranged, overlapping each other, in opposite rows: not spirally arranged.

Division – Part of plant.

Flask – A transparent glass or plastic container used for the propagation of orchids from seed or as mericlones.

Genus – A group of closely allied species. By convention, the first letter is written in upper case: e.g., *Cattleya*.

Grex – All the progeny (plants) arising from a cross.

Hybrid – A cross between two different species and/or hybrid grexes. A natural hybrid can occur without human intervention, e.g. *Miltonia bluntii* (*spectabilis* × *clowesii*). An artificial hybrid results from hand pollination.

Inflorescence – An arrangement of flowers on a single main stalk (spike) of a plant.

Intergeneric hybrid – A cross between two different genera.

Keiki – A vegetative offset, identical to the parent, produced from the pseudobulb and/or inflorescence of orchids such as *Dendrobium, Epidendrum* and *Phalaenopsis*.

Mericlone – A plant resulting from the culture of a meristem.

Meristem – The undifferentiated proliferating tissue found in shoot and root tips of higher plants.

Meristem culture – Meristem tissue is aseptically removed from a plant and grown to produce a mass of undifferentiated tissue. This mass is divided, grown and further divided, the parts then being permitted to differentiate into individual plants, each genetically identical to the original tissue donor.

Monopodial – A growth pattern. A continuously growing stem.

Node – A point on the pseudobulb where a leaf emerges.

Patent – Certain orchid cultivars (clones) are registered as unique and the sole property of an individual or an organization. One may not vegetatively propagate patented orchids without permission of the patent holder. Patented orchids can be used as pollen donors or recipients without permission.

Pollinium – Plural = pollinia. Orchid pollen is borne in compact masses called pollinia.

Raceme – A flowering shoot (inflorescence) in which the growing region at the tip of the shoot continues to produce new flower buds during growth.

Seedling – A plant that has yet to bloom. A plant raised from a seed. A seedling is an unique individual, similar to but not identical to its parents.

Seeds – Reproductive units produced from the union of genetic material contained in ovules and pollen.

Species – The basic unit of biological classification. By convention, the first letter of the species name is written in lower case. A group of individuals that have many genetic and visible characteristics in common and that exchange genes through pollination. Species become separated by barriers to gene exchange such as different blooming seasons or different flower structure.

Spike – see Inflorescence.

Spray – A simple or branched inflorescence.

Sympodial – A growth pattern where shoots arise from the base of older ones.

Bibliography

BANNOCHIE, I. and LIGHT, M., *Gardening in the Caribbean*, Macmillan Publishers Ltd., Basingstoke, England (1993)

GREEN, TED, The Genus Spathoglottis in *The American Orchid Society Bulletin*, 58 (11): 1121-1125 (1989)

KENNY, JULIAN, *Native Orchids of the Eastern Caribbean*, Macmillan Publishers Ltd., Basingstoke, England (1988)

PRIDGEON, ALEC, ed., *Illustrated Encyclopedia of Orchids*, Weldon Publishing, Sydney, Australia (1992)

PRIDGEON, A.C. and TILLMAN, L., eds., *Handbook on Orchid Pests and Diseases*, American Orchid Society, West Palm Beach, Florida (1990)

Sander's List of Orchid Hybrids, 5-year Addendum 1986-1990, The Royal Horticultural Society, London (1991)

SEATON, P.T. and PRITCHARD, H.W., The Do's and Don'ts of Orchid Seed Storage in *The Orchid Review*, 98: 172-174 (1990)

SEATON, P.T. and PRITCHARD, H.W., Observations concerning the storage of orchid pollen and seed, in *The Orchid Review*, 98: 394-395 (1990)

STOUTAMIRE, WARREN P., Orchid Seeds Versus the Mails in *American Orchid Society Bulletin*, 61 (6): 578-591 (1992)

The Handbook on Orchid Nomenclature and Registration 4th ed., International Orchid Commission, c/o The Royal Horticultural Society, London (1993)

THOMPSON, P.A., *Orchids from Seed*, The Royal Botanic Garden, Kew, London (1977)

WARREN, RICHARD, New Guinea Orchids – II: The Antelope Dendrobiums in *American Orchid Society Bulletin*, 59 (3): 252-259 (1990)

WISLER, G.C., *How to Control Orchid Viruses: The Complete Guidebook*, Maupin House Publishers, Gainsville, Florida (1989)

WITHNER, CARL L., *The Cattleyas and their relatives: Volume III. Schomburgkia, Sophronitis, and Other South American Genera*, Timber Press, Portland, Oregon (1993)

YAM TIM WING, Breeding with Vanda Miss Joaquim in *American Orchid Society Bulletin*, 62 (8): 800-809 (1993)

Index

A-frame support 10, 18
Air pollution 32
Antelope-type Dendrobium 38
Aphids 26, 28
Awards 24

Bacterial Rot 30
Bacterial Spot 31
Bark chips 3
Baskets 2, 17
Bean Yellow Mosaic Virus 28
Beds 15
Black Leg 30
Black Rot 29
Brazilian Miltonias 17, 42
 Pl.12-2
Bud blasting 32
Butterfly Orchid 44

Cane fires 32
Capsule 23 Pl.6-4
Cattleya alliance 36, 51
Cedros Bee 43
Charcoal 3
CITES 32
Clay tile 3
Columbian *Miltoniopsis* 42
Containers 17
Convention on International
 Trade in Endangered Species
 32
Cowhorn Orchid 37
Crock 17
Crown rot 1, 31 Pl.13-1
Community pot 24
Compost 13, 15
Cymbidium Mosaic Virus 28

Day length 12
De-flasking 23-24
Diseases 27
Dormancy 5
Dry gardens 6
Dry Rot 30

Equitant Oncidiums 44
Ethylene 32
Evaporative cooling 8

Fan 8
Fertilizers 3, 5
Flamboyant (*Delonix*) 13
Flasking 21, 23
Flower quality 25
Fungicides 21, 31

Housing 9
Hybrid 24-25, 58

Import regulations 33
Insect growth regulators 27

Jewel orchids 42

Labels 17 Pl.6-4
Lady-of-the-night 14, 36
Leaf blotch 29
Leaf spot 29
Leaf type
 quarter-terete 48
 semi-terete 48
 strap-leaf 17, 48
 terete 11, 48
Leopard Orchid 35
Light 10-12

Index 63

Mealy bugs 27-28
Mericlone 20
Meristem 1, 20
Microclimates 7
Misting system 6, 11 Pl.14-4
Monopodial growth 1, 21
Moss 3, 4
Mounts 17, Pl.8-2
Mule ear-type Oncidium 14, 43

Natural hybrid 38, 43
New Zealand Sphagnum Moss 3
Nun Orchid 37 Pl.4-4

Odontoglossum Ringspot Virus 28
Oncidium alliance

Perlite® 4
Pests 26
Pesticides 31
Phalaenanthe Dendrobiums 39-40
Photoperiod 11
Physan-20® 31
Pigeon Orchid 14, 38
Pollinia 22 Pl.6-3
Pollination 22
Pollen storage 23
Posts 16
Potting materials 3
Potting tools 29
Promix® 4, 46
Pseudobulb 1, 3, 21

Rafts 17
Red Lava Rock 4
Reed-stem Epidendrums 15, 23, 40, 41 Pl.6-2

Relative humidity 8
Reverse osmosis 7
Rockwool 4

Sanitation 27-31
Scale insects 27-28
Seed 22
Seed storage 23
Seedlings 5, 24
Shadecloth 9, 15
Shadehouse 6, 9-10 Pl.14-2
Slugs 11, 18, 26
Snails 26
Spider mite 27-28 Pl.13-4
Stem propagation 20-21
Sterilizing tools 20, 29
Stigma 22 Pl.6-3
Storm damage 31
Stress 32
Styrofoam packing material 4
Sympodial growth 1

Terrestrial orchids 2
Thrips 26
Tree fern 4
Trees 13-15
Tri sodium phosphate 29
Twisty Top disease 27 Pl.13-2

Virus 18, 20, 26, 27-29

Water 3, 6
Watering guidelines 7
Water quality 6-7
Water storage 6
Weeds 10, 32

Plant Names Index

ANGRAECUM *(Angcm.)* 34
Angcm. distichum 34
Angcm. eburneum 34
Angcm. sesquipedale 34, 54
Angcm. Veitchii 34
AERIDES *(Aer.)* 34, 54
Aer. odorata 34
ANECTOCHILUS *(Anct.)* 42
Anct. formosana 42
ANSELLIA *(Aslla.)* 3, 35
Aslla. africana 12, 35, 54 Pl.10-1
ARACHNIS *(Arach.)* 15, 35, 43, 54
Arach. flos-aeris 16, 35, 49
Arach. hookerana 35
Arach. Maggie Oei 35 Pl.8-1
ARANDA *(Aranda)* 15, 21, 35
Aranda Christine 35, 43
Aranda Noorah Alsagoff 35
ASCOCENDA *(Ascda.)* 4, 17, 21, 35, 47, 54
Ascda. Cholburi 43
Ascda. Hilo Rose 43
Ascda. John De Biase 35
Ascda. Mem. Choo Laikeun 47
Ascda. Pralor 35
Ascda. Princess Mikasa 35
Ascda. Red Gem 47
Ascda. Royal Sapphire 35
Ascda. Su-Fun Beauty 35 Pl.7-3
Ascda. Surin Pl.9-2
Ascda. Yip Sum Wah 35
ASCOCENTRUM *(Asctm.)* 15, 35, 43, 54
BLETIA *(Bletia)* 36
Bletia purpurea 36, 54
BRASSAVOLA *(B.)* 36

B. nodosa 14, 36, 55
BRASSOCATTLEYA *(Bc.)* 36
Bc. Maikai 36
BRASSOLAELIA *(Bl.)* 36
Bl. Richard Mueller 36
BRASSIA *(Brs.)* 36
Brs. verrucosa 36
BRASSIDIUM *(Brsdm.)* 36
Brsdm. Betty N. Shiraki 36
BROUGHTONIA *(Bro.)* 36, 37
Bro. sanguinea 19, 36, 55 Pl.15-1
Bro. sanguinea alba 37
CATASETUM *(Cstm.)* 24, 31
CATTLEYA *(C.)* 1, 2, 4, 17, 20, 21, 23, 24, 29, 36, 37, 55
C. amethystoglossa 37
C. aurantiaca 37
C. bowringiana 36
C. dowiana 21
C. granulosa 47
C. guatemalensis 37 Pl.5-2
C. guttata Pl.4-2
C. skinneri 17, 37 Pl.5-4
C. walkeriana 19, 37 Pl.5-1
C. walkeriana alba 47
C. Pearl Harbor Pl.4-3
CATTLEYTONIA *(Ctna.)* 37
Ctna. Jet Set 37 Pl.5-3
Ctna. Keith Roth 37
Ctna. Maui Maid 37
CAULARTHRON (see DIACRIUM) 37
Caularthron bicornutum 14, 37, 55 Pl.4-2
COELOGYNE *(Coel.)* 17 Pl.10-4
Coel. pandurata 17, 55
CYMBIDIUM *(Cym.)* 14

Cym. canaliculatum var. *sparkesii* 14
Cym. finlaysonianum 14, 55 Pl.15-2
DIALAELIOCATTLEYA *(Dialc.)* 37
Dialc. Amethyst Snowflake 37
Dialc. Snowflake 37
CYRTOPODIUM *(Cyrt.)* 37
Cyrt. punctatum 12, 37 Pl.10-2
Cyrt. andersonii 37, 55
Cyrt. paniculatum 37
DENDROBIUM *(Den.)* 1, 4, 27, 29, 30, 32, 38
Den. anosmum 3, 38, 55 Pl.3-1
Den. antennatum 37
Den. bigibbum 38, 39, 56 Pl.3-2
Den. bromfieldii 38
Den. crumenatum 7, 11, 12, 14, 38, 56 Pl.2-2
Den. discolor 7, 11, 12, 38, 56 Pl.2-2
Den. phalaenopsis 39 Pl.3-2
Den. stratiotes 12, 38
Den. strebloceras 38
Den. superbum 38
Den. superbiens 38
Den. undulatum 38
Den. Kalagas 38 Pl.2-1
Den. Lili Marlene 38
DIACRIUM (see CAULARTHRON) 37, 40
DORITIS *(Dor.)* 40
Dor. pulcherrima 40, 56
DORITAENOPSIS *(Dtps.)* 20, 21, 45
Dtps. Orglade's Puff 40
Dtps. Purple Gem 40
Dtps. White Chiffon 40
Dtps. Zuma White Puff 40
EPICATTLEYA *(Epc.)* 41
Epc. Fireball 41
Epc. Orange Star 41
EPIDENDRUM *(Epi.)* 3, 20, 23, 40
Epi. cinnabarinum 15, 40, 41
Epi. ibaguense 40

Epi. schomburgkii 3, 15, 40, 41, 56
Epi. secundum 40
Epi. radicans 40, 41
Epi. Joseph Lii 15, 41 Pl.6-2
GONGORA *(Gga.)* 41
Gga. maculata 41
Gga. powellii 41
Gga. quinquenervis 41
Gga. tricolor 41, 57
GRAMMATOPHYLLUM *(Gram.)* 41
Gram. scriptum 41
Gram. speciosum 41, 57
HAEMARIA *(Haem.)* (see LUDISIA) 2, 42
KAGAWARA *(Kag.)* 47
Kag. Christie Low 47
Kag. Firebird 47
LAELIA *(L.)* 36
L. milleri 36
L. sincorana 37
LAELIOCATONIA *(Lctna.)* 37
Lctna. Lillian Melendez 37
LAELIOCATTLEYA *(Lc.)*
Lc. Caribbean Clown 37
Lc. Love Knot 37
LUDISIA *(Lud.)* (see HAEMARIA) 2, 42
Lud. discolor 42 Pl.11-4
MILTONIA *(Milt.)* 42
Milt. bluntii 42
Milt. clowesii 42
Milt. spectabilis 36, 42, 43, 57
Milt. spectabilis var. *moreliana* 42
Milt. regnellii 42
Milt. Anne Warne 42, 43 Pl.12-2
Milt. Belle Glade 42
Milt. Castanea 42
Milt. Gayety 43
Milt. Honolulu 43
Milt. Lanikai 42
MOKARA *(Mkra.)* 15, 21, 43
Mkra. Chark Kuan 43 Pl.7-4
Mkra. Princess Mikasa 43
MORMOLYCA *(Mlca.)* 14
Mlca. ringens 14, 57

ONCIDUM *(Onc.)* (see PHYCHOPSIS and TOLUMNIA) 1, 2, 4, 17, 20, 21, 23, 36, 43, 48
Onc. ampliatum 17, 43, 57, Pl.12-3
Onc. bicallosum 43
Onc. haematochilum 43
Onc. lanceanum 14, 43, 57
Onc. luridum 43
Onc. maculatum 36
Onc. papilio 3, 4, 31, 44 Pl.12-1
Onc. sphacelatum 3, 17, 36, 44, 57
Onc. splendidum 43 Pl.15-3
Onc. Florida Gold 43 Pl.12-4
Onc. Noel Schoenrock 43
Onc. Pepita de Restrepo 43
OPSISANDA *(Opsis.)* 49, 50
Opsis. Dusty Purple 49
OPSISTYLIS *(Opst.)* 49, 50
Opst. Memoria Mary Natrass 49
PAPHIOPEDILUM *(Paph.)* 1, 3, 17, 23, 31, 33, 44, 46
Paph. chamberlainianum 45
Paph. glaucophyllum 45
Paph. niveum 44, 45
Paph. philippinense 44, 58
Paph. Acteus 45
Paph. Astarte 45
Paph. F.C. Puddle 45 Pl.11-2
Paph. Miss Faith Hanbury 45 Pl.11-1
Paph. Utgard 45
PERISTERIA *(Pstra.)* 33
Pstra. elata 33
PHALAENOPSIS *(Phal.)* 1, 3, 4, 17, 18, 20, 21, 23, 24, 27, 31, 32, 39, 40, 45, 58
Phal. equestris 40
Phal. lueddemanniana 45
Phal. schilleriana 45
Phal. venosa 45, 46
Phal. Bamboo Baby 45
Phal. Barbara Moler 45
Phal. French Delight 45
Phal. Golden Amboin 45
Phal. Hakalau Prize 45
Phal. Hakalau Spirit 45
Phal. Hawaiian Classic 45

Phal. Lippeglut 46
Phal. Mahalo 45
Phal. Marquesas 46 Pl.1-2
Phal. Misty Green 45
Phal. Oberhausen Sun 45
Phal. Pago Pago 46
Phal. Zuma Red Eye 46
Phal. Zauberrot 45
PHRAGMIPEDIUM *(Phrag.)* 46
Phrag. besseae 46
Phrag. longifolium 46
Phrag. Eric Young 46 Pl.11-3
PSYGMORCHIS 3
Psygmorchis pusilla 3
PSYCHOPSIS (see ONCIDIUM) 44
RENANOPSIS *(Rnps.)* 47
Rnps. Lena Rowold 47
RENANSTYLIS *(Rnst.)* 47
Rnst. Queen Emma 47
RENANTHERA *(Ren.)* 20, 47, 58
Ren. imshootiana 33
Ren. monachica 47
Ren. storiei 16, 47 Pl.7-1
Ren. Brookie Chandler 47
Ren. Nancy Chandler 47
RHYNCHOSTYLIS *(Rhy.)* 47, 49, 58
Rhynchostylis gigantea 47, 49
SCHOMBOCATTLEYA *(Smbc.)* 47
Smbc. Harry Dunn Pl.4-2
Smbc. Meringue 47
Smbc. Snow White 47
Smbc. Trudy Fennell 47
SCHOMBURGKIA *(Schom.)* 47
Schom. humboldtii 7, 14, 47 Pl.4-1
Schom. thomsoniana 14, 47, 58
Schom. tibicinis 47
Schom. undulata 47
SOBRALIA *(Sob.)* 13
Sob. macrantha 13
Sob. violacea 13
Sob. xantholeuca 58
SOPHRONITIS *(S.)* 37
SPATHOGLOTTIS *(Spa.)* 36, 48
Spa. plicata 48

Plant Names Index 67

Spa. unguiculata 48, 58 Pl.6-1
TOLUMNIA (see ONCIDIUM) 44, 48
VANDA *(V.)* 1, 2, 4, 12, 15, 17, 20, 21, 29, 30, 35, 43, 48, 54, 58
V. coerulea 33, 35, 49
V. dearii 49
V. hookeriana 16, 48
V. sanderiana 48, 49
V. teres 16, 48
V. tesselata 16, 49
V. Bangkapi 35
V. Dawn Nishimura 35
V. Hilo Blue 35
V. Jennie Hashimoto 49
V. Kasem's Delight 35
V. Mevr. L. Velthuis 49
V. Miss Joaquim 16, 48, 49
V. Rasri Gold 49
V. Ruby Prince Pl.8-3
V. Seethong 49 Pl.9-1
V. Seprai 49
V. Thailand Beauty 49
V. Thanantess Pl.9-4
V. Thananchai 49
V. Udom Delight 49
V. Wisteria Velvet 49
VANDACHNIS *(Vchns.)* 50
Vchns. Premier 16, 49
VANDOPSIS *(Vdps.)* 49, 50
Vdps. gigantea 16, 49
Vdps. parishii 49
Vdps. lissochiloides 16, 47, 49
ZYGOPETALUM *(Zygo.)* 50
Zygo. intermedium 50 Pl.10-3

Animal Insight

Changing Lives through
Animal Communication
with
'The Animal Psychic'

Jackie Weaver

Books by the same author:
Celebrity Pet Talking
Animal Talking Tales

Jackie Weaver © Copyright 2010

All rights reserved

www.animalpsychic.co.uk

No parts of this publication may be reproduced, stored in a retrieval system, or transmitted in any form or by any means, electronic, mechanical, photocopying, recording or otherwise without the prior permission of the publisher.

ISBN 978-1-4782-0968-3

Psychic Book Press.com

First published 2009

Second Edition 2012

Cover Image by Personaldesigns © Copyright 2012

Artwork by Jackie Fennell – www.jacksart.co.uk

Interior artwork Jackie Fennell and K. Hobson

All rights reserved

For Bob, Sally and Rolf,
and all the people that
believed in me and helped
me on this wondrous journey.

I would like to say thank you to Jacky Fennell whom I first met as animal communication client, but who has since become a great friend and has kindly adorned this book with some of her wonderful illustrations. Also to Louise, for inspiring and encouraging me to write this, and to Sally and Jan for their wonderful help also.

"If you are a psychic and an animal lover, this is the book for you. If you are not a psychic, nor an animal lover, this is still the book for you! The stories will help you to understand how animals think and communicate and how the psychic faculty works. The underlying theme of this book, as in life, is love. Jackie Weaver loves all animals and loves her work. This is a heart warming, intriguing and most enjoyable book."

William Roache MBE

Aka Ken Barlow, Coronation Street.

"This book really goes to show how wonderful animals are and how they really can communicate with people. Jackie takes you on an amazing journey to share her insight into the animal psyche. She undoubtedly manages to change animals' lives and achieves things most people would never have dreamt possible – a real eye opener."

Jacky Newcomb

'The Angel Lady'

Contents

	page
Foreword	7
A Weight off their Minds	11
What Made Toffee Tick	13
A Bed for Life	17
All in a Heartbeat	19
Best Foot Forward	23
An Irish Comedian and his Slippery Mate	25
Jumping for Joy	27
A Lasting Impression	31
Untold Damage	32
A Cat in a Flap	27
And the Beat Goes On	29
If the Truth be Known	44
Built up Apprehension	47
Trailer Damage	49
In the Fields of Heaven	50
A Real Video Nasty	52
A Dream of a Ride	53
With the Best of Intentions	55
Total Recall	56
Completely Bamboozled	59
A Cat's Prayer	62
A Fleeting Reminder	64
Letting Go	66
Cutting Corners	68
Steady Up	69
Enlightening	72
A Seasoned Visitor	73
A Move Misunderstood	84
Secret Love	87
Some Generosity Required	88
Making Huge Strides	89
Under Pressure	91
Life's Timing	92
The More Condensed Version	94
Not on your Nelly	96
Live TV	98
In Poor Taste	100
No Space Required	102
Privacy Please	106

Jackie Weaver

A Word from the Wise	107
Attention Please	108
All at Sea	109
Before his Time	110
Private Call	112
Not the Old Stick	114
A Kennel to Dine for	117
A Jigsaw at Christmas	119
Sally, Our Angel	122
Nodding Off	125
Rebel with a Cause	126
Buzz Off	129
TV Debut	130
By Coincidence?	132
Postscript	137

Introduction

It is sometimes hard to give a job title for the work I do and impossible to say how it happens, but it does. I am often referred to as an animal behaviourist because the majority of the people that come to me are experiencing some form of behavioural problems with their animals.

It is the way I get the answers, and try to sort out what is going on, that raises some eyebrows and does take some believing. It certainly differs from the standard animal behaviourists, but everything I say and do is absolutely genuine and true, as are all the cases and wording in this book.

I have altered some names to give anonymity for the owners and their animals, but many have asked for their names to remain the same. If you want to classify me then I would come under the description of Animal Communicator but people so often refer to me as 'The Animal Psychic' the name has stuck!

As the majority of people have no idea what either of these terms mean or how it works, it is my hope that this book will give you a clearer understanding, and the amazing things it can achieve.

I am in my forties, a former veterinary nurse and married to ex-flat jockey Bob Weaver, who is now a horse dentist. We live in a gorgeous little hamlet in South Shropshire, England, with our little rescue Collie, Sally.

For many years I held the horses for Bob for their dental work, but this came to a stop when I was diagnosed in 2005 with cancer - non Hodgkin's lymphoma, and not just one type of it but two! (I never have been one to do things by half!)

By the time I was diagnosed, I was classed as stage four, which means it had invaded most of my organs. To say I had an uphill battle was an understatement. It had spread to my liver, spleen and bones and I was extremely ill by the time they diagnosed me. I was sent to Cheltenham General Hospital and given the strongest amount of chemotherapy my body could take and, amazingly, after a few weeks, I started to feel slightly better and convinced them to let me go home. Chemotherapy is not the easiest treatment to take, but it is not nearly as bad as I thought it would be. After three treatments, my liver scanned clear, this was a huge step forward and I truly believed that I would be fine and, after another five lots of chemo, I was in remission.

It was a difficult time, but definitely not all doom and gloom. At the point of losing my hair, my friend Amanda suggested we should all shave our heads! Talk about turning a negative into a positive! With the local press in attendance, Amanda, Bob and I, met at the hairdressers, and did the deed.

The Shropshire Advertiser put a 'before and after' picture of me on the front page, with the cracking title, "Hair Today, Gone Tomorrow!" Donations came in from everywhere, and we raised £3500 for the cancer unit! I feel that the love, laughter and positive thinking really helped pull me through.

When they did finally get me into remission, I asked my consultant if he had thought it would leave my liver etc. as well as it had. His reply was,

"No, Jackie, we only gave you four weeks!" Quickly followed with, "You should do the lottery; you have no idea how lucky you are!" I laughed, and thanked him with all my heart for saving my life. That conversation has played so many times in my head, I am truly grateful and now realise I was saved for a reason.

For many years Bob and I had recommended an Animal Communicator, (Julie Dicker, who has sadly passed away) to our dental clients that were having problems with their horses. We did get many a strange look, but the people that sought help, got it, and were very pleased they had. When I met another communicator who came to talk with our animals, much to my surprise, she told me she knew I could do this too. She showed me how it worked and I felt like someone that has been shown the keys on a piano, and then was able to sit down and play 'The Moonlight Sonata', I feel so blessed! To be able to give help, love and healing mirrors the three elements that pulled me through, and certainly transformed my life.

Amazingly, for the medical profession, this psychic gift has been recognised and recorded in writing after one of many of my hospital visits. I even talked with one of the other doctor's secretary's dogs, so I sent a note to my consultant to say, "Thanks, I have done the lottery and won it! As you know, it isn't money, but I wouldn't swap this for a million pounds!" And, I seriously mean that. It's so true to say 'there are some things money can't buy'. Once someone has opened your eyes, so to speak, you start to understand that there is so much more out there than you ever could have imagined. We are most certainly always loved, protected and guided from afar. These revelations I have now become used to, I had no idea that we have guides and guardian angels; whether they are of human or animal spirit, they are there to watch over you and help you. A classic example of this is when you are driving, coming to a bend in the road, you are suddenly aware that there will be a car taking it rather wider than they should be. You instinctively keep over as far as possible; that was a guide protecting you.

Animals are wonderful to work with as they are non-judgemental and are honest (most of the time) and are also extremely forgiving, loyal and intuitive. I rely on animals to be honest with me and I, in turn, treat them with the honesty that they and their owners deserve. I make absolutely nothing up, I just pass on what they tell me, they don't gossip like people can and often give wonderful advice for their owners too!

Most people recognise that hypnotism does exist and is often used successfully in the form of hypnotherapy. My work also goes into the animal's subconscious; therefore, the animal can do as it pleases whilst we are chatting. During a conversation, I manage to find out where their fears (I say fear, as most problems, as with humans are based on fear: fear of rejection, fear of being hit, etc.) have come from. Things can often be buried deep in the subconscious but still affect their daily lives.

I get it out in the open, and rationally explain things to try to allay their fear. I then get them to give me a word, or words (which I call a 'bonding key') for the owner to say at the relevant time. This bonding key is designed to prompt their minds to remember the explanations and reassurance I have given them during our communication.

Sometimes I work in the presence of an animal but this is not a necessity and most of my work is done at a distance, as bizarre as that may sound. It is wonderful because I get to sit in my lovely warm office, chatting to animals from all areas of Britain and abroad. There is nothing weird or spooky about this. Many people are clairvoyant/psychic which literally means 'clear seeing' and sensitive to things beyond the everyday range of perception. .

Clairvoyance and psychic work involves using a different part of your brain (this is sometimes activated by trauma or near death experiences etc.) and, for me, it is simply having a 'chat' with your animal and telling you what they say. Distant communication with the animals is achieved by tuning in to them telepathically by looking at a photo (although I can to do it by description only, but a photo is far more personal). I only ask for their name, age, and how long the owner has had them. I introduce myself to the animal who then starts giving me information in the forms of vision (like a video replay) words and sounds, physical pain and emotions. I know that maybe this will sound impossible when you read it, but if you have done this first hand, you will know it is totally possible, and I hope by the end of this book you will realise that too.

I spend my life saying, "You just couldn't make it up," and this book, I hope, will show you that. For the people that are reading this and have had communications done with an animal and experienced the beauty of it firsthand, I do hope you enjoy reading my cases and their results.

My original website was called 'animal-insight' for two reasons; firstly, because I can 'see' the pictures in my head whilst talking to an animal and, secondly, I get such an insight of how animals think and why they often behave as they do.

When I work, I do this in a three-way conversation, usually on the phone. I always say, "Remember, if he can hear me, he can hear you," and often animals do reply or comment on what their owner has just said.

When working to solve a problem, I need to get information 'straight from the horse's mouth', so to speak, and after reading this book I hope it will have shown you, that in so many cases their logic is not the same as ours. I often tell owners to look on this like a talk with a child. We can ask them their likes, dislikes, experiences and about any physical problems they may have. It turns into a wonderful personal experience, and sometimes you will be amazed at the smallest detail of something you do so kindly that they notice and appreciate.

Animals seek love, loyalty, happiness and fulfilment, just as we humans do. I am so lucky that they can share it with me, so I can share it with you. Once an animal has been given the opportunity to have a voice it is often noticeable that they know they have been 'talking'. People are frequently amazed at what their animals have told them, through me. They find it so much more meaningful being able to talk to their animals with the clear knowledge that; if they can recall it to me, whom they have never met, then their animals can certainly do understand what is said to them.

Throughout this book I have scattered my 'Animal Titbits'. These are the answers that animals gave to my various questions; I couldn't let them go by without a mention. They gave me such pleasure with their wit and wisdom. I hope they do the same for you.

Animal Insight

Weight off their Minds

My normal opening conversation to someone asking for a communication is a quick 'hello' and so forth, followed by, 'I only need to know the animal's name, age, sex and how long you have owned them.' (I do this with good reason because, if someone is unsure or even sceptical, when I start to give them information, this stops any doubts about them having 'fed' me that information already.) So when Cybil, Polly's owner, arrived at my house for a reading, I was a bit flummoxed, as during the dispensing of coffee, she uttered,

"She will fib to you!" I think I looked a bit bemused and taken aback, but explained to her that some animals can fib although it's a rare occurrence, and checked that she still wanted to go ahead, which fortunately she did. Cybil came accompanied by her friend who had been to me before, so then handed me a photo of Polly, this lovely five year old, Flat Coat Retriever cross, who was jet black, with ears pricked in expectation.

We must all have laughed for an hour non-stop; her dog was so on-the-ball with such a wicked sense of humour. If she had been a child in the classroom, she would be the one to sit beside to make the time pass and learning seem less dull! Anyone reading this who knows about Flat Coat Retrievers or who has ever met one, will know that they are in a league of their own when it comes to exuberance and amusing qualities. You can imagine how the conversation went with this particular Retriever!

As I tried to tune in to Polly she gave me a picture of someone wearing a variety of outfits in the oddest of colour combinations you could imagine. I looked across at Cybil but she was dressed in jeans and a blue jumper, so nothing out of the ordinary. I got Polly to repeat the picture and then I had to say it as it was, albeit as carefully as I could! I waffled something to the effect of,

"Would you say that you have been known to wear clothes that really didn't match, or even clashed, so much so that people might even comment on it?" This was met with hoots of laughter,

"Yeah, I don't care what I wear with what, the first thing that comes out the drawer will do!" This was succinctly confirmed by Polly with the remark,

"See, told you I didn't fib!" causing much laughter all round. I asked her about her health, and she said she had no problems, but then added,

"I am very good at the vets you know!" I passed this on, and Cybil quickly interjected with,

11

"Ha, told you she would fib!" I asked her if she really thought that Polly was that far off the mark. Cybil then explained that actually, on the whole, Polly is good but that there is one part that she really isn't good about. Well, in for a penny, in for a pound I thought; let's find out the real truth here!

Polly immediately obliged by giving me a picture of her struggling, which to me was like someone was trying to put her onto something. She was straining on her leash and having no intention of obliging. Using my logical brain I thought: was I looking at the surgery table? I suggested this, and Cybil said,

"Well you are nearly right, but it's the weighing scales so you were very close!" (These scales are usually a slightly raised platform with a digital read-out) As Cybil was trying to tell me her thoughts about why Polly didn't like it (perhaps it was slippery) I suggested that we should really ask Polly herself what the real reason for her objection was. And this was her reply,

"If I get weighed, and the truth is known, I might get less to eat!" I couldn't disagree with that answer, or the logic behind it, and really neither could Cybil. This also made her realise that why, even in the house when she has tried to use her own scales, Polly would make it impossible to pick her up by doing the impression of a turtle on its back frantically waving its legs in the air. She'd do absolutely anything to make sure getting lifted upon them was not an option! Polly said that she wasn't overweight, and on checking that fact, it turned out she wasn't. Polly, obviously listening intently, followed this up with, "So why do you want to keep weighing me?" This point was taken on board so we then assured her that there would be no more weighing, and if the need ever arose, the vets would have to do the old fashioned thing, and hazard an educated guess!

I later found out from her friend who had accompanied her, that Cybil had been slightly worried about what her dog would say, so hence the instant, "She will fib," remark. This didn't happen and she really enjoyed the chat, nothing personal or embarrassing was revealed, animals are certainly *not*

like that. I never hear, "Mum was kissing the postman!" or anything that would cause offence.

This is why I just love working with the animals, as they will do their utmost to make their owners feel good, show such loyalty, but obviously understand fashion more than we realise!

What made Toffee Tick

I cannot take credit for the above title. It had been used in an advertisement by the Riding for the Disabled (RDA) to highlight a fundraising evening I was doing for them. Their manager Celia Baker, who was also in charge of organising the event, thought it up. This is the story of how I came to be involved in this evening.

Many people are sceptical about my work, so I was amazed when, during a phone call regarding horses' teeth, I was asked for my help by Celia! Celia is the manager of the RDA Centre but is also affiliated with the adjoining Equine College, and, in a respectful way, I would describe her as 'old school'. Everything must be done properly, and when she asks for something to be done, she expects it to be done today, not tomorrow. This is how life used to be, and to be honest, most people over the age of 30 would wish it could go back to that! Put it this way, if Celia was a matron of a ward it would run like clockwork, be sociable, but you'd know where you stood too!

Once we had sorted out how many horses needed their teeth doing, she said,

"You're the talk of the county, you know!" which rather took me aback. She carried on to say that she had heard many stories about me and my work and had been finally convinced by her friend, whose horse I had had a casual chat with whilst Bob was working on its mouth. To be honest I had forgotten how the conversation went, but it was quickly relayed back to me, and it made me smile. The owner concerned listened to the various things that her rather cheeky lad, Folly, an ex-racehorse had told me. She had been polite enough to nod here and there when appropriate. When he said he was really bothered about the flies that kept going in his ears and biting them, she laughingly said,

"Well, he hates me putting the cream in them, so unless you can convince him otherwise, there is not a lot I can do about it!"

So into negotiation I went: I put it to him that he can't complain if he won't accept help, so how would he like to do this? He said that although he didn't like it, he now realised what she was doing with the cream, but, more to the point, it held him up from going out in the field! He volunteered, that if she could do it quickly, he would try and put up with it. I did my usual thing of asking him for a 'bonding key' and his was, "Two minutes Folly, just two minutes!" I thanked him for our chat, and his dental work completed, Bob and I left the yard.

The next day, Folly's still rather sceptical owner got out the tub of fly cream and stood outside his stable door. So, with admittedly some lack of sincerity, she said the agreed words and was stunned when Folly put his head forward and down, and stayed dead still. As fast as she could muster, she dipped her fingers in and managed to put a layer of cream onto the inside of each ear. Then in her own words she stood back and thought, 'Oh my Lord!' She then obligingly put Folly out into his field - after all he had given her his two minutes - she shut the gate, rushed to the house and phoned Celia, starting with the words, 'You'll never believe this...!'

I was really chuffed with this result and appreciated Celia giving me the update, and then asked what she wanted me to do for her. As usual I asked her not to give me too much information about the problem, and she asked me when I could do it. I suggested,

"This afternoon if you want?"

"Oh thanks," she replied, and overheard her say to someone in the background, "Oh great! Jackie's going to come over this afternoon." I interrupted her and said,

"No, I'm not coming over, I'll do it over the phone, could I call you back in about an hour?" Celia stuttered slightly and said,

"But you can't see the pony, how are you going to do that?" I said not to worry, found out his details, his name, which was Toffee, his age and his description, and I said we would speak later.

I tuned in with Toffee, a stocky 15 hand bay horse, a good Irish Cob type being of the right height and build to be able to carry children and adults alike. I asked Toffee to tell/show me something to validate I was talking to him. He gave me a few things, but as there are many horses at the centre, I needed something more. He then gave me a picture of him standing with something in front of his feet, together with the strong sense of not being willing to go over it. Celia was trying to work out what this was, and I heard the girls behind her confirm that he was fine about crossing the long narrow drain at the back doors. I overhead them and said that it was not as

Animal Insight

wide as a drain, in fact it was something like a hosepipe or an electric tape. With that she exclaimed:

"Gosh Jackie, you are a witch!" I roared with laughter and said that that would be her description but not mine, and that maybe she should not call me that to other people! But actually she has introduced me several times as 'Jackie the Witch', but from her I take it as a term of endearment!

Anyway, Celia explained that at the weekend the horses had trashed the electric tapes attached to posts that were supposed to be keeping them separated into certain groups. They had all gone off and had found the grass field that was, until then, undisturbed, as it was to be for their winter hay crop. Now, when I say all the horses, it was all of them except Toffee who was left all on his own, standing behind the tape that was left on the ground. Although these electrified tapes do give a low-grade zap, Toffee was too scared to try and even jump over it!

We chatted to him and covered various things, but whatever Celia was trying to get at he was not bringing to the table, so to speak. So I asked her to give me a bit of guidance to get the issue out into the open. She said to ask him about the school - they have a lovely indoor, sanded area that the horses are able to take the disabled children and adults around. They are led by the army of wonderful volunteers under the strict guidance and directions of Celia herself.

I asked Toffee to show me what he did in the school and he showed me a vivid picture of him taking off like a scalded cat, and that was exactly it. But it only ever happened at one place in the school. He would walk round the school but when he got to a certain area; he would just turn tail, dragging his handlers with him. He was so strong and determined; they were at a loss as to how to stop this happening and, more to the point, why. I sensed that this reaction was to do with something outside the school rather than within it, so I asked if Celia could get round the back to exactly behind the area that was spooking him, so off she went with a mobile phone in hand.

I asked Toffee to help us by showing me what it was that he was so frightened of. He repeatedly gave me a sound, no pictures, just a tick, tick, tick sound which I passed over to Celia. She looked about to see if maybe a branch was rubbing on the roof or something, but nothing, but I insisted and asked: "What goes tick, tick, tick?"

"Oh no, no it couldn't be!" was her astounded reply.

"What is it?" I asked.

"It's the electric fence power unit, but he can't hear it, it's through a concrete wall at least a foot thick!"

"Oh yes he can - I can hear it from him, and I am 25 miles away!" When she got over the shock and gathered her thoughts together, she asked if we thought we could do anything about it, and I said it was worth a try, but as usual I didn't promise anything.

Often during a chat, an animal shows things for a reason. One of his first pictures was the unwillingness to step over something. We now realised why he would not go over the electric tapes; there was obviously a serious fear here but he needed to be able to go down this side of the school where there was no tape, just a machine through a foot of concrete that could not possibly hurt him. We asked Toffee what could we do to assure him that he would come to no harm; what would he like us to do?

He asked if it was possible for it to be switched off whilst he was in the school, and Celia thought that this would be fine, no problem at all, but Toffee insisted on the belt and braces approach and also insisted on a sign to go on his stable door in big letters saying, 'Have you switched the electric off?'

We met him on his terms and asked what bonding key words could we give him, and it was very simply to walk him past and say, 'It's ok, Toffee.'

Although he did have some other insecurities we left it at that to see if we could at least get over this pressing issue. With his stable door now adorned with the sign and the electric unit switched off, Celia instructed someone to lead him past. Off they went, down the side that he is not worried about and then as he approached the 'tick, tick' area he yanked back from his leader and proceeded to run away. Celia suddenly realised that she had forgotten about the words he wanted, which prompted her to shout quickly,

"It's ok, Toffee!" And amazingly he pulled up from his frantic trot. Celia then took him herself and said the words at the appropriate time and place, and although he was very tense he walked on. This was a huge step forward, so she tried again and again, and, to her amazement, each time he got better and better. Soon it was the turn of a rider to try. Firstly they led him and he went past, and in no time they were able to ride him freely on a loose rein.

This change was remarkable, but as there are so many volunteers, the number of times there was sudden panic as someone attempted to take him down the previously 'no go' side of the school, that it led to this story being repeated on many occasions.

I often explain my work as getting into the subconscious to change things, and hope that the animal's conscious will allow itself to be overridden now that the logic/fear has been explained and understood, as with people trying to stop a habit, sometimes it works and sometimes it doesn't. Fortunately for Toffee it worked.

I did mention that Toffee had other issues; at the end of the day animals are individuals just like us, and they are suited to differing types of work the same as we are. We had explained and sorted out his worries about the electric fence unit, but in himself, he felt it was too much responsibility to carry these disabled children and adults. They had little or no balance, and although well supported by leaders, he found it very disconcerting. Unfortunately, he showed this by using his weight to barge people out of the way when he got worried; really not ideal in this environment. He was eventually sold and has now got a very good home as a happy hacker, and there is one thing for certain - he will never break out of any electrically taped paddocks!

A Bed for Life

Cheska, a beautiful roan Spaniel, whose eyes were showing the depth of her anxiety, had been lucky enough to be re-homed to a very loving and experienced dog owner called Annie. After a year of trying to sort out difficulties with Cheska, Annie really was at her wits end. Cheska was not being bad, but Annie could see the dog's distress and could not get through to her and soothe her feelings. To compound the situation, Annie kept seeing visions but didn't quite understand why or where they were coming from. (This is a typical example of someone who didn't recognise their own clairvoyance and I didn't really understand what it was until I was told too.) They were of Cheska but in a former home – she saw horrible images of brutality and neglect that sadly turned out to be real. During the chat, Cheska relayed them to me too, confirming their reality, so we now knew the extent of the damage done.

Unfortunately, this is not an isolated story; some breeding bitches like Cheska, do get punished when they fail to produce a litter. These poor dogs are really just a financial commodity where love and respect is not part of the equation. Appallingly, one of Cheska's owner's deranged reasons for beating her was for dirtying in her kennel - but then if you don't let a dog out for days on end, which they didn't, this inevitably will be the result. So Cheska now had a total fear of doing what is a natural occurrence.

Having been so badly beaten, mainly to the head area, this left her very defensive - but with such a desire to be stroked too, it broke my heart to feel her pain. We talked it through and I asked her how she would like the reassurance she needed, i.e. to know it would be a safe stroke coming her way. She wanted Annie to instruct people to touch her under the chin first, this way she would know that they understood her fear and then she could trust them.

Another misunderstanding was traffic, which to a dog that has been kennel-bound is quite understandable, so I asked her to explain the fear more precisely. She showed me an image of her shying away and said that she was frightened of cars hitting her, and gave me a most fearful heart pounding in my chest. Logically thinking, how would she know that there are roads for the cars, and pavements for us? So Annie and Cheska went off to do traffic watching, and Cheska now realises that there are rules for cars and that she is not in any way unsafe when walking on a pavement.

All the baggage that these poor animals carry weigh them down so much that they get in that catch 22 situation. They are so scared of making a mistake that they overreact in certain situations and then they make a mistake. I explained that we all make mistakes too, we humans certainly do and quite often too – also, we humans often have husbands, and they are always making mistakes!

Many people do not give me an update on their animal's progress after a reading, but Annie wrote to me within a couple of weeks. I was so touched because she said that the difference in Cheska was 'immediate and amazing'. Apparently she was so much happier and more settled, and had started to relax in people's company without that terrible fear.

During our next chat, Cheska had described the new bed that she really wanted, just to make her feel totally at home. Annie said she would go out that weekend and buy her one. Annie sent me another letter, with photo enclosed, showing how Cheska was so pleased with the subsequent new bed, and told me how she had sat down in it before Annie had even decided the proper place for it. I was so delighted for them both.

I had another chat to Cheska about six months later, and she truly is a changed dog. She was so chatty and very secure with Annie and her family, and simply loving life. The other thing to note is that the horrid visions that Annie was picking up from Cheska have never been shown since.

This was another very emotional case, but we got there and I will be keeping in touch with her owner. Incidentally, Annie found me through an article written about me in a paper about a year previously. For the headline, they had actually called me 'Mrs Doolittle' which had caught her eye. It was a large article explaining how I work and how I came to do it, in the hope that it would inspire others, that sometimes when the chips are really down, that miracles can happen, so never give up hope. She had cut it out and kept it, even though at the time she didn't even own a dog! I truly think that hand of fate was working again.

All in a Heartbeat

Sid was a ten year old Labrador cross, who was an absolute dream to talk to. He was not a very large Labrador, but jet black with a dash of white on his chest and with bright amber eyes that look deep into you. His owner, Sal, had heard of me, and, although I had not done any work for her personally, had recommended me on various occasions. Through her kindness, this had led to other owners and their pets getting help.

She had a couple of worries about Sid so we decided to have a chat and see exactly what was going on. This would give him the chance to say what he wanted, and didn't he just do so! He was just so switched on and very much on the same wavelength as his owner, very sweet and very appreciative of his life with her.

At various points throughout the conversation, he took my breath away, quite literally, and when asked what was causing this he told me about his heart. I am always wary of potentially serious medical indications that are passed over to me, as I don't want to alarm or worry their owner, and I spend my life saying, "I do not diagnose, I just say what I am given or told by the animal themselves." Sal told me that she knew he had a slight heart murmur, but as Sid indicated this to me several times, I suggested that maybe it should be checked again. He also had a growth under his tail, and although not terribly large at that moment, it was in an awkward place and looked as if it could present a real problem in the not too distant future.

A couple of weeks later, Sal sent me through an update, saying that she was now rather worried about this lump, so had been to the vet's surgery to get it checked out. The vet thought that the lump had increased in size and if it was to enlarge much more, this could create another problem. Due to its unfortunate positioning, a lack of skin in that area might make it hard to stitch it back together. Whilst there, Sal mentioned Sid's heart and asked if the vet could check it again for her. He put his stethoscope on Sid's chest, listened acutely before concluding that he thought the murmur basically sounded the same as it had before. That day Sal's luck was in; the vet had a new scanning machine on trial, and offered to check Sid's heart out for free. It turned out Sid was right; there was actually more of a problem than first thought. Although this was not life threatening, it meant that the anaesthetic for the lump removal would have to be very carefully administered, and monitored throughout the procedure. He was also prescribed a course of drugs prior to his operation to help improve his heart function.

Sal was so worried but felt in her heart she was doing the right thing. She decided to let Sid have his say, so then she would know for sure. He was in complete agreement with her; he felt that the operation should go ahead and now, whilst they still had the chance to stitch it together. He was most relieved that they were now fully aware of the extent of his heart condition, and said he would be very brave and calm about the whole thing. Sal immediately phoned the vet practice and booked him in for the following Monday.

That Monday seemed never ending for her, but at six o'clock, she let me know that he was home, safe and sound, wrapped in a blanket, snoozing! I sent him healing energy as he said it was throbbing a bit but he was feeling fine, and the vets had been ever so kind as they really liked him.

Within a week, Sid was completely recovered and very bouncy, to the extent that the vet even remarked on how amazingly well he was. To top that, a friend visiting a few weeks later even questioned whether it was actually Sid! He is feeling so much more comfortable now and I hope it stays that way for many a year to come.

In addition, after ten years of being terrified of fireworks, that November Sal realised that I had also been able to allay his fears about them. His fear was that they could come into the house and hurt him, so I explained why they couldn't. I pointed out that they are just in the sky, and that there are windows and doors; so nothing uninvited can come into your house. He gave me words for his bonding key which was, 'It's okay, they can't come in,' so Sal duly used them and with that he settled back down and relaxed in his bed.

I don't tend to keep in touch with many owners, but Sal is one of these people that differ. She is so caring and tries selflessly to help others, and has been a link to quite a few of the cases that I have done, namely 'Completely Bamboozled' that you will read further on. It also turns out that she rather enjoys writing herself, and has very kindly helped me with this book by being my unofficial proof reader spotting my numerous mistakes for me.

During the Christmas period, I was passing close to where she lives, so popped in to meet her and the adorable Sid. True to his picture he really does have the most beautiful eyes that just make your heart melt. He is actually quite shy of new people, so he weighed me up, and then came over to greet me. I asked him if he knew who I was and he said,

"Yes, you're the lady on the phone!" Technically he was correct, Sal and I both laughed; we would never have thought of it like that! He looked so well and spent his time dodging the new puppy.

In life there are some animals that are just unique and get right into your heart; well, that's Sid in a nutshell.

"I would still be able to hear with them on!"

A confused, but hilarious answer from a three year old trotter being asked what he thought of his blinkers!

"You made me a promise, and it was true."

Such a personal statement made to me by a horse that had her barriers up and didn't want to know people, but trusted me enough to try, and is now enjoying being loved again.

"Do you know they are a girl and boy sheep, but they don't have babies you know, funny that!"

A very observant line from a gelding talking about his two field companions, not realising that the boy had actually had the same operation as himself.

"I would be better with five legs."

From a horse that was a bit of a careless jumper and often landed on his nose.

Animal Insight

Best Foot Forward

I had a most entertaining afternoon at a local secondary school that I had been invited to; they had their own equine study group and thought that what I do would be an interesting concept to show the pupils, and hopefully enlighten them.

If you thought I wasn't nervous, you couldn't be further from the truth. Adults can be sceptical, but a group of teenagers?! I thought it might be a struggle, but fortunately this invitation came because one of the group was a dog walker for someone whom I had done work for. He had seen the difference that communication can make to an animal's life and behaviour when problems had arisen.

Surrounded by many eyes fixed on me, they gave the impression that they thought I was going to be someone very strange or magically mysterious! I quickly explained how I got into animal communication and how it worked, and that it is nothing scary, it's just like having a conversation with another person. One of the teachers produced a photograph of the family's pony. This was the animal voted for by the group, and incidentally, the teacher's daughter was one of the pupils in attendance too.

I set about introducing myself to this pony, a small welsh mare well into her 20's that was fortunate enough to have had the same home for most of her life.

Rather surprisingly, during the introduction, another teacher entered the room with a brown and white Springer Spaniel, who had obviously not quite grasped the concept of what a lead is for. The word *lead* really gives it away, but I think he would have called it a pull! Undeterred and oblivious to the disruption caused, she proceeded to put him a wire dog pen under her desk.

Well, as much as I shut my eyes to try and concentrate on the pony, this dog puffed, panted and generally moaned. Just as I was thinking to myself: *this is really not helping me*, she suddenly said,

"Is he bothering you? Shall I take him back to the car?" With much relief I replied,

"If you wouldn't mind." She bent under the desk, opened his cage and clipped his lead back on him. He then proceeded (at his usual hasty speed) across the classroom towards the door, at which point I suddenly heard, clear as a bell: "Feet! Feet! Feet!"

"Hang on," I shouted over. "Is he having a problem with his feet?"

"Oh, yes," she replied, complete with a flabbergasted expression.

"Better bring him back then and I shall have a word," I suggested.

With apologies to the pony, I explained that this dog was determined to have his say whatever, and promised to come back to her later.

As usual I set about striking up a conversation with the dog. I never go straight to the problem/issue because you wouldn't do that with a person you didn't know, would you? It would be too rude. Now bearing in mind that he was a one-year-old Springer Spaniel, he thought rules would only apply to him when he got to about five! He was finding life and all that he shouldn't do, totally hilarious, which was great entertainment for the pupils. I then asked him what was wrong with his feet; he showed me a picture of lines pointing upwards, about 3 cm long. I described the picture to the pupils and we decided it was probably stubble; the remnants of a cut down corn field.

"Ah," said his owner, "Are they pricking his feet?"

"I don't know," was my reply. "That's your assumption, but let's ask him."

He disagreed and said that the stubble didn't hurt his feet, but he showed me the action of something coming out of this corn stubble and into his feet. He repeated it several times just to make sure I saw it, but I was flummoxed and admitted to the owner that I had not got a clue what he was talking about, and maybe she knew? She was none the wiser either, but said although she had been to the vets twice about the problem she would take him back again. I suggested that she asked if there was there anything that can come out of the corn and into his feet? I said it was probably best that my communication with the dog not be mentioned, so to hear what the vet suggested himself.

The next day she put the burning question to the vet, to which he replied,

"Oh yes, harvest mites."

She quickly replied, without thinking,

"Oh, so that's what he was telling Jackie about!" Fortunately the vet and I know each other quite well, so he just nodded with acknowledgement, but her comment was also overheard by the nurses who were in fits of laughter, but also amazed at the accuracy of what I had been able to explain from the dog's descriptive pictures. The Spaniel got the relevant treatment and the problem was solved.

Now back to the classroom.

Following on from my chat with the Spaniel, I had really got the students' attention and so I went back to my talk with the pony, who turned out to be so sweet, loyal and loving. At various intervals, she insisted on telling me loving things to pass on to her owner, the teacher, who was struggling not to shed tears. She was amazed and so grateful for all the information I had passed onto her.

As a last thing, I asked the pony if she had any helpful advice for his rider, the teacher's daughter. Most times you would expect to be shown how they are ridden/looked after, but the pony suggested that she should get her bedroom blinds fixed, as they really were such a source of annoyance to her. Her mother looked blankly at me, and then looked over to her daughter whose face was a picture as she admitted that,

"Yes, okay, they don't work properly and they never hang straight!" I found the whole reaction hilarious, but it goes to prove that they know a lot more about you than you realise.

I believe that we all carry pictures in our heads and that our animals see them, so they know what's going on. I can remember a horse informing me that her owner had a sore back, to which she readily agreed, and the horse then told me it was her mattress that was at fault and that she should turn and rotate it. Her mare supplied me with a perfect picture of the mattress, even down to the detail of the material that was sewn in under each button. Seeing as she had never been in the house, let alone the bedroom, that image must have come from her owner!

I think it was a truly educational afternoon for the high school students, and hopefully they will never look on animals in quite the same way again. They were kind enough to send me a testimonial for my website, which I put up with pride, and I feel that if this can reach youngsters it will enhance their lives for good.

An Irish Comedian and his Slippery Mate

Most of the animals I talk to have a sense of humour, but King, a handsome bay Irish bred horse, had us in stitches. He had been bought by his owner for her boyfriend, and to save his embarrassment we will call him Phil. This horse was a great example of letting a few cats out of the bag, so to speak, but in a totally inoffensive way.

As soon as I started talking, King took over the whole thing and wanted to show me the many things that amused him. He said,

"I really like it when Phil tries to do sitting trot, I go up and down as much as I can to bump him out of the saddle!" and, "When Phil goes to canter me, I really push off from behind to see how far I can send him up my neck!" He even repeated to me that Phil's instructor was constantly telling him to, "Sit up, sit up." What tickled us most was that Phil's girlfriend had bought him a lovely pair of long leather riding boots, but these were really pinching his calves. King took great delight in informing us that apparently Phil mumbled complaints about them all through his lessons. His girlfriend had no idea how uncomfortable he had found them, but she did now!

I thanked him for chatting to us and asked if there was anything else that he wanted to tell Phil.

"Oh yes, you know that whip you lost…it's down the field." A quizzical look from his girlfriend confirmed that; yes indeed, Phil was the one who had lost the much searched for whip. End of that conversation.

We took a coffee break and I listened with pleasure to the mirth he had created, and I am sure King would have rewarded himself with a rosette for the horse with the best sense of humour ever!

Whilst there I also had a chat with their dog, a Rhodesian Ridgeback, who was well built and lying very contentedly on his equally big bed. He had injured his leg and they didn't know how. He showed me the problem was up in the shoulder area and that he had fallen down some concrete steps. Following the description, we realised they were actually the ones leading up from the back garden. As big as he was, he was a real softie and was keen to let me know that it was still rather sore, but was certainly enjoying the attention he was getting.

After we had discussed his likes and dislikes, and checked out his physical complaints, I thought I would ask if he had any helpful advice for them before we finished the chat. He showed me a visual of their lovely winding wooden stairs, and suggested that putting rubber mats on them would be far better, and safer. Just as I was thinking how sweet and thoughtful that was, they were quick to explain to me that that bit of advice was actually to his advantage. Those stairs lead up to the bedroom where he is not allowed, and as the stairs are slippery, he knows he can't climb them. We did give him ten out of ten for trying though.

It is a visit that I will remember for a long time, such fun and laughter, and I would love to have heard the conversation when the dog went up the yard later that day. Maybe he would have a discussion with King about how they could get down to the field, and with a bit of luck, find that whip!

Jumping for Joy

Gerry was a ten year old horse from a yard in Scotland, a deep chestnut colour with a big frame but very poorly muscled. To say this horse had emotional baggage would be the understatement of the year. He was so depressed and mentally shut down, it was very difficult to get a word out of him, let alone discuss how he felt.

As I have explained previously, it's a three-way live conversation and in this instance, as emotional as it was, the owner was really able to help. She explained to him she loved him and had got me to talk to him so we could try to help him. This encouragement worked and he began to relieve himself of all the horrible things that had happened to him (I did offer to just acknowledge them myself but his owner wanted to know everything, so I described all that went on). He imparted some rather disturbing pictures, but we held it together and assured him that there was no way that this would ever happen to him again. Most importantly we assured him that it was NOT his fault, akin to the way a child who has been mistreated, manages to reason they have somehow brought it upon themselves.

It transpires he was a 'failed' show jumper; he had injured his leg and was no longer of use to the previous owners and quite frankly, financially worthless. With the hand of fate Ann Marie was guided in his direction and bought this poorly lame horse and had spent a lot of money trying to get him sound. All she wanted was to have him as a pleasure horse and just give him a nice life. I take my hat off to her; there are not many people out there that would really take on such a financial and emotional risk.

She had now owned him for a year and the physical side had improved but still with a way to go. Sadly, personality wise, he was so difficult and so shut down that he did not respond to any form of affection. He was totally defensive, to the extent the only time she had been able to give him a hug was when he was sedated by the vet for x-rays.

After a lot of persuasion, he eventually opened up and I was able to explain things to him to reassure him, and he gave much more in-depth information that explained why he was wary about his back legs being touched. He gave us bonding keys and Ann Marie used them when needed, and for the first time since she had owned him, she saw him relax and not run away from people, herself included. He used to pace round the box when she was in there, he told us why and I told him that he would never be in any danger with her, so it is totally unnecessary. The bonding key he gave us was, 'I'm tired now, Gerry', so she let him pace the box a couple of times, with her moving out of his way, said the words, and to her amazement he stopped. Our healing journey had started and a huge corner had been turned. He passed over all his physical problems for me to acknowledge, and was assured that a chiropractor was going to be booked.

A couple of weeks later she told me he had even started neighing to her when she came to the yard and seemed to be happier in himself. Although she had been bravely hacking him out before, he had stopped shying at so many things and was even carrying himself like he now had a sense of purpose.

Alas, within that week, she contacted me again as his behaviour had totally changed, he had become boisterous and unruly, and could I help...

I was travelling down the motorway and as Bob (my very obliging husband who tows a caravan beautifully, thank goodness, as towing scares the daylights out of me!) was driving, I decided to talk to him there and then. I tuned in with him and was quite taken aback; from the horse that had been so depressed, he was absolutely full of himself. He had developed the 'sweet shop syndrome', as I call it; it is just like a deprived child being let loose in a sweet shop, sometimes manners and thought go out of the window, as they tend to grab instead of asking. Having been downtrodden for years, he suddenly felt free and showed me himself running round the fields, bucking and shaking his head. He was also being silly like putting his ears back and pretending he was going to bite people. He certainly never bit anyone, but it was just an ignorant source of amusement to him. We quickly realised he was behaving like a silly teenager who did not know where the boundaries were, and what was acceptable and what wasn't.

Animal Insight

We went through the various things and used another bonding key, which was every time he did something stupid/childish, Ann Marie would say, 'Gerry, that is NOT acceptable behaviour', and true to his word, this reminded him that he could show his cheeky personality but with certain rules being applied. We also told him to look at how the other horses behaved, and within a few days he got the message and returned to a much calmer horse.

To have been involved with Gerry and his transformation has been wonderful. To hear things from Ann Marie, like, "People cannot believe he is the same horse," makes my job so worthwhile. She says she now at last has a connection and an understanding relationship with her horse. Having spoken to Gerry, other owners on the yard could see the difference and got me to talk to their horses too. Some with little problems and others because they just wanted to know what their horses had to say.

As I have said before, animals are like us with all different personalities, and this yard gave us such an insight to this. The amazing thing was that the horses would go and chat to each other about what they had been telling me!

I really do spend my life saying, "I just say what I see," but sometimes doubt my interpretation of the visual I have been shown. So when Ava, a very pretty and poshly spoken mare told me that Nugget, a pony sharing the field, was whispering in her ear, I thought this was a lovely, but surely imaginary, picture from her. I laughed and told them about it, and surprisingly, Ava's owner, Kate, backed it up and said that she quite often sees the two of them close together and actually it does look like that! So, for fun, I asked the mare what Nugget was saying to her and this was the reply:

"Oh Ava, you are the prettiest horse here, and if you wanted to give me some of your food, I wouldn't mind!" This gave us such a giggle and Nugget's owner said that would be absolutely typical of him.

I have also chatted to Nugget, who is aptly named, not just because of his colour but he is worth his weight in gold. If you think he is an angel, you couldn't be further from the truth, he is a little monkey. Everybody on the yard knows him, because he is one of those that gets into and up to everything he shouldn't - but they can't help but love him! In fairness to him, when he has to do his 'job' he does it well, it is just the in-between bits that he does in the name of having a laugh.

Nugget does really like Ava, but gave us some interesting information about their conversation in the trailer after shows. She tells him she always does so well, and, with him being small by comparison, he obviously couldn't do as well as her. Well what a fib that turned out to be! If the truth be known, she had been eliminated so many times (owner's fault) and he actually had won many rosettes. Nugget just laughed, and pointed out that firstly; the trailer did belong to him and secondly; wait till the next show and he will ask what really happened. On the subject of ownership of the trailer, this had been squabbled about also, together with playing at pretending to bite each other when travelling together. Nugget was pleased to be proven to be correct, it was his trailer as he had insisted all along. We asked Ava why she thought she owned it. As she always got loaded first, in her mind this would be the right protocol, due to it being hers!

Back to the rosette conversation, I mentioned Ava's owner's fault (freely admitted) because there had been a few eliminations and things were not going smoothly. I asked Ava if there was anything she could think of to help improve their chances. She told me that she would always jump if at all possible but could I ask Kate, 'to walk the course twice!' It transpires that Kate's memory for the order of the jumps is not good, so she agreed that if she walked it twice, it really might help.

Approximately a year later, and during updating chats with them all, we found that little Nugget had a molar problem that had been overlooked. He had to then have an extraction, but now, once again was able to enjoy one of his favourite pastimes - eating! Ava and Kate have sort of got it together; she now can do a round in the right order, so maybe, just maybe, one day she might get one of those imaginary rosettes.

As for Gerry, he has completely transformed. He stands tall and proud, so much so that his owner has got a lad to compete him at show jumping. He is jumping big tracks and loving it, and his rider knows that we chat, so I have had to do a few reassurances there too. Ann Marie still hacks him out and gives him all the love and attention, which he has rewarded her with by the bucket load.

A Lasting Impression

Maddie, a wispy little female Collie, beautifully coloured with dashes of sandy brown mixed amongst her fluffy white coat, was only seven months old when I first spoke to her. She was rather young compared to the majority of animals I talk to, but even the very young have a voice.

Maddie had a huge confidence problem, and the only person that could touch her was her owner. As soon as anyone else put their hand out to stroke her, she backed away immediately and went into her over-anxious mode.

Susie, her owner, is another one of our dental clients, very open-minded and over the years we have enjoyed many an interesting conversation. This led us to tell her about Julie Dicker; another animal communicator (who has now sadly passed over) but who had helped Sue's friend with a horse, giving valuable insight that she desperately needed. When I started doing communication, Susie asked me to see what I could find out from Maddie.

This was a typical case of people trying to think of obvious explanations - has she been hit on the head or has someone smacked her on the nose etc. I quite often tell this story on demonstrations and let people offer their opinions, but I have yet to hear the right answer. The answer I got from Maddie was so different, nobody came close, and I was as surprised as everyone else.

This all stemmed from when she was six weeks old, yes, six weeks, you wouldn't think they would notice much, but she did. She was born on a farm and was dutifully reared by her mother, but not handled by humans at all apart from being sexed. This was when they were new born, and bear in mind that puppies' eyes don't open until nine days old, so at that point she had no idea what her mother looked like, let alone a human being. The first physical human contact she had was by someone who picked her up by her scruff (the loose skin on the back of their necks that the mother uses to carry them around) to have a look at her.

This in itself certainly doesn't sound traumatic and generally would not be, but, unfortunately when the person put her back down to choose another to inspect, they didn't place her completely to the floor and she was dropped roughly six inches to the kennel bed. This, to a six week old little pup, was a long way, probably equivalent to a few feet for, say, a toddler child. This was not done out of malice, just ignorance and not realising the effect it could have. Most people would think at that age they were just little beings and probably notice very little, but now I realise too, that that is not the case.

So, we had established that although she was now a lot bigger, she thought that people were still trying to reach over and take the scruff of her neck to lift her up and maybe drop her again. I explained that she was grown up now and this was never going to happen and that it was an accident when she was a baby. I assured her that she had a home for life with Susie, and these explanations did indeed increase her confidence. She is now eighteen months old and although very much more settled, she is only happy for people to stroke her under her chin and down. She clearly would rather people did not try to put their hand above her head. This has worked well, at least she can have physical affection from many people; it is on her terms so she does not feel threatened by them, and so can relax and enjoy it.

This case is one that I really believe that without the existence of animal communication the situation would have never been resolved. I feel very fortunate that I was in the position to be able to help change Maddie and Susie's life for the better.

Untold Damage

On a bright autumn day I decided to accompany my husband, Bob, on his daily duties. I rarely go out with him nowadays and, for the life of me I cannot remember the reason why I did. I now know it was no coincidence me being there, as I very quickly found out my help was needed.

It was around midday, and for once, not raining, as we pulled onto a farm that my husband had visited many times before. Bob set up in the barn, and started working on a horse at the far end. I went and stood at the building's entrance to enjoy the sunshine, when I saw this gorgeous coloured pony being led up towards me, so stunning in fact, that I remarked on this. I was met with the reply,

"I know but she has got so many problems, it's so sad." And with that, the words seem to just fall out of my mouth. "Well maybe I am the person that can help you." So she asked me why and what did I do?

Once again, I thought I was going to get that, 'Did she fall out of a tree and land on her head?' look, but I started to explain anyway, and with that she said,

"Oh, yes, my mum was a medium, I totally believe in things like that." I sighed with relief, because if someone already believes in the spirit world,

Animal Insight

it makes my job so much easier to comprehend, and the more open they are, the easier the conversation flows.

This bonnie little mare was called Smudge, and her owner Helen, who is very sensitive and intuitive, suggested we took her for a graze and we would have her chat out in her paddock. Helen thought this would be better so we could talk with privacy, without the intrusion of others.

Well, talk about an outpouring! This poor little mare had been so cruelly treated and could not understand what she had done to deserve it. She showed me the most awful pictures, to the extent of being hit round the head with a metal pole, and pulled down to the ground by her left ear. This explained why she was so head shy and wary of even the slightest hand movement in that direction. This disgusting treatment had not been dished out because of any riding issues; it was all about breeding problems. It became apparent, that her previous callous owners were determined she was going to be bred from, regardless of whether she had hormonal/physical discomfort problems or not.

In total fear and out of self defence, she would kick out at the stallion, so they roped her back legs which resulted in her falling over and damaging her right hind. This immediately answered the question why she was so worried when you handled her legs. She was exhibiting a slight lameness but not enough to put your finger on, but she constantly rested that leg, and wouldn't let the farrier have that foot to shoe. I asked her what she thought would help, and she explained that she thought it had 'never drained properly from the injury and that the cells were thickened'. She asked for magnet boots to be used to boost the circulation. The boots certainly worked, and she now willingly gives it to the farrier to be shod.

A horse's stable should be like their bedroom: somewhere they can relax, sleep and generally feel comfortable. Although Smudge was happy to go in her stable, if Helen entered with a bridle, she would do the 'wall of death' impression. I asked her to explain her fear, and she said that she associated the bridle with being taken back to the stallion and the abuse that she had faced there. To get round this, Helen now goes in with a head collar and rope, grooms her to show that she is going to be ridden, then she is then happy to have the bridle put on; another problem solved.

Amongst her many fears was the trailer; she broke sweat and trembled as soon as she went in. Again, this was triggering a memory of her being in stock back at the stud. (Many studs have these to restrict the mare's movement either to be covered by a stallion or for various health checks etc.) I understood her thoughts, but assured her Helen just wanted to travel her to take her to nice places where the riding would be better. Coupled with the trailer issue, was the fact that Helen was trying to put protective boots on her, which was acceptable for the front legs, but definitely not the hind. Again, this was triggering the hobbling memory, so once again it was all made clear to her, and Smudge asked if Helen could refrain from using the word 'boots', they were 'leg protectors', and true to her word she let her put them on.

Once Helen had mounted her for a ride, she was a very happy pony and seemed to enjoy having such a purpose in life. She had obviously not read the green cross code, because stopping at junctions seemed immaterial to her, so we did have to have a quick safety talk with her too!

Within a couple of months the difference in Smudge was clear. In fact she was so settled that Helen thought it would be wonderful to get the children a little pony, so they could ride out together, and it would also be a companion for Smudge too. After trailing through adverts and going to see various ponies, they came across a showy little boy called Tickles. He was quiet, very handsome and seemed to be the perfect choice, and was certainly a head turner.

Although this did lead to some insecurities by Smudge, they settled down and all seemed to be well. Helen was aware that Tickles had been out of work for the past couple of years but was led to believe that he had simply been outgrown. When he started to look 'pottery' in his gait, she quickly realised that he was laminitic. (Laminitis an extremely painful condition of the foot, in human terms the nearest would be akin to the effects of gout.) Sadly, it can cause irreparable damage to their feet, so I was asked to chat to him and see what he said.

Tickles confirmed her thoughts, he had had laminitis on several occasions and could they please take him to stand in the stream at the bottom of the fields? Helen was totally unaware of the stream, but the farmer confirmed there was one there and said she could take him down there. This cooled his feet and got him his wish and the children's too, as they shrieked with joy at this pony paddling game.

Tickles was also showing some other physical problems, so I body scanned him and immediately he gave me the feeling of my mouth being offset, with an ache in his jaw and pressure at his poll. (This is on the top of the neck behind the horse's ears.) Helen called on Bob for his dental services and apart from his teeth being so very sharp, he had a nasty sore in his cheek, where a large back hook had come up and was pushing outwards into his cheek. This certainly explained his objections to having his bit put in and the right side of his face being touched. He also had a few chiropractic problems which were sorted and he was far more comfortable.

Animal Insight

As his health improved, he was getting more spirited and rather faster and keener than he had been.

This was rather a worry as he had been bought as a lead rein/first pony for two very small children. As he and Smudge were happy together, Helen changed a few things, and hoped he would quieten down. Roughly a month later, I got the most frantic phone call, saying,

"You'll never believe what has happened." But with that I 'saw' immediately and said,

"They have had a kicking match haven't they?"

This sadly was the truth, and it was not a threat and push, but a real double barrelled event, being repeated by Smudge herself. By the time Helen had separated them, the mare was so distressed, as unfortunately Tickles had suddenly taken it upon himself to offer her some male affection. As he went to her back end, it brought all those horrendous memories flooding back and she just went berserk, fortunately no serious physical injuries occurred, just a few cuts and scrapes.

A very hard lesson learnt, but once they had separate paddocks and she had some assurances from us, all seemed well. Although by now, Tickles was proving to be quite a gutsy pony and obviously wanting to be doing far more than the boring quiet things, suitable for four and six year old children. Helen being of a very light build decided to get on him and see exactly what he was like. He loved it, but got so excited and they even popped a few jumps, which would have been superb fun for a confident child but really not suitable for little ones to learn on. With a lot of discussion, Helen decided that as Smudge would obviously never tolerate a gelding and that as he needed to do more, so she would put him up for sale. It didn't take long to sell him at all, he was tried by a very confident child who pushed him faster and faster and Tickles obliged and didn't put a foot wrong. He flew his vetting with flying colours and off to his new home he went.

Helen's little boy Tom was really sad, as he had enjoyed playing with Tickles and had amazingly not been put off by his erratic turns of speeds. Helen then spotted an advert giving the words equivalent to a mother's dream, she just had to go and see her, although a four hour drive. Most importantly, it was a *her*, in no way did she want to risk a repeat performance, and so two girls together should be fine.

Little Bluebell, was exactly as they had described and with baited breath, the family had to wait for all the usual things to be checked but within ten days, she was theirs. On arrival, she settled as if she had lived there all her life, but the bonding between her and Smudge was not going well. Smudge was being aggressive so once again we had to try and sort it out. We explained to Bluebell that Smudge had had a hard life and unfortunately she did have an upset with the last pony. We asked Bluebell to be patient, do her own thing and not take it personally. With that, the little pony said she felt sorry for her, as she had only ever known love. This was so true; she had been in her last home for most of her young life and they truly adored her, hence her owner making sure she went to a loving home, as this one certainly was.

After a few weeks when it looked like they were settled, Helen put them in the same paddock. Big mistake. Smudge got very agitated, the little one spent her time trying to befriend her, but to no avail, in fact it was having the opposite effect. We established that Smudge, did not want to have a relationship with any horse at all, but if they had their separate paddocks, she would feel secure and that is the way she would like it to stay. As far as Smudge was concerned, Bluebell was just her 'Mate' ('Mate' was said with a real emphasis on the 't' at the end of the word, this I would describe as her trying to give the effect of what you would call someone that just happened to be working on the same building site as you!) This has worked exactly as she said, in fact they are often seen grazing, mirroring each other down the fence line, but as long as there is that boundary, Smudge is totally relaxed and Bluebell accepts it as it is.

By now, the children had shortened her name to 'Bell' and although a godsend, she still had a couple of quirks which Helen wondered if I could help with. One was quite innocent, but was making it impossible for Tom, the six year old, to lead her in from the field. Every time he would try to clip the rope to her headcollar, she would instantly try and rub her head on him and would either knock him over or send him flying! We had to ask what an earth was this about. She showed me her favourite 'scratchy' spot, high up her neck, and for years people had rubbed it. She responded to this kindness, with various head angles and pursing of the lips, and as strange as this sounds, she said it actually gave her a 'buzz'. It was like she was addicted to it, so at every opportunity she would try to get people to do it. Helen admitted that she would often do it to her too, as Bell pushed into her to get it and realised how much she enjoyed it. Now we knew the reason, I set out to try and undo her over-zealousness.

I said to her, "Imagine if you were in your field and a really big horse came up and started rubbing themselves on you, they would just knock you over and it would be quite frightening," she agreed this would be so, so in turn I explained, "in actual fact, that is exactly what you are doing to this little child, when he is trying to catch you." She seemed to take it on board, and the bonding key phrase was, 'No Bell, it's like the big horse syndrome,' (her offer, not mine, what a mouthful, so it would have to be said by an adult). The next time her son went to catch her, Helen repeated the phrase and she just stood and let him clip her up and lead her out of the field, no problem. I have to admit I was amazed at this result and how quickly she stopped the habit.

Things are now totally settled, Smudge knows she is totally safe and is now considerably more relaxed and will be going on fun rides this summer. As for Bell, she is doing her job looking after the little ones, and Helen's son has various words she has offered for him to use to help her understand him. My favourite one she gave was for him to use for a faster or slower trot, was: 'trot up' and 'trot down', which for a five year old makes perfect sense, as us humans would say, 'speed up' or 'slow down'.

There have been quite a few ups and downs over the past year, and sadly Smudge is an example of how emotionally damaged some animals can be, thus exhibiting strange behaviour from time to time. Although she has vastly improved, I don't think she will ever truly get over her former years, but thank goodness she landed up with Helen who has had more patience than many. She has now got the best chance of having a loving normal life; that she really does deserve.

Apart from being in the privileged position to help with her horses, I did mention at the beginning about Helen's mother, who sadly had passed away about nine months before we first met. Through the amount of the work needed, we have formed a good friendship, and she recently accompanied me on one of my charity nights and videoed the evening for me. Apart from me being able to help her animals, most importantly I was able to pass messages from her mother to help her grieve and go forward. We are both positive that her mother had something to do with organising our meeting in the first place.

A Cat in a Flap

Whilst on one of my outings, a lovely lady and her daughter sat down in front of me saying they had a problem, and hoped I was the person that could solve it.

She owned an exotic breed of cat, but for the life of me, I cannot recall his name, so for the purpose of this story I have called him Precious. A choice I think he would have thoroughly approved of, because he was certainly that in himself, and to them. After telling us how wonderful he was, what he loved to do, and how fantastic his owner was, she decided to get him to cut to the chase, and said could I please ask him about the new cat flap.

His owner explained that she had just spent nearly £300 to have a special cat flap fitted; it was one that worked by reading from the animal's unique Identichip. (These are microchips, about the size of a grain of rice that a vet can inject into their neck. They are mainly used for lost animals, so when found they can be scanned and their owners contacted and informed of their whereabouts.) As smart as this new cat flap was he would not go through it, and as he had been using a normal cat flap since a kitten, they really couldn't fathom it out.

During the chat with him, it was clear that he had a life of Riley and wanted for nothing with the best quality cat food money could buy. The problem was; the other cats in the neighbourhood had discovered about this and were coming into his house to help themselves, bringing with them fleas and unwanted disturbance. This was the reason for installation of a very expensive cat flap that only his Lordship could use - if only he would. They had tried all the various bribes, when her daughter piped up,

"I don't think he likes the beep." I stopped her there before she gave me any more information and said that I had better ask him, as that might or might not be the case.

I asked him why he wouldn't use it, and with a feeling of total angst he said,

"I can't, I can't, I don't know if I will make it," and gave me the impression of someone on starting blocks ready to do a sprint.

My brain logically tried to work out what this meant and I asked his owners, "Is there a limited time for this to open then lock again, as he seems scared that he won't make it through in time?"

"Yes and no," came the answer, with an explanation that was very much needed by Precious and me, as until now I didn't even know that these Identichip reading cat flaps existed, let alone how they work! They enlightened us.

"There is a time factor; when he pushes it, it beeps, and when it comes back to rest, it will then lock after 30 seconds." I ran this past him and asked if that is how he understood it, his reply was,

"Oh, I thought I had 30 seconds from the beep to get through, or it would come down and lock. I really was worried that it might get my tail if I was not fast enough."

I set about explaining to him that he had got it wrong; when he pushed it and heard the beep, as long as the flap was ajar, he could take as long as he liked to go through. It only locks when the flap is back in the closed position for 30 seconds. I said, "Please try it, it is perfectly safe. You know you were telling me about all your delicious food and your wonderful warm, cosy home; well this is designed to keep those pesky cats out that keep sneaking in!"

I wished them the best and, as usual, said that I cannot make any promises but hopefully he would take it on board. When I got back from my weekend, a lovely email had arrived telling me that that afternoon they rushed off home and, on their arrival, Precious was so excited to see them. (Occasionally animals will make it quite apparent that they know they have been communicating.)

He was asked if he enjoyed his conversation with 'the nice lady' (that did tickle me) and hoped he understood that it was all done to make him safe. With that, with a head swish and a flick of his tail, he proceeded to the cat flap and straight through it!

Even though I say it myself, I really feel without animal communication this would have been one mystery unsolved, and one very expensive cat flap back in its box.

And the Beat Goes on

I truly believe that everything that happens does so for a reason; however difficult and sad, or on the other hand, how lucky and fortunate. Many animals, and people, go to Heaven before the naturally expected time. My personal belief on this is that they are needed in Heaven sooner to help others still here on this earth. My work is all achieved with the help of my guides and I would be truly lost without them.

Spirit guides are not exclusive to clairvoyants; we all have helpers from up there guiding us. Don't you often think, after the fact, you just knew something wasn't right? That is an example of your guide trying to look after you, and inform you; to help you make the right decisions.

I believe that our lives are mapped out and the paths are set that we should walk. I think if we walk them as well as we can, then we should not reproach ourselves if we make a mistake. Mistakes happen to give lessons for us to learn from, and to help us through our life's journey.

Animals often seem to come into people's lives as if they had chosen the owner, rather than the other way round. How often have you been in the right place at the right time and found the most adorable pet you could have ever wished for, even when you swore you wouldn't have another!

I have had many examples of animals that have come into people's lives for a while. Sometimes it is only a short time (sold, re-homed etc.) but they were there to teach you something, or highlight something that you were not aware of.

Through my work, I have gained a true insight of how intuitive most animals are, and how much they know about what is going on. Again, this is my own opinion, but I am sure animals have guides too; why should guides be exclusive to human beings?

A while ago I was asked to chat to a horse called Drummer. He was a stunning coloured lad that stood 18 hands high (human equivalent of way over six foot) but the most gentle of beings. Alison had owned him approximately four months, when they came to grief whilst setting out for a ride.

Drummer, for whatever reason, and totally out of character, bucked so violently that Alison had a crashing fall that actually led to a serious fracture of her hip joint. This fall had left her so shaken, confused and in severe pain, that she came to me looking for answers. Her memory of the actual event was failing her, so she wanted to know what had actually happened, why, and what she could do to help her horse, as there was obviously something very wrong.

I introduced myself to Drummer and we got chatting. He took this opportunity to show me how wonderful their relationship was, and all the kind things he appreciated that Alison did. Eventually I got onto the subject in question, and asked him to show me exactly what had happened. He gave me a clear visual of Alison leaning slightly right, as she was pulling up the left saddle flap to tighten his girth. With that he exploded, and passed me over the most severe pain, like someone gripping and twisting behind my right shoulder area, this would have equated with the front saddle position on his right hand side.

Animal Insight

She said that made total sense, as that is exactly what she was doing, and the incident had occurred very much at that time.

With relief this proved that it was not malicious, which had never been contemplated, but was good to have this confirmed: so we knew we were looking at a pain issue. I body-scanned him and he gave me clear pictures, showing his pelvis tilted down left, pressure halfway down his neck and many muscle related problems. This was all backed up by him showing me that his stride had been slightly rigid; as had been the case since she had owned him. Generally horses will loosen off with work; he had been so kind to behave so well, considering how uncomfortable he must have been.

Poor Alison, who was still trying to recover, was concerned as she had not been physically able to visit him. She was worried that he would be feeling neglected, or worse, guilty, for what had happened. I talked to him about this and both fears were allayed.

She organised for Drummer to have treatment; the chiropractor found exactly what he had described and this definitely made him feel a lot better. Within a couple of months he was careering about in the field and even managed to hurt his leg. Alison was mending slowly but at least was able to go to the yard to see his happy antics.

So, during another communication which was to check out the problem with his leg - it seemed to be a slight strain and nothing more he assured her he would be sound (horse terminology for being physically okay) in a week, and he was! He was ready to be ridden again, and although he was enjoying Alison's visits, he wanted to know when she would be ready also.

It wasn't that much further down the line, that Alison got the shocking news that she actually had the onset of osteoporosis, more commonly known as brittle bone disease which occurs due to lack of bone density. She was advised to be careful and not risk a fall; so riding a horse would really be very foolhardy.

As she was in her early forties, with diet, supplements and a change of exercise, she could improve the condition considerably. Having been given this worrying news, she came back to me, having realised she would never be able to ride him again. She felt that the fairest thing to do would be to sell him, to let him make someone else happy and give him his working life back.

It was the middle of 2009, the economic climate was very poor and sadly, the horse market was stagnant. People were seriously struggling with life's bills, let alone keeping horses, so she had agreed to sell him for far less than he was worth. Some people who replied to her advert said they were willing to travel a long way and wanted to come that Sunday.

They would buy him untried and un-vetted, this being the process done by a vet, where the horse is checked in several ways to make sure he has not got any physical problems. (This, I have often equated as going to a betting shop and putting a lot of money on a horse racing that you really don't have full knowledge of. Would you really take such a gamble?)

With a heavy heart she got me to explain to him that she had no choice and that these people would give him a home. Immediately my guide prompted me to ask if they were dealers, as we didn't want to make any promises that wouldn't be kept.

This, in turn, prompted Alison to recall their conversation, in which they admitted that if he didn't suit them, they could sell him on, although said in a way that made it seem very unlikely. I didn't say much more, but felt I had made her aware. Although this did make me feel uneasy, I felt it was not my place to say anymore on the subject.

Drummer was so wonderful and understanding; he just wanted to be happy himself and ultimately let Alison know that he was absolutely fine with her decision. At this point he did drop in that he 'might have a bit of a think about their lorry!' Funnily enough, he was a cautious loader but after a while would always go on. I thanked him for all the chats we had had over the past few months and wished him the best of luck on Sunday. I also took the opportunity to say how much I had enjoyed the conversations with Alison; she is a truly unselfish owner and kindness itself.

On Sunday evening, an email popped into my inbox, with the title, 'Don't laugh, but he is still here!' Sure enough, he really had thought about the lorry (and the people) and point blankly refused to go on!

After an hour of trying, they gave up and said they would have to leave him, but they would come back with an even bigger lorry to collect him. Their assumption was that maybe the lorry was not quite big enough for him, but unfazed, they said they really did want him and would contact her as soon as they had arranged something.

Later that Sunday afternoon, Alison was suddenly overcome with the feeling that this was not right and she had to act quickly to stop the sale and think again. This was achieved by a phone call, apologising but saying she had changed her mind. She was now back to square one and what was she to do? Later that day, she recounted the 'refusing to leave' story to a local lady whom Alison used to ride for. She immediately said,

Animal Insight

"I think I know someone on our yard who may want him, leave it with me, I will find out." Gosh, Alison could not believe her luck, and sure enough this lady was very quick to get back to her. Unfortunately the original man did not want him, but the owners of the livery yard loved the look of him and were interested themselves.

As Drummer had been off work for at least four months, it would have been rather irresponsible to ride him there, so they decided they would come and see him and pick him up, if they still liked him.

They duly arrived the next day, and he did his usual 'I am not too sure' approach, and then proceeded to head into their lorry. He travelled quietly and arrived at his new home, with not a hair turned out of place. I am sure there was some divine intervention - such a wonderful result; her friend gets a wonderful horse and Alison knows he is totally safe and literally just down the road!

Alison has since been to visit Drummer in his new home and was delighted that he was loved and cared for as much as she could have hoped. He really did land on his hooves! The new owners have said she is welcome to visit him and have promised to send pictures of him once he is back in full work.

I hope this story highlights just how perceptive animals can be, and what they are aware of. This lovely horse was certainly wary of these buyers, to the extent he refused to load. Alison then bumps into her friend, relates the 'refusing to leave' story and her friend then buys him, and he willingly goes with her. I think this certainly sums up the saying 'there is no such thing as coincidence!'

Most importantly, as I said at the beginning, some animals come into your life to show you things. Had Alison not fallen off and needed x-rays, she would not have know that she was harbouring what can be a most debilitating condition. If it had not been discovered until years later, the chances are it would have been irreversible.

As hard as the parting from this wonderful horse was, he did come into her life to show her something she really wasn't aware of. As a result, she was able to seek professional help quickly, and as she is young, her bone density should improve enough for her to, maybe one day, even ride again.

Jackie Weaver

If the Truth be Known

To be honest, although I know animals can speak, I hope by the time you have finished this book that you will be in no doubt either. If an animal really does show resistance, it is usually for a genuine reason. It is then up to us to explain what is happening and why, and sometimes to maybe question our reasoning.

It is worth considering that maybe this animal is really trying to let you know something, but in his or her own limited way. If we could all hear their voices, there would be so much less misunderstanding and confusion out there, the picture would be so much clearer for us all.

Judging by some of the animals I talk to, some would be just like people that really don't know when to be quiet, and others that would tell tales on their friends. I assure you, it does go on; there are some animals that are also just as happy to shift the blame and fib as we humans are sometimes guilty of doing.

One such conversation that has stuck in my memory still gives Pam, a very dear friend I am fortunate to have, and me a giggle when mentioned. It was during an informal chat with the lovely Marigold, a dainty and rather delicate Lurcher who was about twelve-years-old. She belongs to Pam and shares her home with another three dogs.

We had a lovely chat, one of those ones that were filled with the 'Aww' moments. At the end I asked her if there was anything else she would like to tell Pam. Well, she seized the opportunity by conjuring up a picture of diarrhoea in rather vast quantities, splattered over a large rug (fortunately without giving me the smell accompaniment) and exclaimed,

"It wasn't me!" I instantly thought, how terrible. Had she been falsely blamed? But this theory was quickly dispelled when my friend came back with a classic answer of,

"Well there were only the two of us at home that weekend, and I can assure you it wasn't me!"

This incident was also clearly etched in her memory; it transpired that her husband had been away for the weekend with the other dogs, and was bringing guests back with him to stay the night. It was only about an hour before their arrival, that Marigold had presented her with this unfortunate problem, and although there were no stains on the carpet, the incident was clearly etched in both Marigold and Pam's memories.

Another example of fibbing would be from a seven year old pony called Smithy. He ended up having a chat with me and his owner because of

Animal Insight

something that was said during a communication I was having with his owner's other horse, Merlin.

Merlin informed us that Smithy, this small but stocky pony, was saying he was a rig! (This is a horse that still has one testicle remaining (usually retained up inside) so still providing the hormones as if he were a stallion. This is quite uncommon really but can be the cause of aggressive behaviour.) A rather odd thing to say I would agree and Merlin also wished us to know that he didn't believe a word of it. With such a bizarre conversation taking place our curiosity was heightened, so it was decided that we should give Smithy the chance to give his side of the story. Smithy was very obliging, and certainly not shy, he was actually very forthcoming when asked,

"Smithy, did you tell Merlin you were a Rig?"

"Yeah, I'll admit to that," he answered.

"Why did you say that?" I questioned.

"Oh, it's not true, you know, but I was thinking if Merlin thought I was a rig, he would be more wary of me."

I related this curious, yet clever answer back to his owner. It then came to light, that when the horses first met, they had a rather serious clash, and to be honest, had never really become friends since. So, now we know, this was akin to Smithy pretending to be a black belt in karate to try and scare someone off. It didn't really work, because as I said, Merlin reported it to us in the first place, and told us at the time that it wasn't true! But 10 out of 10 for trying on Smithy's behalf and we told him so. At least Merlin mainly ignores him now, probably thinking 'If he thinks we would believe that, then we would believe anything!'

"There are no such things as obstacles, these are things made of your own objections."

A very profound statement by a cat trying to encourage her self-doubting owner to go on a training course that she says she wants to do, but finds every excuse not to.

"I'm that good; he just sits there smoking whilst we do the track."

A young trotting horse expressing his reliability, which led me to carefully establish if his wife knew about her husband's smoking, fortunately she did and we had a great laugh.

"I'm not that well put together you know, rather like a cut and shut."

An ex-racehorse describing himself and recalling a description that was quite often used about him, but now in a new home and having such fun.

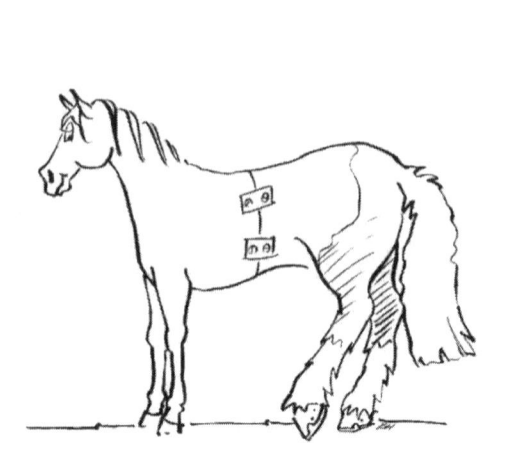

Animal Insight

Built up Apprehension

Bruno was an 18 month old black German Shepherd dog, a real masculine specimen, with a long gleaming coat, defined facial features, and with such presence. His owner, Mary, a middle-aged lady, contacted me as things had hit a real downhill slide. Mary was now totally beside herself, as she really could not work out what was going on.

I tuned in with him and he told me that things used to be okay, but they're not now; this indicating to me that he had not always been this way. I asked him when he thought things had changed, his answer was three months ago, Mary confirmed this was actually right, and with that, he showed me pictures of scaffolding, ladders and generally the impression of builders. I sensed that this wasn't at his Mary's house so asked if there was building work going on nearby, but she said this wasn't the case. The pictures were repeated, so again, I asked if maybe she walked past a builder's site or something similar, again this was met with a 'No,' so I asked her to note it and said we would move on.

I worked as I usually do and got him chatting which he was quite happy to do. Eventually, I asked Mary to give me a direction in which she wanted me to go, and she said he had had a change of behaviour and could I ask him why. With that comment, he showed himself lunging forward and gave me the feeling of aggression associated with it; here lay the problem.

I asked him to take me back to the point where he felt 'the change' had taken place, and again he showed me ladders, waste skips and generally a builder's picture again. This time it was coupled with a picture of what seemed to be him being tied up outside a shop. Gingerly, I put this forward and asked Mary if she recognised any of this. She said yes, she tied him outside the shop every morning after his walk, to buy her daily paper, and then suddenly gasped,

"Oh my goodness, the builders are working in the shop next door!"

Ah, at last, now I understood why he was desperately trying to show me builders. I told him that we now knew where the builders were, but what had they got to do with him? It turns out, that they had noticed him being tied up every day, and passed some comment, to the effect of, 'Look at that Alsatian, somebody could take him from there quite easily you know!'

The conversation could be taken in various ways; perhaps that one of the builders thought Bruno would be easy to untie and snatch or, maybe, they were just genuinely worried that someone else would see him as an easy target to steal. We will never know, but it was enough to worry Bruno as he then realised just how vulnerable he was tied up out there.

I have to remain impartial during communications, but personally I would never tie a dog up outside anywhere. I feel that you are not in a position to protect them, and sadly, in this world people can be very mercenary, and a beautiful pedigree animal is often not looked upon as a pet, but as a quick buck, or sometimes worse. If anybody took our Sally I would be devastated to say the least, so we aim never to put her in a position where we would not be able to protect her, as best as possible.

Now we understood why he kept giving these builders pictures (I always say what I am shown, even if at that point they seem irrelevant, but typically, further on in the conversation, their meaning becomes apparent). I asked her if she could recall a day when she came out and he was severely distressed, straight away she knew when this was. Mary said when she came out, there was a teenage lad standing next to him, whom she thought was worrying him. She had, in fact, told him to leave the dog alone, but it transpired (from Bruno) he was a kind lad and had been actually trying to help calm him down. Mary then felt dreadfully guilty, but it was an honest mistake.

I did all that I could to make Bruno feel safe, and to try and undo his defensive behaviour. I found out his biggest fear was to be parted from his owner (and her housebound father, to whom he was a loyal companion) so in his mind he reasoned that if he acted aggressively, then nobody would want him. This being very similar to a child that has been bullied, they often can turn and start to dish it out, in order to avoid it happening to themselves. Logically, I can totally understand the animal's reasoning, and it is not the first time I have heard it either.

We got some 'bonding keys' from him and hope that he will learn to relax and again enjoy his walks as he did before. He has been promised, in no uncertain terms, that he will never be tied up outside anywhere again, and that Mary will keep him safe, as his happiness is paramount to her.

Trailer Damage

Beau was a magnificent show horse, who stood about 17 hands high. He was a flea-bitten grey, of a heavy hunter build with a huge presence. Beau's owner, Ella, wanted nothing but the best for him, and came to me in the hope that I could unravel the mystery for her. She knew Beau had problems, but he wouldn't accept help and try as she had, she could not get through to him.

Ella had only had him about a year, and throughout this time had noticed a huge deterioration in his attitude and physical well-being. He had got to that stage where even their interaction was looking like a complete lack of co-operation. Beau was actually at the end of his tether; even being touched made his skin twitch with the discomfort.

I will give him his due; as soon as we started to talk he saw the opportunity to let us know exactly what was wrong, how it had occurred and how to cure it.

On asking how his physical problems had occurred, he showed me a moving picture of what appeared to be him in a trailer. This looked like it had either crashed or had to brake so hard that it had actually given him whiplash.

I asked Ella if she could remember this incident, and she told me she knew exactly what I was talking about. Logically, I was waiting for her to tell me about an accident or mishap, but actually, this was down to a purposeful deed by the previous owners. They ignorantly admitted to their actions, by imparting their wisdom of how to stop a horse moving in a trailer, telling her, "You just slam the brakes on, that soon stops them!"

How cruel and thoughtless people can be, so for a minute, think of it like this; you get a horse to trust you, load him into what is very much a tin can on wheels. Whilst travelling, he does move about a bit, and sometimes gets slightly unbalanced; for this, you punish him by slamming him into the front breast bar only then to be ricocheted backwards, and so easily achieved with the power of some ignorant foot on a pedal. It really doesn't bear thinking about does it?

I explained to him that this was not his fault and it would never purposely happen again, and how appalled we both were at what had happened. Now we understood how it had occurred, we needed to fix these physical problems that had seriously got the better of him. He was so precise about them: three vertebrae in his neck were misaligned, his right hind foot sometimes dragged, wasted upper left rump muscles etc.

Again, I mentioned that I didn't diagnose but would tell you what he showed me. Surprisingly, his owner said she knew all that as her chiropractor had found the same. The issue was that Beau refused point blank to let the chiropractor touch him, in any shape or form, to do her treatment. I asked him what we could do to get round this situation and he surprised us with his totally positive answer. He said, most confidently,

"That's easy, we all know where the problems are now, so just give me Bute ('Bute' is the abbreviated word commonly used for Phenobutazone, which is a form of anti-inflammatory and painkiller which is available is powder form) and some calming powders and things will be fine!"

I expressed to her, as I do to many such clients, that I couldn't make any promises that this would work, but was telling her, what he had told me. (Not every any animal changes, but a high percentage do.)

We covered lots of other things and I felt very hopeful that matters would improve and he would get the treatment he needed.

Within a couple of months, Ella contacted me to say,

"Beau is like a different horse." They followed his advice and he let the chiropractor treat him with no resistance at all, and his physical problems are now a thing of the past.

He is so much more relaxed and is enjoying life. Ella told me she was taking him to the Royal International Horse Show. Unfortunately, he didn't win anything that day, but to actually be able to be there, ride him and show him off, was in itself prize enough!

In the Fields of Heaven

Although most of the animals I talk to are horses, dogs and cats, Shaun's owner Di, contacted me as she desperately wanted to let her animal make his own decision. Shaun turned out to be an eleven-month-old pet lamb, aptly named with tongue in cheek. He was so cute, with his little white face randomly scattered with black speckles, but was very undersize for his age.

As soon as I tuned into him, immediately he gave me the feeling of being very bloated, with very uncomfortable stomach pressure. Di said that is exactly what his problem was and nobody is quite sure what was causing it.

I started chatting to him, and believe you me, he really was as sweet as little lambs look. I eventually asked him if he knew what his problem was.

Animal Insight

He said he was born with it, and as a newborn his mother rejected him, as often happens in nature when the mother senses that their offspring has been born not quite as they should be. Shaun pointed out that he had always had problems drinking from a bottle, due to a small hole that was a deformity in his mouth/throat area. Di said that it made sense as he would 'blow up' after a feed but go back down again within a few hours, this sounded typical of an animal swallowing air whilst drinking their milk.

Having amazingly survived to eleven months, he was now a bit more mature and he was grazing as well as eating concentrates. Sadly, although he was still on small bottles to help maintain his weight, he was ballooning up even more and looking ever so uncomfortable. Her vet had suggested putting a valve into his rumen (this is done from the outside, through his skin and then into part of his gut) which would be visible from the outside where the gas would be releasing. This was to try to let the air out in a controlled way, and this was the question she wanted him to answer, as the operation was his choice.

He was very quick to reply, saying, he thought 'it would be excruciating', and that he 'had had enough treatment, but thank you anyway'. As sad as his statement was, Di said that is exactly what she thought his answer would be, but felt that it was important to hear it from him, just to make sure.

"Where do we go from here?" she asked. I had a quick think and decided to ask him what the best way would be to manage his condition for as long as would be possible. He was so clear as to what caused him the problem, he pointed out that when he eats grass, this produces gas which exacerbated the situation. He thought he would be better off coming back down from the sheep area and said,

"I would like to live in the farmyard like a pet." He could try to live on milk and sheep pellets which his body could tolerate to a certain degree. He knew he wouldn't be here forever, but said he had been here on earth to teach her many things and enhance her knowledge.

Holding back the tears, she said he was absolutely right and we thanked him for that.

Shaun got his wish and spent his last few months as a pet down on the yard, near to the house as he had asked. I felt very honoured to have been in a position to help him and let him have his say. Sadly, although not unexpected, his stomach could take no more and he passed away.

He is buried in their garden with a rose called 'The Shepherdess' planted above him. What a wonderful, apt name, and I am sure it will bloom and grow as he will in Heaven.

A Real Video Nasty

Blondie was a four year old Quarter Horse imported from America. She was named due to her glowing cream colour with an extra white mane, just to complete her look. Her owner, Elaine, was doing a wonderful job with her, but there were clearly some fear issues. She was hoping that through communication we could delve deeper to help sort them out.

This was one of my early cases and was very emotional for me to do as Blondie was obviously very depressed. As sad as she was, she was willing to talk, thankfully, and she showed me many very vivid pictures. After passing on her pitiful feelings to me of weakness and worthlessness, I asked her why she felt like this. She then took me back to America to when she was about two years old.

Firstly, she showed me herself being pulled round in circles by long rope/lunge lines, so hard and so fast that she really struggled to stay on her feet. Then she gave me a very clear picture of this huge western saddle looming towards her. This was followed by images of a big man, about six feet tall, getting on her. Under his weight she basically sank in the middle, and he then proceeded to sit at the back of this western saddle, (which was far too big for her), with his legs forward, using them harshly to bully her into moving.

I have to admit that these images brought tears to my eyes on seeing them, but at least I was then able to explain to Blondie that all happened back in America. It was over two years ago and she was now in Britain and owned by one of the sweetest of owners, who loved her dearly. I went on to explain that Elaine understood that Blondie had problems and was in no rush to make her do anything. By the end of the talk Blondie had cheered up and I also did some emotion healing with her - this is achieved by mentally closing the door on bad past issues and reassuring them that they are in the past and can never come back.

As I mentioned, this was one of my early cases and Elaine is a dental client of my husband. When he was booked to go the next time to do their teeth, I went with him to meet this little mare in person.

I should point out that throughout the communication with Elaine, she kept saying that she understood exactly what I was describing and what I was talking about. Then on arrival at her house she offered us coffee and asked if we would like to see the video of Blondie that had been sent over from America. I hadn't been aware of this video; it had been sent to Elaine when she was interested in buying her.

My husband, Bob, and I sat there watching this video, completely dumbfounded. The images I was seeing on the TV screen were just exactly as Blondie had managed to show me - even down to the signature way he rode her so cruelly. There was a fair amount to watch on the tape, but I could only manage a few minutes. The emotions were flooding back to me, I had already relived it once, and I couldn't bear to do it again. Elaine then explained that that's why she bought the horse, as she just knew she couldn't have left her there. Thank goodness for Blondie that she didn't!

Blondie was already a far happier horse, and when I went to see her she was lying down quietly in her stable and amazingly she let me sit down beside her, then she lifted her head and put it in my lap, she stayed like that for a while. There was actually enough time for Elaine's daughter to go and get a camera and some photos, which can be found on my website. As sad and emotional as it was for all of us, it really did help prove to me my clarity of 'seeing' what animals want to show me.

A Dream of a Ride

One of the most beautiful experiences now etched in my memory, was with a big handsome Dutch bred dressage horse. He was deep mahogany bay, of a strong build but with a gracious head.

Phil, a young groom, had bought this horse that was now in his late teens, with the intention of doing some low-key dressage on him. Sadly, the horse was no longer physically capable of this, but at least he had a lovely home.

The horse and I had a wonderful chat and I assured him that his new owner was not disappointed in him, but just glad to own such an affectionate horse. When I asked him to show me an experience, he gave me a picture of a big indoor arena with rows of people seated down each side. He then proceeded to do the most wonderful uplifting dressage, and gave me a feeling of immense pride inside. This went on for about a minute and I 'rode' the most wonderful dressage paces (kind of like an elegant dance on horseback). This was such a fantastic feeling for me to experience.

I described all this to Phil and it transpired that this horse had been a Prix St George (top level) dressage demonstration horse, who had travelled all over the country showing people what the best dressage horses can do.

It was a truly wondrous sixty seconds. For someone like me, who can only do basic paces, I got to ride like the best dressage riders in the world. They are the select few, and have trained themselves and their horses for many, many years, dreaming and praying of making that elite standard. This beautiful horse took me there to show me, and let me feel what it's like, and understand what he was so proud to do. Just incredible.

With the Best of Intention

I have done demonstrations to raise money for the Cancer Unit that treated me, and always felt nervous before I started, but nothing could have prepared my nerves for the day I accompanied Bob on a visit to do some teeth. Helen, the yard manager, had asked if I could come too and have a chat with a couple of their horses. The yard visit certainly was not the problem, in fact, I thoroughly enjoy them, as most people listen to what each other's horse says (I love to see the reaction of the owners faces) but it was the predicament I was about to find myself in, that really set my nerves jangling.

We arrived on time and, lo and behold, the vet had got there before us. Anyone who has horses will understand this miracle. Bob rushed and got his kit together whilst the vet sedated the pony that offers to show the soles of his feet, every time you try and go in his mouth. I was just standing there, as you do, and a conversation came up about a mare called Ruby, whom funnily enough, I had talked to some while ago. The vet asked Helen how was Ruby feeling now, and this was the reply that made me freeze:

"Shall we get Jackie to ask her?" Helen volunteered.

Well, this was met by my eyes flitting back and forth between her and the vet, and with my mouth trying to soundlessly form discreet words, to the tune of, "No, shhhhh, he's a vet!"

"No, you're okay with this, aren't you?" she boldly said to him.

Well, by this time I think my colour had drained, and Bob was carrying on as if he couldn't hear a thing, and the vet said straight to me,

"It's okay, carry on, it would be good to hear!"

If anyone thinks your stomach can't turn over, well it does, but I had to step up to the plate and ask Ruby for her answer. I quickly re-introduced myself to her, and she said she remembered me from our previous chat regarding an ovarian problem, then with distinct clarity, volunteered these words, "I am feeling a bit better, but my iron levels are not quite up to what they should be yet!"

'Unbelievable!' I thought, could she not have given me something vague like, 'Oh, I have a bit of a sore leg,' not something demanding such accuracy. With that, I took a deep breath and repeated it to the vet.

To give him his due, he was totally fair, nodded and said,

"You are absolutely right, that's what her blood tests showed," and with that he turned to Helen and suggested she increase the supplement to try and sort out the last of this anaemia problem. I smiled and started to breathe again at this point, thanked him for being so courteous and listening to me, and you never know, one day he might even ask for my help.

I expressed the urge of desperation for coffee and disappeared off to make myself a cup, only to be followed shortly by Helen (who seemed totally oblivious to my consternation) and still slightly in shock, I gasped,

"Ahh, I could have died, he is a vet you know!"

She casually replied,

"Yeah, but we had already been talking about you and he knew of the other things that you had got right, and I thought it would be nice to show him it is true!"

I forgave her and thanked her for her kind intentions, and actually it has cured my fear of vets knowing what I do - if they listen, they listen, and if they don't, they don't!

Total Recall

William was a four year old horse that was very sweet but came across as rather slow on the uptake. Talking to him was actually very easy and he gave us a real insight as to the power of memory and incredibly how much they do know, even when they are just a few days old. Now you may be thinking that it would not be possible, but this little horse, who, bless him, is not totally physically right either, recalled it as it was. The owner had missed the actual birth so he was not aware of what had happened, but suspected something had gone amiss.

When I was talking to him, he told me of various problems that he had, although he was not worried by them, and put them to me in a very matter of fact way. An example being: "My legs are quite strong but my hocks (hocks are the large joint that lets their back legs bend, and also lock when a horse sleeps standing up) are quite weak," and many other references in the same vein. Eventually, I asked if he knew why he was different to the other horses.

He passed me a clear vision, showing when he was being born, he got stuck; his head and neck were out, but he was trapped by his shoulders and

Animal Insight

showed me the constriction around his neck. I acknowledged this, told his owners and they asked me if, perhaps, he might be able to give us more detail. He showed me that he could not balance his head left or right, because his neck was so weak, and with his body so wobbly he could not achieve the balance to stand. His owners immediately said that was absolutely right, that's exactly how they remembered it.

Having listened to his owner's, William passed me a picture of them and the vet, all standing over him looking very desolate. This was accompanied by the words,

"It doesn't look good." With that reminder their faces fell as the emotional memory was still etched in there, but quick as a flash he laughed and said, "Ha, but look at me now!"

Animals are so fascinating, and I am sure William wouldn't mind me digressing to tell you this. With his schoolboy sense of humour, it is more than likely he has been up to the same nonsense. During a conversation with an animal, if something sad comes up, rather than letting their owners stay upset, they will go out of their way to then say something to cheer them up (sometimes with an occasional prompt from me). A fine example of this was an owner crying in front of me, so to amend the situation her horse asked me to tell her that often, when she went round to his backend, he would purposely pass wind! She stopped crying immediately and we both laughed, it cheered her up and certainly made my day.

Anyway, back to William - his owners were totally taken aback but said that was exactly how it had been. Logically, we think that it was the restriction of oxygen that had left him with problems; but it was definitely not enough to affect his memory, well, his subconscious anyway.

The owners adore him and he is just like a child that has got some form of problems, but they make up for it in other ways. As I said, he is akin to a naughty schoolboy, especially with the other horses, but they are completely tolerant of him, which he takes full advantage of and freely admits to it as well!

The other thing that they were worried about was that as the other horses were ridden and doing things, they were concerned he was feeling left out. Although he was now four years old but physically rather weak, would he want to do some form of work? He had a quick think and came up with his ideal solution. He would like to do 'pretty things', at the odd show, with the owner's wife dressed up in 'pretty things' too! It would only be showing in-hand (un-ridden), so not much work really, but with lots of attention. A very clever answer from one that's not 'quite right', as you may say, but with such caring owners I am sure he will get his way.

I actually first met this couple at one of my cancer fundraising nights, and having given them the proof that animal communication was real they decided to come to my stand at a horse show. We then were able to have such a special communication, getting the answers his owners needed to hear, but most of all, being able to give this special boy a voice to tell us that in spite of his problems, he is so happy and is thriving emotionally. I thank him for giving us the insight that even from the very beginning, we now know they are listening and understanding.

"If you keep icing the cake, eventually it will sink"

Wise words from a horse for her owner, trying to get through to her that living by striving for perfection all of the time, could sometimes be her undoing.

"I'm a conservationist you know!"

A lovely cobby horse, explaining why he does everything at his own rather sedate pace, subsequently conserving his energy levels.

"I'm the one that lays the double yolkers!"

A real life chicken and the egg statement! This chicken was one of only five, and her owner said she did find the odd double yolker, but how this bird knew what was inside her eggs was a whole new mystery.

Animal Insight

Completely Bamboozled

"Help, my horse is going to 'Horsepital' on Tuesday!" This was the opening line from an email from Meg, about a six year old mare called Bamboozle. Attached was a picture of a very pretty and dainty bay thoroughbred mare. She was affectionately known as Boo or Boozy for short, and was booked to go in for investigation the following week.

I started the call in my usual way and explained that I don't diagnose, I can only tell you what your animal tells me. Then I tried to get Boo to talk about her likes etc., but she was having none of it. She went straight onto her medical problems, and boy, didn't she pass some over to me to experience. I got the intense feeling of pain at the top area of my neck, like pressing towards my head, I relayed this to Meg, to which she replied,

"Gosh, you're scary, but in a nice way," which I thought was a classic response; however, she knew exactly what I was referring to. I then asked Boo to show me herself moving and she kept veering slowly left, she could not hold a straight line. I felt like her back end was not working with the front, on top of this she said she was weeing far more. All these symptoms Meg recognised, so now we had to ask Boo where she thought these problems were arising from?

She immediately told me that there was a vertebra at the top of her neck that seemed like it had extra bone, or the like, under its front end. So, logically thinking, if the front portion is tilted up, then maybe the back of the vertebra is pushed down, thus causing pressure into her spinal column. Apart from the intense pain, it was causing a problem with messages getting to her brain; possibly a neurological problem too.

By this point, although Meg was very tearful, she felt relieved because this is what she had suspected all along, and for the past 18 months nobody had taken her seriously. Several times she had been given the usual stock answer, "Just ride her through it."

I now understood why Boo went to lengths to say, "Don't let them fob you off," and she was happy to go and have the scan she was booked in for the coming week. She knew she would have to be lunged in a circle first, and as uncomfortable as that would be, she would put up with it, just for someone to recognise that she was not awkward and that she really did have a problem.

Boo told us that if her neck was x-rayed, to ask for it to be done from the side, 'As they would see it as clear as day', and that she thought she would be going to Bristol!? There is a big vet school in Bristol, so we wondered if this is what she meant, and also that maybe this case would be written about. This was somewhat ambiguous at the time.

That Tuesday, she was loaded and went to the vet's practice and had a scan, which involved injecting her with a radioactive substance to flow round her blood stream, for the scan to pick up inflammation etc. This would mean she would have to stay there for a couple of days. Boo was fine about this. Meg had made up enough feeds for her to be given and she knew it was a temporary stay.

The scan showed hotspots (areas of damage/change) in her neck and lower back and one hind fetlock (the horse equivalent of our ankle). This looked like they were actually getting to the root of her problem and proof that she did actually did have a serious problem. They went ahead and x-rayed the three areas and then to Meg's amazement, totally dismissed the neck, said there was nothing wrong and that she had a problem with some vertebrae in her lower back. They said that with steroid treatment she would probably be able to ride her again soon!

Well, this diagnosis was totally unexpected and to be honest didn't cover the neurological aspects at all. Boo went home and Meg agreed to start the treatment suggested, as who was she to argue? Meg had told me about the results and treatment offered, and felt she had no choice but to try with the steroids to see if they would have any effect.

Within a couple of days, she called me to say that Boo was acting totally out of character and could best be described as 'angry'. Meg really wondered what she should do, and could I ask Boo why she was behaving so? Again I stressed that I could not go against what any vet had said, but I would ask Boo what she thought. Boo said she still thought she should go to Bristol, and at that point the penny dropped; the original clinic Meg had thought of was near Bristol (not in Bristol, like the vet school is, so hence the misunderstanding) and apparently this vet was a real specialist in this medical sphere.

I only ever tell it as it is from the animal, but with that Meg said she was going to get a second opinion as she felt the mare deserved it. Boo told her, that even if her problem could not be fixed, that she was fine with that and would quite gladly go to Heaven. She stated that she had come to Meg for a reason, and that reason was for her to help Meg learn.

Within a few days she was travelled to Bristol. On arrival at the clinic, she booked in and then went out to unload her. As she came down the ramp and stepped on to the tarmac, the vet said straight off,

Animal Insight

"This does look neurological to me." (This was being indicated by her lack of natural coordination.) Meg asked if he would x-ray her neck from the side to see if anything was wrong, and as sad as the truth was; it could be seen as clear as day, she had spurs of bone coming from the 2nd and 3rd vertebrae, thus causing a tilting effect from it impinging her spine.

Meg's thoughts had been vindicated; there was something very wrong with her, causing the pain and symptoms this little mare had been showing for so long. The vet explained that it was basically inoperable but he would give her huge amounts of steroids and anti-inflammatory drugs and see if they had any effect on her, but basically they were looking for a miracle.

After about five days, she actually did a couple of paces of canter which she had not done in such a long time, but the truth was apparent that she was not ever going to be cured. I had said to Meg, that if she was going to go to Heaven, and she wanted me to speak to her, I would be there for them both.

Boo was totally fine with the whole idea, she knew all about it, and she described how she wanted it to happen and actually said that she was quite excited to go. As a last request, she said she would love a few hours of pain free time, so she could have a last fool around.

The day came, and early in the morning the vet came and filled her with huge quantities of painkillers and steroids, and wow, didn't she have such fun! She ran round and round, like she didn't have a care in the world. After such a long process, with its huge ups and downs, with more emotional turmoil than one should have to bear, Meg was so at peace with the whole thing, that she managed even to take some photos of Boo, pain free, and enjoying the fun and freedom of movement.

I knew the vet was due at 2pm and at 2.45 I heard Boo say, "Thanks everybody, thanks for everything."

Meg sent me an email that day, to tell me that it had all gone smoothly and that Boo did seem excited; in fact she had trotted sideways down to the field. She is now buried alongside another friend that had gone before her. The email just showed me how communication has such wonderful effects, as there was also a photo of her jumping over the electric tape into the next paddock!

Boo told us early on that she came to Meg to teach her things. I always say that 'there is no such thing as coincidence', and it turned out, originally, that Boo was the free in a 'buy one, get one free' and she certainly did change things for Meg. With all this turmoil, it led her to me, and to be honest, only as a last resort. She had never experienced animal communication before, and now realises just how much can be accomplished by something that basically sounds impossible.

I take this opportunity to say that this story has not been written to highlight a vet's mistake, far from it, they do wonderful work, but, the same as doctors, they are only human and mistakes can be made. Through Boo's story, if we have learned one thing, it is that nobody is infallible, this is not about not accepting the truth; it's about really searching for it.

My picture from her was also slightly inaccurate, but I was fortunate that she gave me the correct area of concern. She was right when she said she thought a case would be written about her. We didn't understand it at the time, but do now. Her story has gone far and wide due to internet forums and now here in my book.

So if someone says, 'Just ride them through it,' think of this little mare, and make sure they have all the facts before you do so. This has been a very emotional journey, and I feel honoured that I have been part of it and able to make a difference. Through my work, I have been given proof, time and again, that we, and animals, do go to spirit and live on a higher plain (occasionally reporting back!)

As Meg now knows, you are not saying, "Goodbye forever", you are saying, "Goodbye, until I see you again."

A Cat's Prayer

I really don't know from day to day what type of case will come in, and this one was definitely not straightforward.

Debbie contacted me about a little female tortoiseshell cat called Charley. Sadly, Debbie had to re-home her when Charley was three, and now she was the grand age of 16. Debbie had seen Charley many times over the years and had, on occasion, been her present owner's cat sitter. I talked through the ethics of this unusual situation, but Debbie told me that the current owners had written to her to tell her that Charley had cancer. She had spoken to them about my work and they were happy for me to help, so I followed my instinct and agreed to try to see what I could do.

As usual, I aim to get information to prove that it is the right animal I am talking to, and to be honest this took a bit more doing than normal as she was in a different home. Charley then gave me a vision of her hiding behind some plant pots and then springing out on someone. This was met

Animal Insight

with laughter from Debbie saying that she remembered that game from those days many years ago when she owned her.

I thanked Charley for talking to us, and tried to explain exactly who wanted me to have the conversation with her. To be honest it did take a while for the penny to drop about Debbie, but then she gave a symbol indicating two people separating. I checked this with Debbie and she confirmed that is why the cat had been re-homed. Charley was quick to say that Debbie had felt so guilty about this, but could I tell her she should not have done, it was just life. She told us that she understood at the time what was going on, and was fine about the whole thing.

Charley started to try to say more things for Debbie herself, who halted this with,

"But she should be talking about herself." I did manage to steer Charley away from talking about her, and explained to Debbie that animals do this because they feel there are things that they think you need to know.

I got Charley onto the subject of her health, and she knew that she had cancer, a growth under her leg, but said that she felt it was a bit worse than they actually thought. She said that she felt heavy, which was not about her actual weight; but due to the effects of the drugs that she was on to try to slow down the speed of the growth. She was in no real pain and was quite accepting of the effects of illness and age; explained beautifully by the line,

"I feel like I am in second gear now instead of top!" Also she was unequivocally not sad. This was one of the major things that Debbie had wanted to find out, and the other being if Charley was all right about the treatment she was having. Any worries about this were quickly dispelled, with the succinct answer,

"You know me, if I didn't want something, I wouldn't have it." Debbie chortled and said,

"Yes, that's her!"

Once the health issue had been talked over, she was quick to come back to Debbie. She asked if Debbie had got the money she needed; this quite threw me (I was quick to say if she didn't want to answer the question, then no problem) but asked Debbie if that made any sense. At first she said,

"No, we are financially fine." Charley was quite persistent so I carefully said,

"Again it's not my business, I am only translating for your cat, but had there been an obvious time where money really would have helped the situation?"

"Ah, yes," Debbie said. And then she explained that 13 years ago when she re-homed Charley, money was really rather short and that had made things even more difficult.

I quickly tried to get off the subject as it was uncomfortable for Debbie, but bless Charley,

"It's nice to be comfortable, isn't it!" which I passed over to Debbie. What a way to sum things up to let someone know they did the right thing.

This was a very special reading to do and now I know why it had felt so right to do. Apart from Debbie needing to know things about Charley, Charley needed Debbie to know things too. Charley went on to say she didn't know whether she would make 17, but she added,

"Heck I've had a good innings!"

As I say, there is no such thing as coincidence; Debbie had found my number in a church on a slip of pink paper. I have no idea how it got there but it was put there for her to find. Maybe we're not the only ones that say their prayers?

Sadly within a few months of talking to Charley her words rang true, she didn't make seventeen but was put to sleep on St. Valentine's day. A very appropriate day I thought, as this cat had so much love to give – and, in return, her two separate owners who loved her very much gave it back to her.

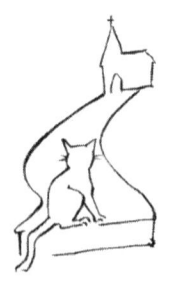

A Fleeting Reminder

I had met Honey's owner, Gill, through a friend who recommended her to me. Gill does wonderful alternative work and she had come to my house to do some reflexology. The visit turned into a social one, we had such a

Animal Insight

wonderful time, talking and sharing our views, she is just one of those people you can meet, and feel like you have known for years.

About six months later, she phoned me saying that she needed help. Whilst nursing her heavy heart about Honey, their Golden Retriever, who was in obvious discomfort, my name had just popped into her head as if someone had said it to her. This is a fine example of how it happens, as angels/guides will steer people in the right direction to help them at their time of need. How many times have you thought of someone and they have phoned, or someone has an accident and the next person that comes along just happens to be a nurse.

Honey, their beloved pet, was fourteen-years-old and nearing the end of her days. Gill wanted me to ask her exactly how she felt physically and emotionally, and what action did Honey want her to take.

Honey quickly reeled off her various ailments. She said how sad it was that she now didn't have the inclination to go and lie in the garden anymore. She went on to say how wonderful her life had been but now she was ready to go, saying she was looking forward to meeting up with another dog. It transpired, this was her litter mate who had died as a puppy, Honey was one of the lucky ones who had been rescued.

Gill wanted me to ask her if she should call the vet out that night, or what did she want her to do. Honey said she wanted to spend her last night at home, in front of the fire with them, and go on her travels the next day. I relayed all the information and wished them well and gave her my love to help her on her journey.

A week later, her owner emailed me, to thank me and say that, as broken as their hearts were, to be able to spend that special last night in exactly the way Honey wanted had made an extremely sad situation more bearable.

I felt completely honoured to be asked to do this and although the conversation about the end of their lives does quite often come up, I find it fairly easy to cope with. Animals are so open and have a complete understanding of the start, middle and end of the life process; they do not have the same fears as some of us.

Life for people would be so much easier if they really did know the truth, that this is not the end for us or our animals, just part of a journey. We are here to learn and help others, death to me is just an enforced separation, but only temporary, because without doubt, we will all go to the same place in the end and are reunited.

This all happened late September; I can remember this as they had not lit the fire yet that Autumn, until Honey's request had prompted it, and to be honest, I thought that was the end of the story.

A few months later, on a beautiful crisp December's day, Bob and I were walking our Collie, Sally, up in the gorgeous woods that adorn our village. Deep into the woods, at the top of a bank, we often stop to look down upon the hamlet in its entirety.

During this break in our walk, I saw what I thought was Sally dashing back past me, but then looked ahead and she was sat there straight ahead of us. Slightly taken aback I said to Bob,

"I have just seen another dog, but who was it?" and, with that, I saw the lovely vision of a beautiful Golden Retriever just walking to my right hand side. I was greeted by the words,

"It's me, Honey. Can you tell her I'm fine?" and with that she was gone.

I knew exactly who she was, and thought what a special moment for my husband and I to share. We finished off our walk and when I got home, I phoned Gill to pass the message on. She was so delighted and said that she had sensed Honey's presence still around her, and thanked me for the message.

That moment is now beautifully etched into my memory and I sincerely thank Honey for that.

This Fleeting Moment story will, I'm sure, invoke some memories with you loving and responsible pet owners. Most of us have had to make the decision to help a beloved animal leave this life to move on up above.

Many people are left with feelings of anguish and guilt, wondering if this was the right action to take. Many also find it so hard to let go of the grief, and would love to see them again. I have written this poem which I hope may help ease you if you still have a heavy heart, or give you strength when you need it again.

Letting Go

Your heart is bursting, searing with pain

That physical touch never to be had again

You only let them go because you so clearly care

They might not be here but they are surely up there

Animal Insight

You feel the pull and the tear of your heart
You feel torn inside and ripped apart
The enormity of choosing what best to do
It was done with your love, as they looked to you

We don't enter into this without thought or care
We do it because the compassion is there
The choice to stop pain and distress of the one we love
Can only be guided by you and the angels above

Many spirits have come through and given me their word
Your tears of sorrow and distress they heard
But they are free and happy and hold no ill will
Whatever was wrong could not have been cured with a pill

The height of pain is a measuring device
It shows how deeply you felt throughout their life
With your love given for this most selfless act
They at least left this earth with their heart intact

Now up yonder and free to roam
This is another level, like a new home
The day will come when you go up there too
They're ready and waiting to meet and embrace you

If you truly did this from your genuine heart
You were so brave and helped them depart
Your love and courage was seen from above
This really was your strongest act of love

If you could ask them now, what might they say?
"In my life, that was actually only one single day,
Please remember the rest, the joy, love and play,
For I look down from above and remember it that way."

As time has passed you may at last feel some ease
Maybe a pet has come for you to please
Animals are not selfish and want you to share
They left that space for another needing your love and care

We are truly honoured to share their in their space
Think back and let that smile adorn your face
The precious time you had could never be measured
Your lasting memories are of those you truly treasured.

Cutting Corners

Donald is a stunning roan driving pony, who has competed with his owner, Laurie, for many years. He loved doing his communication, as did she. He showed me many tricky things he did at trials, and they were in his list of 'likes'; it was wonderful to know he enjoyed his work.

He impressed on us the fact that he absolutely loved cleaning every scrap of food out of his bucket. Laurie laughed and said that his enthusiasm had caused his beautiful white blaze to have a permanent stain on it.

He had a few physical problems which explained why he had difficulty moving in a certain direction, so we assured him the osteopath would be booked imminently. He also brought up that he had had a fall and been very winded. Laurie knew exactly what this was, but was most relieved when he said that she had been more worried about it than him. He confirmed this by pointing out that his attitude towards driving had not changed at all.

Animal Insight

He went further to say that she worries too much about everything, and illustrated this with his own words, 'If the cat didn't finish its breakfast, she would be worried!' This caused great mirth and she said she would try and relax more, but when you love something so much, it is hard.

I am in total agreement with her, I have always been totally over cautious about our animals, to the extent that we now have a saying in our house, 'Belts and braces save sad embraces!'

I asked him what else he would like to add to the conversation and his question made me take a sharp breath.

"Why can't we cheat?" he sweetly questioned. I passed this over, and then quickly stopped Laurie saying anything else, so I could ask him what exactly he meant. He proceeded to explain that the judges are sometimes quite far away and can't see what's happening, so not all horses go the same way! Laurie confirmed that actually there have been rumblings about people taking shorter routes whilst out of view.

I explained that he is far better than that and he doesn't need to cheat and said,

"Look at how much you have won with pure honesty and talent." This goes to show that they really do know what is going on, and probably have a good chat about it amongst themselves!

He finished off eventually, I think he would have chatted all day, by saying what fun he has and that when they arrive at their destination, the first thing his owners do, is go into the lorry and say, 'Are you alright?' He really appreciates this, emphasised by saying,

"Isn't it nice to be treated like a person!" At this point Laurie was trying to hold back her tears, bless them both.

Steady Up

I was talking to a very chatty 17 year old pony, that was so full of confidence and fun you would never have thought there was a problem. He had been a wonderful pony club pony, the type that mothers put their name on a list for. This list is in the hope that when the present family outgrows the pony, they will have first refusal for their own pony-mad brood.

So, to ensure as little information is imparted to me as possible, I ask people to think of a keyword, and this one was 'travelling'. I asked him to show how he travelled to let me know what was going on.

Suddenly, he was making me feel the sensation of being pulled back and sitting down. It felt drawn out, tiring, and like I could collapse; all very disconcerting. It gave me the feeling like I was travelling up a steep hill and not being able to hold myself up.

His owner confirmed that the last time he travelled it was up a very steep hill near to their home, and what I had been describing is actually what he does; he does try to sit down.

What many people don't realise is that it is quite strenuous for horses to travel, they cannot totally relax; they have to use their muscles and bodyweight to keep their balance. When on bends and hills, and especially when the driver brakes hard, for example, this can be very demanding on them.

There was a combination of problems here, not only was he getting a bit older and not so strong, but also the same applied to her towing vehicle. The owner freely admitted that her old Land Rover Discovery was now really struggling to pull up that hill too!

I asked what would be preferable for him and he said he would rather stand herringbone; that means standing on the angle instead of facing forward. Horses often find this a less demanding way to travel, as they can position themselves more easily to gain support, if required.

His owner paid for a transport company to come and take him for a journey in a lorry, just to make sure he was happy travelling like that. She could then sell her trailer, and look for a suitable lorry instead.

Again a problem solved, he got to travel the way best suited to him now, and her 4 x 4 would maybe last a bit longer without trying to pull a couple of ton up a very steep hill!

"Oh, that's the thing that makes you tired isn't it?"

The response when asking a horse what she thought about coming back into work.

"Mind-numbingly boring"

An extremely honest answer from a horse that was asked what he thought of dressage!

"It would be like you going to the top diving board, and trying to make yourself jump off."

An analogy from a five year old horse that had been totally over-faced at jumps when younger, trying to get the point over.

"Oh no, I'm not sitting in that."

Reasoning from a little mare that would not go into the stream. On closer questioning, we found her stable mate had sat down in a river during a long summer ride, and gone home and told her about it, so now she thought it was compulsory.

Jackie Weaver

Enlightening

Whilst visiting a crystal healing/gift shop I ended up talking to the owner's cat, Midge. As Janey was intrigued by what I did, we decided to see what Midge had to say, so she gave me a description of him and the chat began.

He is a very proud and loving cat, jet black, short hair with piercing yellow eyes. When asked what he liked, the first image he showed me was of a cat dipping his paw in a pond. I relayed this to Janey thinking what a cute image, she looked completely aghast and exclaimed,

"Oh no, it's my neighbours pond and they have been blaming another cat for killing the goldfish." We couldn't help but chortle and although this was his favourite pastime, I had to explain that it was not a nice thing to do. To enforce this message, I got him to imagine himself lying in the sun in the back garden and then suddenly, a huge hand came down and swiping him up into the air, and how awful that would be. This I hoped would graphically let him know just how these fish would feel. Bless him; he must have taken this on board as apparently no more goldfish have met their fate. So a job well done; the goldfish and neighbour are happy, as I am sure the innocent cat is too!

Whilst on a return visit to her shop, during the update on the 'save the goldfish' efforts, one of Janey's friends came in. He was very spiritual, and of rather senior years, but ended up joining in the laughter about Midge's secret antics with us. This awoke his curiosity and he casually said he had a problem with his old cat and, 'could I have a word?' His cat was about 15 and suddenly six months ago, had stopped coming into the living room and as much as he and his lovely wife had tried to fathom out why, they just simply couldn't.

After a short introductory chat with this cat, of also rather advanced years, I asked him what was wrong, and he gave me the sound of a slight buzzing noise, like an electrical hum. I asked the owner if they had purchased any new electrical items in the past six months. It took a while as he exercised his memory and recounted all the electrical items he could remember in his sitting room, with a, 'No, we've had that at least ten years,' and an, 'Ah, but no, that's old and runs on batteries!'

Suddenly, eureka! He said they had been given one of those touch on/touch off lamps, but commented that they had rarely used it. I checked with his cat who said he thought the humming sound was due to it being faulty/dangerous so hence the worry about being in the same room as it.

I tried to explain that it was safe but he was still uneasy with that, so it was easier all round just to take it away. The owner followed the cat's instructions, showed him the lamp being removed from the room and said that it was all safe now.

On a later shop visit, I found that all is back to normal and the cat is snuggled up, back in his favourite chair. This is another example of how animals can hear and be aware of so much more than us. Although in this instance, it wasn't faulty, but it didn't sound safe to him so he was just keeping well away from it. Problem solved!

A Seasoned Visitor

I live my life on the principle that, 'What's for you, won't go past you', so when I got an email from another communicator asking if I wanted to take on this job, I thought it was very kind of them. However, having read the contents, I began to think that maybe it was beyond me, but I decided to contact the lady concerned anyway. Strange as this may sound, she was asking if someone could talk to a stray tomcat in London!

This was at about 1pm in the afternoon, so I picked up the phone and asked for Lisa.

"That's me," a friendly voice replied. I was quick to say that she should not get her hopes up as I didn't quite know what she wanted, and I don't do missing pets. (I don't do missing pets because it can turn into a huge emotional roller-coaster, imagine the scenario; a loving owner has lost their cherished pet, and I do manage to tune in to them. Even with the description of their location, it may not be recognisable by anyone. Additionally they could be injured, so this leaves them, the owner and me, completely anxious and sadly in no position to do anything about it.) This request however was different; Lisa was trying to help a stray cat and wondered if we could try to talk to him. I said that I couldn't promise anything but was willing to try. I asked her if she would like to do it now, to which she replied "What now, right now, on the phone?"

"Yes, if that's okay with you," I responded. Although she said she had done communication before, it was later during one of our many conversations that explained why she was surprised at me doing it straightaway, off the cuff, so to speak. The previous lady communicator had had to go into a quiet state to be able to let the animals into her mind before starting a conversation with them. We all work in our own ways, but most people that know me would regard me as quite outgoing and easy to talk to. I find most of my communications are full of laughter; even the sad ones often cheer up and give us something to laugh about, so I treat them like an everyday chat.

Lisa told me that the cat had appeared at her flat just before Christmas 2007, and although she went away for the holidays, he was still hanging around when she got back. I asked her for a description and if she had named him. He was black, slightly longhaired and rather thin but had a distinctive white triangle on his head, and the name she had given him was Jasper.

To make sure that we had tuned in with him, I asked him to describe something that he could see round where she lived and he showed me a path that followed round a building. This was spot on, as this was just outside her flat, but to be sure I asked for another couple of things too, and was quite taken aback with his clarity. Usually the connection is with a pet that the owner interacts with (although if a wild animal it would be to me directly) but this lad was willing to talk to us, even though he was just using Lisa's flat as a smash and grab takeaway!

Firstly, we asked what he thought of his name and were promptly informed that he was actually called Henry, not Jasper! He then explained why he was going through Lisa's cat flap; it was simply to scoff what food was available. He told us in no uncertain terms that he was 'fine' and didn't need any attention or home comforts. This totally rang true, because if Lisa even moved, he was off like a shot, which was very sad as she thought he would benefit from a good home. Henry (as now called) seemed to get on well with her cat Squiggly (a sixteen-year-old neutered male) so the offer was there if he wanted it.

On this offer of a home, he was straight on the defensive and said,

"I have been there before, and that it didn't do us any good!" I questioned him about 'us' and he showed me a ginger cat that apparently he had lived with. They came home one day to find their owners had just simply moved, abandoning them, and so leaving them to fend for themselves. Sadly, he had lost contact with the ginger cat, so was really going it alone, but stated he wasn't sad, just hungry and didn't need anyone. Henry had totally lost all faith and trust in humans and who could blame him?

We chatted to him and found out he was eight; although I would never put money on age answers because some fib and some genuinely get it wrong. We took this opportunity to say we now understood why he would run off. Needless to say, touching was out of the question so I asked what could Lisa do to help him relax and trust her? He showed me a chair that she often sat on, and asked if she could just sit on that chair and solely observe

Animal Insight

him for a month. This would prove that she was no threat to him, and that would demonstrate her trust worthiness.

Coupled with this was a very strange request, especially from a stray cat. He gave me the smell of a lovely fragrant perfume, but a rather musky one at that; this turned out to be the one Lisa always wore. Henry asked if she would not wear this, as his senses were finding it a bit overpowering. I could see his point; domestic cats would maybe notice and even dislike a perfume, but just get used to it, but for a street cat whose life is in the open air, this comment would be understandable. So for Henry, Lisa wore no perfume at all, this was akin to someone going out without make-up on, breaking the habit of a lifetime, but she was happy to oblige.

We chatted some more and thanked him for being nice to her cat and explained that we only had his best interests at heart.

Lisa very kindly sent me a letter thanking me for my efforts, adorned with a simple but very effective and decorative doodle of a cat. Who would have thought a stray cat in London could forge a friendship with someone in Shropshire. We live quite a distance apart, and although we have never met, it just seems like we have known each other for years.

We have had many communications, and after the animal work, they tend to digress into what's wrong with the world etc., but mainly about what touching stories we had heard. Little did we know that this would turn into one in its own right, and thanks to several letters and doodles later, I have pleasure in adorning this story with her own unique artwork. It still amazes me that this started off with someone trying to offer a stray cat a home, to save him from a life on the cold dank streets of London.

A couple of months later she contacted me again, saying that she really thought there was a change in Henry and could I chat to him. We also took this opportunity to chat to her cat Squiggly, to ask him his thoughts, opinions and especially his feelings towards Henry. Squiggly was so sweet and generous, he said that he thought Henry was very interesting and often just liked to gaze at him. Henry being the first stray he had ever met was certainly very different from the cats that he had known throughout his life. He also wanted Lisa to know that, when she was out, Henry was quite chilled out and even ventured around their flat.

Over to Henry then; Lisa was right, he had relaxed and sometimes even batted the cat nip mouse around (with a certain amount of vigour I might add). Best of all, he had even let Lisa stroke him very occasionally when she put his food down for him, and on a few other occasions when the timing was right. This was usually accompanied with his cat 'growl' which he explained was him 'just talking under his breath'.

If Mother Nature had put someone on earth with animal patience, then Lisa must have been her. By now, Henry had commandeered a pink blanket, to show his 'manly affections' to, but Lisa thought if it kept him happy and encouraged him into the warmth, then so be it.

We seemed to be getting somewhere, slowly but surely, although we were beginning to doubt that he would ever be a domesticated cat. He told us that he was just here to show her things, and at that point in time, we didn't understand what he meant. He didn't see much of a problem with his life, and he even showed me his girlfriend, a rather alluring tortoiseshell cat.

It was Saturday afternoon and I had a frantic phone call from Lisa. Her neighbour had come round and asked if Henry belonged to her, as she wanted to have a word about him spraying in the communal hallway. Lisa said also there was a second problem, that could wait, but could I talk to him about spraying fairly urgently? I said that I didn't really think I could do anything but I would ask him his view. I set up the conversation there and then, and sure enough it was as we understood; he was marking his territory. He gave me a picture of a tall plant stand, and true enough, this was the chosen item to mark his scent. She said she could keep cleaning it but as I pointed out, if you take his scent away, he will just want to replace it; so maybe leave a little but use an air deodoriser to freshen the hallway.

The aforementioned second problem was regarding Squiggly, apparently Henry had decided to jump on him, and treat him like the pink blanket in his masculine way! This had been met with dismay and astonishment by Squiggly, who quickly made his escape. Lisa did not want a repeat performance of this behaviour; she certainly would not tolerate that. As usual, I don't assume anything and let Henry give his explanation, so asked him why he did it.

"He asked me to," was the reply.

"Pardon?" I asked if I wasn't hearing this right.

"He did, he asked me."

"Ok, let's ask Squiggly," I suggested

"Squiggly, what did you ask Henry to do?"

"I asked him for a cuddle."

I was starting to see the confusion now...

Animal Insight

"Squiggly, can you please explain to us what you mean by a cuddle?"

"Yes, it's when you lie close beside each other."

Ah, now we know what happened, I would have to explain this one to Henry, but bless him; Henry was listening intently, apologised and said it would not happen again. I did stress that it would be inexcusable and true to his word, Lisa never saw him try again.

It was a serious topic, but to be honest we did have to stifle our laughter. There was no malice involved just a complete misunderstanding between two cats, one very unworldly-wise, and one that is not quite as worldly-wise as he thought.

About seven months passed, it was heading towards autumn and Henry was about the same. Lisa had managed to empty a flea/worming pipette onto him, but physically he was still looking thin and had gained more scars. Having coped with several abscesses inflicted by the teeth of others, the inevitable question from Lisa arose,

"Jackie, how do you think he would feel about being castrated?" 'Oh Lord,' I thought, 'I don't know if we should really go down this route.' Henry really had made it clear that he was not a cuddly house cat, but maybe it was apparent to him that his lifestyle was doing him no favours. I said I would explain to him that if he wanted to be like Squiggly, and live in his home, he would have to be the same, which meant being neutered.

To my surprise he did not throw his hands - well, paws - up in horror, he said nonchalantly,

"Oh right, yeah, I do know that, I will think about it." I left that subject there, as the last thing we wanted to do was alienate him or make him feel under any undue pressure. Lisa and I discussed the practicalities, and she said she had mentioned it to her local vets. The problem was, she could only catch him in the evening and they didn't want him in overnight, due to the spraying aroma. Logistics were not going to be easy!

Lisa and I decided to say our prayers and agreed, whatever will be, will be.

People sometimes ask me if animals talk in accents and in different ways, for example loud, quiet, subservient or over the top. Yes they can, but not terribly often, but the more prominent the accent; the more likely it is to come across. Most often people say, 'I just knew he/she would talk like that,' in much the same way as if you know a person's character you can judge how they would speak to others. Henry was a prime candidate to show this in its essence. Lisa and I were chatting one day and she said,

"Do you think Henry really knows who I am?"

"Why do you ask?" I replied. Lisa explained that the other day she was walking round the back of the flats and spotted Henry with other cats and, typically, as Lisa would, said,

"Hi Henry!" Well, he apparently shot her such a look of scorn, turned his back, and marched off with his girlfriend in tow. I chortled at this scenario, firstly; because I thought if anyone from the flats was listening, they would think Lisa just slightly odd for saying 'Hi' to a stray cat, but secondly; because Lisa has told many people of our work, and although some were polite but obviously not interested, she knows that some people have found it fascinating so would not think this unusual behaviour from her!

Incidentally, she had also told the owner of the tortoiseshell about our communication efforts, and found out Henry's girlfriend was called Serena. Whilst talking to others locally, Lisa also had it confirmed that a house further down had indeed had two cats, one black and one ginger, but they had moved away a few years back, so it was more than likely, that was Henry's original home.

Back to the offhand treatment of Lisa, I quickly tuned in with Henry to ask him why he treated Lisa with such contempt. To be honest I think Lisa was feeling a little bit put out, so it was the least I could do. Henry's reply was to earn him his title of 'Henry the Chav', so if you can read this with a London accent and give him some attitude you will get the picture:

"Henry, do you remember seeing Lisa recently when you were round the back of the flats?" I enquired.

"Yeah, and?"

"Well, when she said hello you acted as if you didn't know her."

"Yeah, I know I did, but I wasn't having her show me up!"

"Show you up? What do you mean by that?"

"Well it's like this; you're out with your mates, and your mother comes out saying something like, 'your tea is ready son'; well all your mates would laugh at you and your street cred would go right down!"

Lisa and I erupted with laughter, but he obviously did feel a bit guilty because although he desperately didn't want to show his soft side, he added, "But tell her I am sorry, I didn't mean to upset her."

He had, on a previous occasion, taken great delight in telling us that he boasted to his mates about his chats with humans, explained in his unique way,

"Nobody else gets to talk to them like I do. I feel real special I do!"

Animal Insight

It was so lovely to know he enjoyed our efforts and quite typical of Henry to point out that the chances of another stray cat in his 'manor' having communication were highly unlikely. This clearly gave him a feeling of definite seniority!

They say there are angels on earth, well this day we would definitely say that Henry had his wings on! It was 8.45am on a Sunday morning and suddenly Henry appeared, a very unusual time for him. Lisa was trying to get ready as she would have to leave soon to catch the 9.00am bus that was just over the hill, roughly five minutes away. That morning he seemed ultra-friendly so Lisa decided that she would spend some time with him and get the next one at 9.15. He played with his cat nip toy and rolled around on the floor, and was very attentive. Time was ticking by, so she thanked Henry, grabbed her coat, hoping to make the quarter past if she got a rush on. As she got to the brow of the hill, she saw lots of flashing lights and police were stopping the traffic. Lisa ventured closer and asked what was happening; one of the policemen pointed over to the demolished bus shelter with a lorry still parked in it. Lisa said, "Gosh what time did that happen?"

"Nine o'clock," came his reply. Her blood ran cold as she suddenly realised she should have been standing there waiting for the 9.00am bus. Fortunately, nobody had been at that stop; but now you can see why we think Henry was doing his angelic duties.

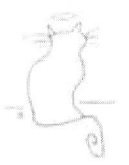

Autumn was quickly heading towards winter and late on a Thursday morning, I heard this very excited voice down the phone…

"You'll never guess!"

"Oh yes I will!" I replied. It was Lisa saying that Henry was in the vets as we spoke and it was just amazing how it had all panned out. Oddly she had had a day off work; Henry had wandered in late morning, and just went and sat on her bed. He didn't move when she entered the bedroom and, in fact, sat there quite motionless. Strange, as that was both unusual timing and behaviour for him. Within a tick, her brain whirred into action, she went and found her cat basket, and headed back to the bedroom where she just walked up to him, picked him up and put him in it, astonishingly with basically no resistance at all.

She quickly phoned the vets, who said to bring him straightaway, so on with her coat and off she went. She sat down in the waiting room along with others and Henry was that well behaved, if you hadn't known better, you would have thought he was a pet cat like the rest. She handed him over to the vets and was told that she could collect him that evening.

Feeling very emotional, Lisa told him she loved him and that it was for his own good. She was elated at being able to get him in for the operation, but she (and I) was desperately hoping that this was the right thing to do. Lisa said that he had sat on the bed so still, as if to say, 'Ok, go on, pick me up then!'

A few hours ticked by with different thoughts of the past nine months seeping in and out of Lisa's head, when she was disturbed by the phone, and a voice from the vets saying, 'Can you please come and get that cat out of here!' Oops, apparently Henry had decided he had done his good behaviour bit, the job was done and he would hiss and spit at everyone that came near him.

Back in his basket, looking wide-awake and none the worse for wear, Lisa took him home. She waited a while to ensure he was okay, but after much constant talking under his breath decided to let him out. Relieved to be out of the basket, he then popped downstairs and out into the back garden. Poor Lisa was so worried in case he was furious and would decide to move on, but her fears were totally unfounded. Sure enough, that evening he was back through the cat flap to be met by one very happy Squiggly, who tells us that, he enjoys their catch-ups when Lisa is out at work. Bless 'em!

The castration was done with good intentions, as I truly believe that if you do things with good intentions and they do go wrong, you should not have to reproach yourself, simply accept it as 'just one of those things', with a lesson learnt if need be. He was his usual self but still spraying. I told Lisa it would take about three months for the hormones get out of his system, so she would have to be patient, and behavioural changes could hopefully follow.

Time had now passed, he had at last stopped spraying and the plant holder had now been thoroughly cleaned, so no more worries about upsetting the neighbour. He did seem so much more relaxed. Gosh, the effort was all worth it, as one night it poured with rain so hard that he even slept in the flat until six in the morning!

Lisa decided we should have a catch up talk with him and see how he felt now, and as she knew, I never make anything up, or change what I am told (although I am tactful where needed). So she knew when we talked about his operation that I would tell it as it was.

Well, he pre-empted my questions and told me he felt fine and the reason he just sat on the bed was because he had decided to 'take the plunge!' He then added that it was so good that he didn't have to fight anymore. The relief for us was immense, and he followed this up by saying that Serena, his beloved tortoiseshell girl, still loved him anyway!

Animal Insight

Having been a vet nurse I obviously knew the reasons and practicalities of castration. I had often wondered if it was right to do this procedure, and how would it affect the older animals that have the operation. This has given me a firsthand account of it and I have never thought about how tiresome it must be to have to fight your way through life. We just accept it's a thing tomcats do, but if they had the choice I bet most of them would go down Henry's route.

We had a fun conversation with both of the cats when Lisa posed a question I would not have thought of, "If you could have chosen your name, what would it have been?"

Squiggly went first, and after some 'umming' and 'arring', came up with, "Elvis!" Once again we were in fits of laughter, at this lovely quiet cat wanting such a name. He explained that it made him sound really interesting, and now when he does venture out, it's a case of 'Elvis has left the building!'

Henry had had time to think, whilst listening to the 'Dude Elvis', and said, "Luther," which we actually thought was very fitting as we immediately thought of Martin Luther King, a man who taught people. As Henry had told us previously he was here to show Lisa things, we agreed that Luther was a thoughtful choice.

I got a lovely Christmas card from Lisa, adorned with yet another drawing and signed, 'With much love your pal and Guardian of their Royal Highness's, Henry - Luther and Squiggly – Elvis', which tickled me. After Christmas I generally use my cards as firelighters but kept this one, with just a couple of others. I didn't really know why, but I just went with my feelings and acted accordingly.

A few days after New Year, Lisa left me a message whilst I was on the phone, it was late in the evening so I decided to phone her the next day. The next afternoon I gave her a call and she immediately asked,

"Did you think of me this morning?" I was honest and replied,

"No, but when I got back in I saw my note reminding me to phone you. Why do you ask?" She said,

"I know this sounds mad, but I heard in my head, clear as a bell, 'Hi Lisa'." I said I quite believed her as to me hearing animals and people 'talk' in my head is quite normal, but told her I didn't know anything about it.

I asked how she and the boys were and, with this, she admitted that she had actually been trying to avoid phoning me, but felt I was the only one she could share her worries with her. She had not seen Henry since just before Christmas and was now very worried, having searched high and low for him, but to no avail. Lisa even went to ask Serena's owner, who then realised it had been a few weeks since she had seen him too.

I immediately thought the worst and felt rather panicked as knew I was heading into a territory I didn't want to go, missing pets or chasing spirits, not quite sure what it was going to be. I felt that I was so involved with this cat, and Lisa, that it would be my duty to do it and asked my guide, Rolf, to give me strength and guidance on this one.

Lisa went through the various scenarios, maybe he had decided to move on etc. but I just knew that he wouldn't abandon his most reliable friend Squiggly, whom he even managed to learn how to cuddle, but in a side by side cat way.

Lisa then said that the last time she saw him, when he came in for his visit, she noticed that he had a bit of a distended belly. He had allowed her to touch it and it moved, rather like fluid would, but he had eaten and then left as usual. With that, I immediately felt very heavy and full in my body, in fact, I felt positively sick, as in nauseous, so I quickly acknowledged this discomfort so it would go. I knew Henry was passing it to me, and just to make sure, he gave it to me again. I was full of pauses as I thought this sounded ominous and would be very emotional but I carried on, then heard the words,

"You didn't see me on bonfire night, did you, Lisa?" Now feeling rather anguished, I relayed them to Lisa, who said she remembered that night specifically as she was worried with all the noise and fireworks and kept wishing he would come in, but he had never appeared.

With that, he then showed me him being clipped by a car wheel on his left side, not so badly as to smash anything but enough for him to recoil. Then another vision, one of something tearing or being weakened inside; but he was able to walk away. Although this did not severely affect him at first, the damage had been done; this was to cause problems with fluid building up in his body cavity.

Although he had still been visiting and eating, he said that he had been slowing down. The day that Lisa noticed his strange stomach was to be the last time she would see him. He also pointed out to us that on his way out, he had paused and looked back at her, like someone does when they love you but are parting to go on a train for example. With tears, she recalled

Animal Insight

the moment, but had not really acknowledged it as anything significant at the time.

Lisa then said she thought he was dead and I said I felt that too, and then she said,

"I am sure Squiggly has just said 'He's dead.'" This might sound completely strange to people who don't do my kind of work, but I totally believed her as animals are extremely intuitive when it comes to a passing.

This statement was met with one straight back from Henry, who left us in no doubt that he had died, when he announced,

"He is right, but can you tell Lisa I can still see the Angel!" I asked him to share with me what he meant; there it was; an angel ornament to the right hand side of her bed. Through her tears she said there is an angel on her right bedside cabinet, but she had bought it weeks after his last sighting. We now realised that he was confirming that he had indeed passed over, but letting us know in such a beautiful way.

He then proceeded to say, with absolute clarity,

"Please tell Lisa she can hear!" ('Hear' in a clairaudient way, like I do) and suddenly the penny dropped, guess who said, 'Hi Lisa,' that morning! Maybe this was also an apt choice of words for him; after all, he did feel guilty for ignoring her previous 'Hi Henry!' He then showed me his body being gently lifted with two hands being slid under him, by what looked like a man in a uniform, maybe a council worker. He wanted us to know that he was safe and to thank Lisa for the biggest thing she ever did for him, by giving him Peace.

I now do believe that this cat was never supposed to stay, that is why he never made himself 'at home', he said he was here to show her things and he most certainly did. With such angelic timing, he arrived just before one Christmas and left just before the next. He chose the name Luther, this means soldier, liberator. Here on Earth he went out of his way to get into Lisa's life and to show things in a different light. If he can see Lisa's bedside angel from up there, maybe he will become her spirit guide, like Rolf my cat is for me.

I thank 'Henry the Chav' for pushing my boundaries, finding me a wonderful friend and giving me a viewpoint of castration for a non-breeding animal. By being liberated from hormones that can make them feel they have to fight and defend like a soldier; when really what they want in life, is what most of us desire - Peace.

Incredibly, since writing this story I got asked to appear on a television show on Sky, called Nick Ashron's Lightworker's Guide to the Galaxy.

This is a programme that highlights 'Lightworkers' who are people that do work to help others, mine being the Animal Kingdom. As anyone in the media knows, scheduling can be pretty daunting to organise, and having twice organised to get me on the show, paired with another guest, it had failed.

So Nick, the presenter, whose daughter Anna's two cats I had chatted to, asked if I would like to bring someone from my book. I chose Lisa, so we met up for the first time and stayed in a hotel near the studios.

We had such a joyous and remarkable time, and, hopefully, did our best to highlight the world of animal communication. I think Henry would have been very proud to hear how he went from being a stray cat in London, to being the central character being discussed on TV Show.

A Move Misunderstood

Susie, a ten-year-old cat certainly gave me a run for my money. She was so argumentative even her owner, Tammy, kept saying, 'Yeah, that would be right!'

She was black, of average size, with a small amount of white on her head, but had a face that I'm sure could frown when the need suited.

Susie lived in a house with four other cats; she lived life on her terms and her terms only. Although Tammy had learnt that this was Susie's way and had long given up any form of negotiation. They had moved house a while ago, but she needed help to find out why the cat's behaviour had become so stressed that she was now refusing to go out.

After getting the chat going and basically letting Susie call the shots, I asked the question about her not going out anymore, and she showed me a rather large and menacing tabby cat attacking her. I told the owner it looked like a tabby cat that was picking on her. Susie said they didn't have a tabby cat, so I acknowledged this, and although we were both rather confused, Susie decided to take me on to a different subject.

The cat then showed me her neck and what looked like a tooth going into it, long, sharp and with a volume of noise to accompany the picture.

Animal Insight

Logically, I thought that this was another fight she was showing me, but actually it wasn't. She had just had blood taken from her neck the day before, and was certainly not amused with the painful and rather undignified process. (The best place to get blood from a cat is from the neck area, and unfortunately they do have to be held in a rather upright position, with their neck tilted back.) If they don't struggle it only takes about thirty seconds to do, but Susie, being Susie, decided this was not for her so a battle had ensued.

I asked her if she knew what the blood test was for and she offered us her version of the result. She stated that her kidney function was a bit reduced but was nothing to worry about; she was very accurate as that is exactly what the vet had said the results showed.

Then suddenly she showed me the tabby cat again, this time smacking her on her head with a paw and then running out of the patio doors. Tammy then exclaimed,

"Ah, the patio doors! Those were at the last house and yes, there was a tabby cat that used to hang around." Now we are getting somewhere we mused.

I explained to Susie, that in actual fact they had moved not just houses but towns too. The horrible tabby cat was now very far away and would never be able to find her. This just goes to show that although we may put a cat in a basket and travel for a period of time to a new destination, how do they know that we are not just on the other side of their housing estate rather than in a different village for example.

Although Susie will always be an argumentative cat - just like there are some people out there who will always moan no matter what - she is now more relaxed and has ventured outside at last.

"Oh don't worry; if it's raining I'd be at the gate!"

Whilst discussing with our horse, Monty, why when I call him he comes, yet makes Bob walk across the field to catch him, I tried to suggest that he was being rather unfair, and what if it was bad weather…?

"You could stick pins in him and he wouldn't bother."

A horse describing his stable mate, who was totally bombproof and easy going, the exact opposite of the one we were talking to.

"Why were they trying to teach me that, when I can do it naturally?"

A succinct response from a miniature pony who confirmed, to his owner, that he really did not want to learn tricks, and this one he was referring to was them trying to teach him to lie down!

Secret Love

Filly was a very fine thoroughbred type mare, dark bay with a very glossy coat. She was bred by Caroline twelve years ago, and over the years they had a lot of fun together. They competed, generally enjoyed themselves, and had a great relationship. She held a special place in Caroline's heart, as she was the last in the line of eventers Caroline had bred.

Circumstances change in life as they did in Caroline's case, and this led her to go and work for a big eventing yard; it was a smashing place to work but, within weeks, Filly began to display serious behavioural problems.

As soon as I started talking to her, she started to make me feel very stressed, and was shouting like a child,

"They jump bigger than me, they compete more than me, I am nothing compared to them!"

It transpired that her stable was inside a large barn, and every time a horse went out, she would throw a complete tantrum, neighing and bashing at her door. This was being done with such force and vigour they were worried that she would injure herself.

When Filly had calmed down, she told me that the horse next to her was making her feel very inferior. He was a very good dressage horse and bragged that he could do this, and he could do that (and believe me they can be mean!)

This had set up an irrational fear that Caroline would decide that she would be better off with one of these other 'talented' horses, instead of her.

We explained that this would never happen, and in fact, most of the horses had only been there a year or so, as usually they were sold on. Whereas Filly; she had been with her owner for twelve years, so there was no need to fear, where Caroline goes, she goes, no question. We did a lot of explaining to help calm her down and asked her what Caroline could do to help prove this to her, so this is what she suggested: at night, before Caroline goes to bed, could she please nip outside and say goodnight to her and ONLY her. This would show how special she was and that the other horses might even take note too, due to them being excluded from this act of affection.

Caroline stuck to her word, moved her away from the conceited horse and snuck out each night for her goodnight duty. Within the week she phoned me to let me know that Filly had completely lost her anxieties and was back to her usual self. Phew, I breathed a sigh of relief, and was glad to hear such good news.

Although I have got used to listening to what one animal will often say about another and most of the time it is very funny, they really are like children and can say things just simply to annoy one another too.

I can recall one occasion when whilst talking to a horse she asked me outright if she was for sale. This took me by surprise as the owner had not mentioned anything about it and I quickly reminded the lady that the horse was also going to be listening to her answer. She paused and then said,

'Yes, she is, well was, maybe is, but more to the point, how an earth does she know? I have definitely not said anything to her about it."

I explained that animals can really pick up on your thoughts but I'd check with the horse that this was the case anyway. But the horse's reply was,

"The dog told me!" I must admit, I had to stifle a laugh and then as I put it to the owner, to top it all, the mare even quoted us the asking price! Sure enough, they did have a dog so the mare's answer was validated. We did laugh, however, imagining the dog listening to this, getting the advert details and running out to the yard to announce what he knew but the mare obviously didn't! He probably took great satisfaction in upsetting her day whilst making his!

I know that filly is still doing really well and even got to go and do some of the more 'serious' stuff too. She is so lucky to have a home for life, she is the centre of Caroline's life as Caroline is in hers.

Some Generosity Required

'Why does my horse refuse to wear a rug in the field?'

This was a question posed to me about Millie, a lovely Welsh Cob mare, black, rather hairy but with a gentle white blaze down her face. Millie was very forthcoming to chat with, and absolutely the apple of her owner's eye. The puzzle was: why if she was happy to wear a stable rug and an exercise sheet, did she insist in wrecking her turnout rug as soon as she was out in the field?

Apart from the huge unnecessary expense being incurred each winter, her owner was fearful that she would get her legs caught up in the straps and have an awful accident.

The obvious answers had been thought over, like: does she get too hot; is she funny about a tail flap; does the wind move it too much? Actually, it was none of the above. Millie was a very broad, big-shouldered Cob, and although her rug had shoulder pleats in them they still restricted her movement.

When the other horses were galloping about she could not move as freely as she wanted, so this was solved by removing it herself, by ripping it apart until she could step out of it. This was why a stable rug was not a problem as they are designed for indoor use only and as for her exercise sheet; it's a light rug that only goes under her saddle and along the top of her back so wouldn't restrict her shoulder movement.

She also told me that the other horses called her fat, and although she was rather more rotund than the rest, she would rather they didn't. (I have to admit, this did cause a certain amount of stifled giggling by myself and her owner as we imagined them bickering in the paddock.)

As I have talked to four other horses on the yard, I did manage to pass the message on about how hurtful words like that could be. One of the other horses was quick to inform me that Millie was bossy, so that's why they called her it. A fair comment I suppose, I didn't negotiate that one any further and left them to their own devices.

This was another great example of how similar to humans their interactions are!

Millie's owner has now researched and found a rug that is generous around the shoulder area and a better fit. Maybe now Millie can keep up with the rest of them, and this might even help her waistline!

Making Huge Strides

My dressage experience is quite limited, so I just describe what I am seeing. I sometimes ask the horse how their rider could make it clearer what they are asking the horse to do. I had a lovely example of this with Jess, a groom, who listened politely to all that I told her from her horse, but didn't seem entirely convinced. On asking her horse what they were struggling with, I was told, 'Extended trot.'

Jess looked at me with amazement as this was so true. As the girl was only about five foot tall, probably less than eight stone, and was riding a seventeen-hand horse, she would look rather like a pea on a drum. To be honest, any sceptic would have jumped at the chance to point out that she would hardly have the leg power to get the horse to extend his legs, but as I constantly say, I can only tell you what they say.

I asked the horse what Jess could do to help, and the mare asked her to say, 'Extend, extend, extend,' at the appropriate time. This could be said out loud, or just simply in her head, either way is fine.

When I was back on the yard a few weeks later, I got the chance to catch up with Jess. She beamed at me and said, "I tried what you said and couldn't believe it. She really stretched out and extended for me. I wish that I had got someone to video it for me, I was absolutely astounded!"

A few weeks later I went on to talk to her dog who proudly told me about the 'doggie dancing' they do together. Her dog also showed me her broken front teeth, which Jess confirmed were apparent. This, until now, had been a mystery as to how they'd been smashed. The dog told us that when she was young she had hurtled down some stone steps and landed on the point of her nose, thus causing the damage still in evidence today. So, from a non-believing groom/owner, she is now totally converted and talks even more to her animals than she did before, by simply using her brain, as they say.

If an animal really doesn't want to do something, I cannot tell them to do it, same as their owners cannot, but I can try to reason with them. Now that more people recognise the fact that their animals can understand, it is well worth trying to explain verbally in order to negotiate. If that fails, that's where we animal communicators come into our own as we can get their version of things (which is quite an easy shortcut if you think about it) and hopefully restart the negotiations.

Under Pressure

Louis was a horse I actually visited in person, as my husband was there to do his teeth. He's a well-bred event horse, dark bay, and of a strong physical stature. Louis had many issues underneath, and to be honest, his eyes looked depressed and his whole demeanour was not that of a happy, relaxed horse.

Straightaway he started to apologise for not being able to take Victoria, his owner, to the levels she had hoped for. This immediately struck a chord; he had been bought for serious money and was sold apparently being able to do a lot more than he actually could. Louis had done a lot of competing but more by 'you will' rather than 'can we' method. When Victoria put him under pressure, he would blow up and throw his weight around in the hope that she would give up, which, to be honest, tended to be the end result, but who could blame her. Although she wasn't a novice rider, sometimes you feel your own safety is more important than trying to finish a competition course.

Louis actually could jump really well, and Victoria was curious to know why, when in a ménage (an area designed for horses to exercise in with a good cushioned surface underfoot usually comprising of sand or rubber or a mixture of both) he will jump happily, but when out cross-country schooling he would put in stops or run out.

Her opinion was that she thought he felt safe in a school (as much as I did try to stop her telling me) but actually that wasn't it at all. The difference was; in the school the show jump poles would fall should he knock them, but cross-country jumps are unyielding, so the fear was of hitting them and hurting himself.

This reminded her of a conversation with the vendor, who stated that he was 'so brave' that they didn't bother with the small cross-country jumps - they just went straight onto the proper stuff! The 'proper stuff' they had mentioned consisted of big fences made from tree trunks and jumps built so solidly that they would last for years and years. This had really overfaced him, and had probably rapped his legs a few times too. Sometimes it doesn't take a lot for some horses to lose their confidence, the thought of pain and fear is enough to do it, whereas others can have crashing falls and go back out competing again as if nothing had happened - again very much like the difference between one person and another.

After explaining to Louis that Victoria was not disappointed and, due to the onset of a medical problem that wasn't apparent when she bought him, major competition was now out of the question, so there was no pressure on either of them to do any form of serious competing at all.

We also discussed his problem about not wanting to jump downhill; this was mainly due to his conformation. He had a high wither (the area at the base of a horse's neck where the front of the saddle would touch) and he felt the uncomfortable pressure of his saddle as it shunted forward into this wither area. (Sometimes even good fitting saddles can be affected by downward propulsion.) As a result he would go slow and crablike to avoid this, so I asked him for his advice how to get round this.

He asked her to hold the base of his mane and sit still; this would hopefully limit her and the saddle's movement on him. On her next ride, she tried this and was amazed when he stepped up a gear and popped off downhill happily.

Louis will always be a quirky horse as that is his nature. Now we have taken away his baggage, and Victoria understands where his resentment came from, they have struck a good balance, leading to a better life for them both.

Life's Timing

Now you are over halfway though my book, I do hope you are enjoying reading it and following the wonderful animals that have shared my working life. I also hope that I have heightened your interest about something you may not have previously experienced. I believe the stories speak for themselves, showing how wonderful animal communication can be, and show you; you just couldn't make them up. I feel at this point I would like to share a couple of my personal views with you.

I am fortunate that most animals that I have worked with have been forthcoming with their information, but on a couple of occasions, they have been rather reticent with me, and I have backed off from the conversation. One had an owner that didn't believe a word of what I did, so the horse could not see the point in participating either.

The other animal however, gave me the complete opposite description of what she was like, and tried to come across as the easiest horse in the world. The truth of the matter was; she was aggressive towards people, and didn't care for the company of other horses either, but could see no wrong-doing in her behaviour. We did eventually manage to identify some things to ensure it was her we were talking to, but if someone can't see the consequence of their actions, negotiation is very limited. This mare was homebred, so her background was known and the other horses there were, by and large, relaxed and happy. She had not been abused or been generally mistreated, and I assure you, I would be the last person someone like that would ever contact.

It is my own personal opinion (you may not agree) that I believe there are some animals born with psychological problems, just like us humans. Why should it just be limited to the physical aspect? She, like some people, had such a temper that she would lash out without thinking and get enraged over a range of very minor things. There are no such things as animal prisons/hospitals for this type, and unfortunately, sometimes we have to face up to the fact that they are truly dangerous, we have to think of our own safety, let alone others, and sadly seek the appropriate action. Saying all that, a huge percentage of behavioural problems are caused by us humans and that is where my work can help to try to undo what has been done. So for any animal that I work with, I do my best to listen to and explain things, and fortunately, most do take that opportunity.

Although communication is as normal as someone going to work and typing on a computer, I never forget how privileged I am for an animal to converse with me. I sometimes get very pressing questions, and sometimes an animal will avoid the issue, just like a person would. I tend to change tack and try again later in a conversation, and that usually works. On the very rare occasion, if I cannot get an animal to discuss a specific thing, then I respect their feelings and tell the owners accordingly.

One thing, I hear so commonly is, 'Oh I wish I had known about this years ago,' and I guess some people reading this may be thinking the same. I truly believe that everything in life is about timing and that things happen at the 'right' time, and not before. We sometimes need to have had that time to gain the experience, to understand what we are looking at now. You cannot change the past, what is done is done, but you are now further on in life and having gained experience, will maybe choose to try another way the next time. As I said, we cannot change the past, for those days will never be lived again, but the days ahead are our future, so long may we go on living life's experiences and using our knowledge gained, in the best way we can.

Jackie Weaver

The More Condensed Version

'There is something special he will want to talk about.' Those were her husband's opening words to me to tell me there would be something very obvious, according to him, that this horse would say. This was after his wife had given me the name and description of their horse, which sadly eludes me now, so for this story I will call him Barney.

That, in itself, was a very ambiguous line, but, fundamentally, her husband didn't believe a word of what I did! As I had chatted to his wife's pony an hour earlier, she really wanted me to do another and he wanted to listen in.

So here I was at a summer fair, with her sat in front of me, and him kneeling beside her with his eyes fixed on me, so no pressure then! I said that I would try, but asked him to imagine saying that to a person; how could they start to guess what he was hinting at? He seemed unimpressed by my reply so I thought I would be quiet and try.

I told them a few general things that applied to Barney, and to be honest, many things can apply to several horses. They have many things in common, as do we people, but her husband was polite enough to nod, and she responded well.

I now knew we were tuned in with their horse, and as I had explained to them (well tried) like I do to most people that I get things from their animal's point of view and what they might perceive to be important to them. (Often people book a reading with preconceived ideas of what their animal will want to talk about and often they are quite surprised with their animal's choice of topic. Sometimes they don't bring things up so I will then ask and see what response I get and even then, if they really don't want to discuss it, I can't make them.)

So, I took a deep breath asked him the burning question. I was given a very strange picture (in fact, I asked Barney to repeat it, as it was that strange) but I said it as I saw it.

"Why is he showing me a picture of a horse that looks like it's been concertinaed?" I asked, with that rising, questioning pitch to my slightly nervous voice.

With that, her husband's jaw dropped, her eyes filled with tears and I managed a breath! It became apparent, that whilst out hunting, someone's horse had run into the back end of Barney. This, in turn, had shunted him into the one in front and, basically, squashed him between them both. This was a very unusual but extremely painful accident, which had caused serious damage to be done to his spine.

Animal Insight

Barney told me about his back operation, what major surgery it was and very invasive. It had, however, left him fearful at the lack of his own strength, but he told us he knew he would 'come right' and did want to work again.

We assured him that there was no rush and he then asked if he could be led off another horse to gain his fitness that way. This was a very sensible suggestion as it would avoid back pressure, so was readily agreed.

Barney said that they would know when he was ready to be ridden as he would stand still to be mounted. Presently that's one thing he just wouldn't do, so there lay the explanation of one of the main questions they were going to ask me anyway.

I wished them well and hoped that Barney would make a full recovery as he had stated. Fortunately, they live fairly local to us and just before this book went to publish I met up with Barney's owner at the local point to point race meeting.

She was aboard one of her other mounts and on loose-horse-catching duty. This tends to involve having a canter up and down a length of track many times during the racing day. Also, it's a great opportunity for meeting up with people for a good old chin-wag and bringing back the odd loose horse that had ejected its jockey.

To be honest, I didn't recognise her but, fortunately, someone said her name whilst guiding a person in her general direction, so I waited a while, then I ventured up to her. When we spoke, I said that she probably didn't remember me but did she remember the chat with her horse?

"Oh yes," she enthusiastically replied. "You're Jackie Weaver, I do remember, and he is doing really well. Although, you know, I have to be honest, I was still sceptical that he would follow what you told me but, I give you your due, it went exactly as he said; I led him many times to the mounting block but he refused to stand still for me to get on. Then one day I led him there as usual, and he just planted himself - didn't move - so I climbed aboard. He walked on steadily and all felt well, so we set off on our first ride for a very long time."

Barney was so true to his word, he said he would get there and he certainly did! In fact, she was delighted to tell me that he had hunted all season. Also, he was back doing indoor show jumping, and had scored nearly 70 percent in his first dressage competition and, as any dressage riders reading this will know, that's pretty impressive.

I talk to so many animals, and do ask for feedback, because often it is like sharing a problem with a friend, and then being left to wonder if everything was resolved. On many occasions I never get to know, but on this occasion I was so pleased to be in the right place at the right time to find out such a great result.

Not on your Nelly!

'Would they like a new friend, a puppy, kitten…?' is a very common question I get asked. The answers are often what the owner thinks, but expressed by the animals, in their own individual way.

There are the ones who are really not bothered like, 'I don't mind either way, it wouldn't upset me, whatever you want is fine by me.'

There are the ones that are so loving and generous with their feelings; this is very common for rescue animals that have learnt to love and trust again. They are more than happy to share their owner, as often they realise that they can help/love another and certainly appreciate what their owners have done for them.

Here's a beautiful line that was given to me about that type of owner, 'Her heart has an abundance of love, so there is more than enough to share round.'

There are also the jealous types, who don't understand the concept of sharing, which is often met with a, 'I wouldn't think so, would you?' with that slight sarcastic undertone, often punctuated with a staccato effect in their answer. This is quickly acknowledged by me and the owner, as we don't want them to get miffed, like they seem to do in their everyday life anyway.

There are the worldly-wise or those born with that nannying instinct who think it would be a great idea. They often say something like, 'Oh yes, I can teach them all they need to know,' which is often followed up with, 'but also I'll let them know what is acceptable and what certainly isn't.'

Then there was the one, that, whilst intently following the three-way conversation (and, might I say, having a 'whale' of a time) listened to this question posed by her owner. Before I could even put it to her, she stated loudly and clearly,

"Not on your Nelly!" With this outburst, we melted into fits of laughter and her owner said,

"That is nothing short of what I'd expected."

This was Bess, a five year old, black female mongrel, looking very much like a small Labrador, but with that tell-tale white on her chest, suggesting she wasn't. She had exhibited the most marvellous sense of humour and was relishing the unexpected attention she was receiving. If she was a person she would have been on a stage somewhere entertaining the troops.

She delighted us with her mirth, expressing how she was the life and soul of the party and how much she loved other dogs that, in return, love her. Bess also told me that dog training really was not in her list of 'likes' but assured me that she and Eva, her equally hilarious owner, had an understanding. This, I would describe as 'rather testing Eva's patience', but done in such a style that the laughter kept getting in the way of the proper instructions!

Eva loved the fact that she was so gregarious and thought that she should go to a rescue centre and find her a friend to play with. The new friend would share in her hectic doggie life, filled with walking, playing, feeding and sleeping; the latter being achieved after several hours of very energetic behaviour, or by the warm Aga that seems to entice her there.

Spring arrived, so one glorious sunny day Eva decided to drive to a large, bursting-at-the-seams rescue centre. It was half an hour's drive away, so she popped Bess in the car and off they set.

On arrival she went to reception, explained about the home she and Bess could give a stray, and enquired if she could be taken round. So, with forms filled out, she set off round the kennels, doing her utmost not to link eyes with these poor creatures, most of them reaching out to her and some sadly cowering to the back of their kennels.

She knew that one would gain her attention and it did. She was a lovely young bitch about the same size as Bess (that 'medium' category that covers Collies, Springer Spaniels and the like), seemed friendly and became a possible candidate for becoming Bess's new friend.

Eva asked if she could take her and Bess for an introduction wander in one of the walk enclosures, to see how they gelled. They duly set off, Eva expecting Bess to do her usual to see how well her new 'friend' would play with her. She was waiting for Bess to jump like she was on springs, and run about in those ever decreasing circles, but there was nothing, and I mean nothing! Bess acted like, 'dog, what dog, I see no dog,' and completely went out of her way to ignore this poor innocent animal.

It didn't take Eva long to realise that Bess didn't want to know and decided that this maybe wasn't to be after all. Eva left the centre, rather perplexed, full of apologies and with some guilt for having maybe raised that little dog's hopes, but at the end of the day, Bess was her priority.

Live TV

Percy is a ten year old Springer Spaniel, owned by a lovely lady, Lauren. Lauren was organising a holistic fair and I'd phoned to ask if I could book a space. This was done on the advice of my friend, Penny, and although I was really unsure if people would want to talk to me, she persuaded me it would be fine.

Lauren had never come across an animal communicator before, but she also thought that people would be very interested in what I had to offer. I gave her an outline of what it was about and when she mentioned that she had a dog, I offered to have a chat with him for her and show her first hand.

Percy is a complete livewire, as you would expect from a Springer and although enjoying life with her and her children, when her new boyfriend came on the scene things started to change. Steve, the boyfriend, had tried every which way to get on Percy's good side but still the dog was showing aggressive behaviour towards him.

We established that this was mainly in the house, and even more so if he tried to go upstairs. This was a complete 'no go' area, confirmed by the picture of a long velvet stair curtain drawing Percy's defence line. On asking Percy's point of view and why he was being like this, he explained that Steve kept going away and one day he might not come back. He was worried that it would upset Lauren, just like it had during the break up of her last relationship, which he had been witness to.

It became apparent that Steve came from quite far away and was splitting his time between Lauren and his mother, so this was factually true but Percy saw this as non-commitment. I explained to Percy that this showed how caring Steve was, because as much as he liked Lauren, he still wanted to spend time helping his elderly mother. I reassured him it was nothing for him to worry about, and that if their relationship doesn't work out, there is nothing he can do about it. The responsibility does not lie with him, so stop worrying about something that may never happen.

That night, Lauren and Steve went home, and I am sure had a good chat about the fact that animals do have a voice like us humans, and it's just a shame that only certain people can hear it. They arrived for the second day of the fair, and were excited to tell me how very affectionate Percy had been towards them both. Also they could see how much more relaxed he had become.

However, the chat with him was not all doom and gloom, far from it. Although the above was a serious issue, he did chat away to us with a

Animal Insight

certain exuberance, very much like Lauren would have expected. Me too, as I have yet to find a quiet Springer; I love chatting to them, they are so outgoing.

One thing that he did was to keep giving me the repeated picture of a garden shed door. As I can only say what I see, and as strange as this was, I said questioningly,

"Why does he keep showing me a shed door?" The reply was immediate,

"Ah, Guinea Pig TV!" It turned out that Percy spent many an hour just sitting tuned into his favourite motion picture, courtesy of their furry pets housed in the garden shed.

A few months later Lauren phoned me again, she had picked him up from kennels and taken him for a walk. On returning home, she noticed a large wound, but had no idea how he had got it. Having checked the car over, she then immediately phoned the kennel owners who were equally mystified. They had gone and checked his kennel, and said there was no blood, so Lauren could only presume it must have happened elsewhere. She gave me a limited outline, which is totally the way I prefer it, so I set out to try and unravel this mysterious injury; as to where and how he got it.

Straight away, Percy showed the gash on the inside of his right hind leg but fortunately did not seem to be upset by it in the slightest. He then took me over his journey. This was into the forestry, parking the car, jumping down from it with total ease and no hesitation, haring round at breakneck speed as usual. Then suddenly I saw it, he had gone onto a short sharp broken wooden stake that had caught him under his right hind leg, and opened it like an envelope. As bad as it looked, he said there was not a lot of bleeding and it wasn't that sore. Sure enough, he couldn't have felt much, as he had jumped back into the car without a problem - mystery solved.

He had to go to the vets and have it stitched up and was amazingly well behaved, although this might have been something to do with the treats he was promised on his return home. He was totally unfazed by the whole episode, and popped off down the garden ready for his next guinea pig epic.

I would also like to take this opportunity to thank Penny for persuading me to do the fair. I had only met Penny a matter of weeks before when she had a stand at a local show selling crystals etc. We got chatting, I had an 'animal chat' as I do, and she suggested that I should go to this holistic fair. I was so nervous, that Penny, bless her, offered to come with me for moral support. We had two days there, and it was wonderful. I met lots of people and chatted to many animals. I have had such fun and enjoyment at these holistic fairs since. Without their grounding, I would never have gained the confidence to be able to go out and do demonstrations. In life, people can be so generous and wonderful; they will go out of their way to help you, and that is Penny to a tee

In Poor Taste

During a chat with Jane, whom I have known for several years, I was updating her on my madly changing life. Jane wondered if I could have a chat with Tess, her beloved, although rather mischievous Jack Russell. I thought this would be great fun and although most of my work is done at a distance, she's a friend, so it was a chance for a good chin-wag and sampling of her latest home-baked goodies.

So on a cold autumn day, with rain cascading down the windowpanes, we sat in Jane's lovely warm farmhouse kitchen hugging our steaming mugs of coffee, ready to start the chat with her dog. Tess, a cute black and white eight year old female had made the effort to greet me with her usual great enthusiasm as I entered, but then proceeded to jump back up onto her sofa, snuggled into her blanket and showed no interest in my presence whatsoever! (Remember, this is working into their subconscious, so of no consequence to the communication.)

As much as I tell people not to give me extra information about their animals, there seems to be an overwhelming urge for people to say something anyway! Just as I was starting to tell Jane how we would do the communication with Tess, she suddenly blurted out,

"I wonder if you can see her heart condition?!" I burst out laughing and said,

"Don't tell me your name, Jane, don't tell me your name." (My personal reminisce of that classic line from the 1970's sitcom Dad's Army, when the enemy asked Pike for his name and his Captain shouted out, 'Don't tell him Pike!') After much laughter and apologies from an over-keen owner, I went back to the conversation I was about to have with this little girl.

Tess chatted away telling me all that she liked, which included visiting the neighbours, which fortunately truly adore her too, and an insight in to her personally invented caravaner's game. On her farm, they have the occasional weekender who parks on a small patch of field, and much to Tess's delight are of keen stalking interest. On a morning, she will sit quietly and patiently, just waiting for them to open their door, and smell that fresh country air, and – bingo, up she rushes, full pelt and barks at

Animal Insight

them, makes them jump out of their skin, then turns tail and heads back to the house. To be honest, this has been happening for years, and Jane is well aware of it, and admits that Tess does look very proud of herself! We decided not to bother to try to change things, after all, they only have the occasional tourist, and I am guessing Tess has now lowered the odds of ever seeing the same one again.

She was also keen to express her extreme dislike of the rain, which in her words, 'Feels like needles hitting me!' Jane recognised this, realising now why it was such a struggle to put her out when it was raining, so decided to add a waterproof coat to her Christmas list, although due to prior confession we told her we didn't know if she deserved it.

Tess also talked about her health, and sure enough she showed me a picture of fluid round her heart, which generally indicates to me a heart condition. With this picture and remembering the earlier remark, I knew this was exactly what she was showing me. She then showed me some tablets and then a picture of her doing a wee – this I thought indicated diuretics; tablets that remove excess fluid. Jane said that that is exactly what the vet had given her for Tess, but as she refused point blank to swallow them, she had taken them back. I explained to Tess what the tablets were for and how they would help her, and I asked if she now wanted to start taking them. She agreed and said if Jane could cut some cheddar cheese up into six cubes and put the tablet in one, she would eat the lot!

Jane duly went back to the vet's, fortunately fairly local to her, to re-order the tablets (with some vague explanation about how she just thought she'd give Tess another try with them) and followed the request by slotting one into a random cube. She watched with amazement as Tess proceeded to gulp them all down quite happily, apparently not even noticing the edible pill case.

I spoke to Tess a few weeks later and she said that she felt 'a lot lighter' and Jane confirmed that her breathing was much improved. Jane thanked me, saying she was most delighted and very relieved, as she was well aware that without the tablets, Tess's living years would have been severely decreased.

A couple of months later, there was a panic phone call from Jane because Tess was refusing the bits of cheese. After a quick word with Tess I then asked Jane if she had changed the cheese. She quickly replied,

"Yes, I have found some lovely organic cheddar for her." This was obviously not to Tess's liking, so she asked for the cheap processed cheese to be bought again. Panic over, and problem solved!

It has now been a couple of years since that communication, and I am pleased to report that Tess is fit and well and still taking her tablets. The vet, whom I also know, now knows the story behind the re-try, and Tess seemed most impressed with her Christmas present too!

No Space Required

Whilst working at another holistic show, I met Myra, an international and very well respected clairvoyant. She, apart from giving wonderful readings, is qualified in hypnotherapy, numerology and so much more, and to be honest, subjects I know so little about.

The more people I meet, the more I realise that there is a whole new world out there, full of ancient information that has been overlooked for centuries. There is so much more to know, and when understood, it can often make our lives so much easier. If you swim against the tide, you will get nowhere, and more than likely go backwards. If you go with the flow of it, you can move on and, hopefully, learn how to make the best of it.

Whilst we were having a coffee break, Myra mentioned that her little cat, Helena, had been a bit poorly, and nobody really knew why. They had recently moved and thought this might have something to do with it. Myra gave me her description and soon we were having a three-way conversation.

Helena assured me that she was fine about the move and was enjoying the open spaces. I asked her to tell me why she had been ill, and immediately she showed me her drinking from an outdoor water source. Helena said that it was that water that had made her ill, but she had learnt her lesson and wouldn't drink from there again. Sometimes water courses can get contaminated with fertilisers, toxins etc. but at least she was now aware of the dangers.

Animal Insight

She also wanted Myra to know that she was not impressed with their new vet; in fact she thought he didn't really care and just wanted their money. Myra confirmed that she and her partner, Simon, had indeed got that same impression too. The vet had come across as rather disinterested and uncaring with it, so they promised Helena they would find a new surgery to take her to in the future.

Although this little girl began with a very rough start to her life, she was more than content with her life now and came across as very appreciative of the love and understanding she got. She certainly was a very gentle and knowing soul.

One question that did come up was, 'Why will she not come into the sitting room?' Apparently, she always used to sit with them, but since moving there, she just sits in the room next door. With Helena listening, she immediately volunteered sweetly,

"Oh, I thought they wanted their own space, so I was keeping out of the way!"

"Oh, no!" I explained, "They miss you terribly and want you back in the sitting room with them." Myra thanked me for telling her that and we finished off the short chat.

Simon drove up for the second day of the fair, came straight up to me, and introduced himself. He gave me a hug and thanked me immensely, happily informing me that Helena had spent the previous evening in the sitting room sharing the fire with him.

Through this lovely job I have, I have met up with them on a few occasions since, and apart from them being wonderful company, I am fortunate that Myra has done a lot to inspire my confidence. We can't technically explain what we can do, but we can do this wonderful work, and as long as it brings happiness, healing and harmony for others that is good enough for me. If people do not believe, and sometimes even choose to berate us, I have learnt to see it as their loss and problem, not ours.

Although my work is predominately with the Animal Kingdom, occasionally a human spirit will drop into a conversation. I have no problem with this, it will only happen when it is right, spirits know if the person down here wants to hear from them.

I will not dwell on this, as it is not my field, although I am honoured to pass information on when given it. Whilst out holding a horse for my husband on a dental visit, I landed up having a chat to the lady's horse after it came up about the type of work I do.

Various things were said, but the horse wanted to bring our attention to a specific ride in the woods that had occurred about three months previously. The lady smiled, and recalled, with a slight degree of sorrow, that it was the last time her brother had ridden this mare, and sadly he passed over shortly after.

Suddenly, I could see and smell cigar smoke whirling round the stable, and thought, I think we have a visitor! Now, if you don't think I am very careful, but also nervous, I most certainly am. These are people that have been someone's loved one, so a huge amount of sensitivity is required to check that you are hearing, what you think you are hearing. I gently enquired,

"Did he used to smoke cigars?"

"Oh yes," was her immediate reply, so I quickly asked (silently) for something else giving verification that it was him. He told me to tell her, that he thought she was doing a great job with the stray cat. This stray was only a recent caller, so now we knew it was definitely him. We had a short chat, but what made us laugh so much was the fact that down here, he was a complete non-believer, and thought it was a load of bunkum!

He was pleased to take this opportunity to come through and then said,

"How funny, when I was down there, I didn't believe a word of it, and here am I having a conversation with you!"

With the dentistry finished, and a coffee much enjoyed, I was glad to have been put in the right place, at the right time, to give her messages from her brother that were obviously very welcome and comforting too.

So the next time you hear someone berating the likes of us, just think, it really does take guts to say what we are given to pass over to a person.

I try my best to get it right with animals down here on Earth, which are often equivalent to somebody's child, and loved to the same extent. So for the genuine clairvoyants/mediums out there, I take my hat off to them, as their work is so often with the loved ones who have passed over. The pressure to get connection and let their relatives hear from them once again, is immense, but there are good people out there day in, day out, striving to achieve this in order to bring some form of comfort/reassurance to loved ones left down here

"Get off that island girl and start swimming."

Encouragement from a horse for his young, slightly insecure owner who had said that her life was boring and didn't know how to go about changing it.

"I'm like a sewing machine that's going wrong, and the more up and down it goes the worse it gets and the more damage is caused."

A depiction from a horse that had back problems and was struggling to keep up at the trot with others, so eventually he would get himself in a stew and would start spinning round.

"I am not putting my head into a wind tunnel."

Explanation from a cat that would come in the cat flap, but refused to go out through it.

Privacy Please

Champa, an indoor cat, was a six month old Bengal, and simply stunning to look at. His exotic breeding gave his coat the colouring and pattern resembling a tiger in the wild. His owners were very spiritual and worked as healers amongst many other amazing things they did.

They had heard of my work and asked if I would like to come and work at a holistic fair that they were organising. They didn't quite understand how I worked, so I offered to talk to Champa for them, so they would know firsthand.

I do tell people, the more open you are, the more open your animal can be. This young man was just exquisite to talk to and was so in tune with his owners. He said most adorable loving things and gave us many moments of 'oohs' and 'aahs'. This was such fun and by the end, they totally understood how I worked, and then were able to explain it to other people too.

A couple of months later, Karen, his owner, asked if I could have a quick word as there was a little bit of a problem. Champa seemed to be ignoring his litter tray and deciding to 'go' elsewhere, so I tuned back in with him and asked him why. Immediately he showed me the corridor leading to their bathroom and then a visual through their bathroom door. Strange I know, but I can only say what I see. This turned out to be where his tray was, in their bathroom, and had been there since a kitten. He showed me a picture of him in it, and then I heard, 'Oh sorry, Champa!' this being an apology for being disturbed by someone else needing to use the bathroom.

Champa explained to us that as he was now a mature, grown up cat, he understood what 'it' was about and remarked,

"To be honest, I think it is rather embarrassing!"

With that he showed me a cupboard door, and a mixture of brooms and odds and ends. Karen recognised that as their hall cupboard, and enquired,

"Why would he show us that?" We quickly found out, this clever little man wondered if it was possible to put his tray in there, with the door jammed slightly ajar. This was not a problem, so we assured him his tray would be moved to the privacy of the hall cupboard.

He was delighted with this idea, and insisted on telling us that it was called 'Champa's bathroom'. He made only one mistake after that, definitely not his fault; someone had accidentally shut the door.

I was so fortunate to meet his owners and they took the opportunity to run the question about castration past me. They desperately did not want to upset him, so I gave them a copy of 'The Seasoned Visitor' story, which gives it from a cat's point of view. They made up their minds, booked him in and had him neutered. Hopefully his life will continue in peace, with every day filled with love and adoration from his owners.

A Word from the Wise

I think life, in general, is fairly challenging for most of us, so I decided to ask above if they could clarify it to help me to understand. I love what I was given and would like to take this opportunity to share it with you. So in future, however steep the hill you may be trying to climb, you might just find it really was worth the walk. So here is: A Word from the Wise...

Over many years I really felt that I should give up so many times, life just seemed to be a grind, but now I am happy and fulfilled. One of my various guides, Caesar, a very wise old owl, put it quite simply for me to understand. Love, joy and happiness are the elixir of life, just as water is to our living.

So life was like digging a hole! Immense hard work, and as much as I dug and the deeper I went, I just never seemed to get much further. But over the years I continued to dig and although many times lost the will to carry on, somehow I did.

After so long, and having had to dig way further than I had ever thought I would go, suddenly a trickle of water, then a spurt, then the hole started to fill up. This huge hole, called 'My Life' continued to fill and I floated up to the surface with it. Now this was a very deep large hole I had laboured over, so the chance of it ever drying out and leaving me without the elixir of life would be very unlikely. Had it come so easily, in say, just a few digs and water had appeared, then although life would have been so much easier, the chance of it being everlasting would have been slim.

So, Caesar points out: however hard things are, the more effort you put in and the further you push yourself, the likelihood is you will be rewarded by the bucket load. With a lot of water you can drink it, wash with it, grow things with it, swim in it, and most of all – share it with others.

So, I now can truly say: "It really was worth the effort!"

Attention Please!

Betty was a little black show pony, very girlie but flashy with it, complete with a rather rotund belly that has to be very carefully monitored. She was an absolute hoot to chat to and made us laugh from start to finish. She was the ultimate little girl's dream pony; one you could clamber all over, dress up in various outfits from the jousting pony impression, to a Christmas fairy, but most of all she is a pony who just loved to be the family pet.

She was such a joy to talk to and only had a few problems, which were actually when she was doing her showing classes. She would enter the designated show ring and walk round the ring happily with other ponies, with no problems at all. After she was in the line up (that's the time for judges to look at them, just like Crufts really) she would then need to come out to do an individual show of trotting up and down. This is when the problems arose; she just didn't want to move.

On asking her why, you would have thought it might be, 'I don't like to leave the others,' but, once again, that would be our presumption, and true to form, it was not that at all. Funnily enough, it was actually because she was so polite and didn't want to pull out in case it wasn't her turn. I told her how sweet that was, and in no way was it rude, but so lovely that she had such good manners. I got 'bonding key' words for her owner to say, to remind her for the next occasion.

Her owner's next question was, 'Why, when she (eventually) would be going round showing herself off nicely, would she then slow down for no apparent reason?' There was a good reason for this too, she noticed when the judge had turned away to look at the next pony to come out, so her reasoning was, 'If he is not watching anymore, I need not bother showing myself off anymore!'

We got round this by telling her that other ponies watch too, not just the judge.

I had a lovely update and she is much improved and showing herself off for all to see.

During the original chat, for fun, we also asked her to give us her version of what she thought all this showing is about, and her answer was, "The horse version of musical chairs!" To be honest, I couldn't have come up with a better description myself.

All at Sea

Travel problems with horses are fairly common; we do ask such a lot from them. We just expect them to go into a big lorry container that is all fitted out for two or several horses, or into a trailer, being the smaller and narrower means of horse transport.

If you were to think about what we are asking, it is totally foreign to what a horse would ever naturally think of doing. So for a horse to go into a lorry, allowing the doors to be closed, and to feel confident that all is safe and well, is a remarkable feat of trust.

Whilst chatting to a young Belgian bred dressage horse, of striking appearance but with a rather sensitive nature, Mary, his owner mentioned there was a travelling problem.

As usual, I asked him to show me what he does whilst travelling and bizarrely I started to feel seasick! I could see a constant flashing, which to me I found incredibly uncomfortable, I acknowledged the feeling so it would stop me sensing it. I described to Mary what I had been experiencing, physically and visually, and told her had made me feel more anxious the further we went. This was confirmed, that the further they travelled, the more distressed he got.

After using my logical brain, I asked what kind of windows does this lorry have and could these be the source of light flashes? It transpired that it had slot windows; these being about four inches high by ten inches long all the way down the side. The horse could not see properly out of any of the windows to be able to focus with the movement, thus creating a strobe effect and causing untold anxiety.

Mary took all this on board and said she would never have thought about the effect windows could have. She repeated these findings to her trainer, who had witnessed firsthand the hot, sweaty and distressed state the horse had got himself into whilst coming for a lesson. Her trainer agreed that this could well be the reason, and pointed out that she had actually had not only one but two bad travellers since she had bought that lorry.

The lorry was replaced with one that had large windows and the problem was solved. Logically, after a lot of thought, we could have probably worked this one out, but it was quicker to get it literally 'straight from the horse's mouth'.

Before his Time

On one of my charity evenings, apart from raising some much needed funds, we had an absolute hoot chatting to a horse called Oscar who, when asked to describe himself said, "I'm a superstar." So throughout his chat, time and again he went to great lengths to ensure that everyone knew it as well.

I also spoke to an agility Collie which had us in hysterics, with his various antics but especially when trying to get me to imitate a strange high pitched squeak that apparently was his owner's doorbell. The owner informed me, and the audience, that it was supposed to make a sound of a bird. With that, her Collie replied with great emphasis,

"Do you really think *that* sounds like a bird?"

"Mmm, come to think of it, maybe not," she giggled, with a slightly reddened face. By this time her friends were in a state of collapse in the front row, and to be honest my jaws were aching from laughing too.

I did a couple of more horses and managed to show the differences from one animal to the next, confirming they are just like people with their own personal opinions and preferences.

Animal Insight

There was also a farrier in attendance who really wanted me to chat to his horse, and although it was now about 9pm, with the encouragement of others, I agreed to have a quick chat. The conversation went well, and I pinpointed which leg his horse was lame on. This was met with relief from me, as a farrier's knowledge of the anatomy of legs and feet, is second to none.

Acknowledgement from people in a profession like that gives credence to the accuracy that can be achieved in the work that I do, although the horse gave us a different opinion from his vet, as to its cause.

We covered various bits and pieces, and when I asked him,

"What would you like to ask your horse?" I also had to comment that there are really some questions you maybe shouldn't ask in public, and this following question was one, but the farrier was insistent, so I asked his horse the following: 'How would you describe your owner?' Without a pause his horse replied,

"Not really a morning person!"

This was met not only with laughter and a knowing look from him, but also acknowledgement and some hand clapping from his customers in the audience too. I rather think he will be booking afternoon appointments for them from now on, although his horse was kind enough to add, that he did get less grumpy as the day wore on.

This really emphasises the saying, 'Be careful what you wish for!'

Jackie Weaver

Private Call

On several occasions the subject of riders singing whilst aboard their horse has been brought up. This tends to be accompanied with stifled giggles from me, as I try to confirm this musical mention in the kindest possible way.

Owners tend to laugh when the subject comes up too, sort of like somebody talking about you singing in the bath. I do understand where these horses are coming from. Can you imagine sitting in a room with someone that really can't sing, but insists on trying? Well imagine the magnification if they were actually sitting on your back. But as forgiving as animals are, when explained that their riders are doing it as a sign of being relaxed and happy, they tend to accept that, although some ask if they could do it a little more quietly please!

There are owners out there who can sing and their animals really appreciate this. When you look on them like I do, like 'little people' or sometimes 'very large persons', you can then comprehend why sometimes they complain about mobile phones also. Some of the ringtones are horrendous to me, let alone for an animal to listen to, and the use of mobiles can cause problems too.

Recently I asked a dog why he kept running off when out in the woods with his owner. She showed me a few pictures, which represented constantly chatting on her mobile. I put it to her carefully, and she did confirm that she liked to 'walk and talk'.

His logic was, as she was showing him no attention, he might as well just go off and do his own thing. We talked this through – it was a logical point, so she agreed to limit her calls. He also asked if she could confirm to him the time was especially for him, by calling across to him every so often. That would be easy enough to do, so he really would know that she was concentrating on him and nothing else!

The next day it worked and he didn't run off, he obviously enjoyed their 'private' time together.

This again highlights the difference between one dog and another. This lad had taken it personally that he did not have her undivided attention, but as soon as he gained it, he felt it was better to be with her than without her. It would be the same with a child I am sure; if you ignored them for long enough whilst doing your own thing, it would make sense that they would start doing their own thing as well. As with animals, their own ideas are often not the cleverest or the safest too. We, as parents or animal owners, have the responsibility to give them attention and make sure they are safe

"I have skin like delicate paper."

An informative comment from a rather precious horse trying to ensure his owner groomed him ever so gently.

"What was the point of going there just to come back?"

The answer our Collie, Sally, gave, when my husband wanted to know what she had thought of her ride on the steam train he had taken her on at a tourist location. I don't think she felt the enthusiasm for the bygone era, but it was worth her £1 ticket for such an innocent reply and the expression on his face.

"I'm a clothes horse you know!"

I promise this is totally genuine; I would never have made the connection. It was from a very mollycoddled horse that was showing me his owner standing back admiring him wearing yet another new, up to the minute, latest designer rug she had bought for him.

Jackie Weaver

Not the Old Stick

Some horses/ponies have attitude. Rolo, a six year old gelding, had it by the bucketful. I was talking to him and trying to get him to tell me about the nice things in his life, which was met with a barrage of words signifying that he didn't care and didn't do affection as it would be totally pointless because it doesn't get you anywhere. I was rather taken aback, but the owner said, that was him to a tee, and informed me that he'd had at least five homes in his short life. Something was amiss, and this could be why they had found him in a horse market six months ago. Rolo looked like a purebred highland, stunning dappled grey, complete with the dorsal stripe (this darker stripe runs along the top of the back to the tail) so why was he being sold at a market? Even with their alarm bells ringing, Tara and Peter decided to buy him anyway.

At first Rolo showed me a complete array of bad attitude on the yard; pushing, shoving and generally being totally uncaring and ignorant. Although in the beginning he was not unsafe to ride, things had gradually gone downhill and then reached crunch time. Tara had done all the usual checks, and had her saddler visit to check he wasn't in pain from ill-fitting tack. Over a coffee, the saddler steered the conversation round to me and suggested that I may be able to give her some answers.

I let Rolo vent his spleen, and now totally understood his lack of 'giving' to people. In his mind, there was no point, with a despondent, 'I will get moved on soon anyway,' being passed over to me. Once he had got this all off his chest, I asked him to show me about the fall Tina had from him, as she could remember very little about it. Clear as a bell, he showed me them going downhill, then gave me the feeling of someone sticking a poker in each side of my shoulders. I relayed this to her, and she admitted that the saddle could slide forward (hence getting the saddler) so maybe it had pinched his withers/shoulders just once too often. She couldn't have been more right, and sadly, as she was a slightly nervous rider, she admitted that this had really frightened her.

It is not that uncommon for a saddle to slide forward, the horse will often slow down going downhill and feel like they have the handbrake on. This is a good indication for people to get their saddler to check and alter, or even change the saddle. If the saddle is fine, then it is time to look at the horse's physical demeanour, as a horse should be able to move up and downhill with the same ease. His 'attitude' was still coming across to me, and I kept telling him that his owner Tara had contacted me because she loved him and wanted to find out why he is anti-people. He took this on board and answered my next question, 'What has changed so much?'

Animal Insight

"Size is key," was his cryptic reply. So I used my logic brain, and asked Tara if he had changed size. She replied that he had 'ballooned' in the last three months.

Ah, now we were getting somewhere, I thought, and at least he was being civil to me. They had owned him for six months, and as this month was January, had they been over-feeding him due to winter weather, perhaps? (Too much food to horses/ponies can have a similar hyperactive effect like E numbers can have on children.) I put this to her but it was not precisely like that. Feeding was not in their control, as he was being kept on a farm with others, where they had ad-lib haylage (a rich form of hay) from a large metal ring feeder in the field. Well, to a 14.2 pony, this was just irresistible (like me and chocolate) so he had just eaten and eaten himself to the rounded barrel shape he had become. This was the way the horses were all kept there but, fortunately, they were thinking about moving him. This would make life easier, as Tara could control the amount he had to eat.

Sadly, as anyone with ponies knows, they can get fat on fresh air, so owners have to be very watchful. It really is a careful balance of not too little, but not too much. This is very unfair, as grass is the most natural thing for them to eat, but we don't keep animals in the way nature intended, with our neatly kept and fenced paddocks covered in rich grass. They tend to be covered with grass so they don't have to use energy in the search of forage, as they would in the wild. It is a constant weight-issue battle, rather like us with ready meals, very convenient but not really doing us any favours either.

By this time, he had totally dropped the attitude and was even trying to be helpful! He knew his saddle had now been re-fitted and even suggested that there was something that could be put next to his skin under his saddle pad to stop the saddle slipping. I suggested one that I knew to be a good non-slip type, and Tara was kind enough to email me at a later date to let me know it had really worked.

We covered many other things, like his dislike of flapping black plastic that unfortunately seems to adorn many country hedges. Originally this wrapped the bales of silage for the farmer's cows, but seemed to take on a life of its own when set free. I did comment that he now seemed rather happier and less moody than when we had started. I wished Tara luck and hoped that maybe he would learn to trust them, but did have my doubts.

As ponies are of a smaller height than horses, they are generally deemed to be more suitable for children. However, sometimes this is not the case, and some are only suitable for the confident, strong riders, and not novice children still trying to learn the ropes. Sadly, often looks come too much into the equation rather than suitability, and I did wonder if it had any bearing on why he had been re-homed several times in such a short life.

In March an email popped in with Tara's address on it, I confess to opening it with slight apprehension but it was just simply asking me if I could have another chat with Rolo. I must admit I was thinking I might be in for another rough ride, but booked it in and gave her a time for the call.

As usual, I tuned into him before the call, and was given the words, 'Things are better and I am even being affectionate!'

To be honest, I was pretty surprised and hoped that this was correct, so with my heart in my mouth, I rang Tara's number. I said my hellos and then repeated his words to her, although with a somewhat questioning tone to my voice, but she merrily said,

"Oh yes, he really has changed and is so much happier, ask him more!"

I was so chuffed. Here was this lad chatting away with mirth! Only two months previously, he had told me that people were really not worth bothering about, and made me feel like I was getting on his case. He told me he gets to go faster and was jumping,

"It's all such fun," he gushed, and really seemed to be relishing life. This would have been a complete turnabout for Tara, knowing she had become very nervous of riding him. Actually, once his attitude had changed, he had managed to worm his way into her husband, Peter's, heart, who had decided to ride him and see how they got on. Rolo took the chance and decided to try, and wow, what a reward! They had such fun, hacking out, jumping and generally having a bit of a 'yeehaa' as he put it.

Tara was so pleased with the result, but wanted me to establish if Rolo thought she would ever be able to ride him again. I asked if she really wanted the answer; she agreed, and bless him he instantly gave his response,

"No, I think she would be too frightened, I really need a brave rider."

Not the words she really wanted to hear, and she expressed that she wanted confirmation, so asked him to help explain why.

"If Tara was driving and hit black ice, she would panic and steer everywhere," and with that line, she immediately agreed with him. But then Rolo added about her husband, "But if Peter had been driving, he wouldn't have, and even if he had gone in the hedge, he would have just laughed!"

I would say that is a classic way of summing up the difference between two people's degree of nervousness.

Tara laughed, and said that she was resigned to it now, but this left them with a problem. She had been riding Peter's 17-year-old horse that was doing a marvellous job of looking after her and restoring her confidence; but lately, Peter had been talking about joining a riding club and had mentioned that they really should think about swapping back over. We asked Rolo what he could say to help avoid this happening. Confidently he piped up,

"Don't worry; he wouldn't want to ride the old stick when he has got a young flashy thing like me to show them!"

We laughed and laughed, because it's true, some men would rather be seen on the 'flashy one', as it would look so much cooler than the 'old stick!'

So with that bit of manly advice from one to another, I wished her well, and expressed how happy I was that Rolo now had such a great life with people that loved and trusted him. This really goes to show, never give up hope.

A Kennel to Dine for

People ask me to chat to their animals for lots of reasons, and sometimes people even buy a reading as a present for someone. So I was pleased, although somewhat nervous to say the least, to be asked to do a visit for Neil, a clairvoyant, to surprise his girlfriend.

This was to chat to their two cats and their old and slightly deaf dog. The reading was arranged for a Saturday morning, so later that day Neil could whisk her away to an undisclosed destination for another birthday treat.

I duly turned up as arranged and thought she would be surprised, but whilst trying to dissuade her from taking the dog off for a walk, Neil had spoilt the surprise. She was excited and intrigued, so went off to get a pen and paper to note everything down. I tell all my clients to do this, because so much gets talked about, and if they didn't take notes, most would go away and find they couldn't remember half of it.

We started with the cats and it was great to be able to show their different personalities; they really were like chalk and cheese. We had great fun getting the cats to describe each other and to get their views. We also asked to find out what they thought of the dog, and what he does in life – all from a cat's point of view!

Jackie Weaver

The dog, a golden, but slightly faded Spaniel was a darling to talk to, very sweet and very loving towards Neil's girlfriend. He really came across as a genuinely wise old man, just exactly how they thought he would. I think all three animals made her birthday extra special in their own vocal way, such a personal present indeed.

I had probably been there an hour and a half when Neil said it was time for him to go to the 'dreaded kennels' ahead of their weekend away.

"Does he have a problem with the kennels? If so, shall I have a word with him about it and see what I can do?" I enquired. Surprisingly, Neil said,

"Oh I don't think we should, we might upset him." I expressed my opinion that if he felt that badly about them, and it was obviously such a wrench for Neil to send him, to please let me try. I couldn't promise anything but would see if I could make things easier for them both. With a bit of reluctance, Neil agreed.

I asked the dog to tell me what he thought about the kennels, and he admitted that he had nothing against the kennels themselves, but he thought he would have far rather gone for the weekend with his owners.

This I could understand, so I explained to him that there are some places that dogs are just not allowed to go, but had he been allowed, they most certainly would have taken him. It would be very unfair just to leave him at home with nobody to feed him or look after him, so Neil paid these lovely kennel people good money to look after him and keep him safe. I also gave him the option of letting us know if anything would make him feel better about the situation. Quick as a flash he showed me a picture of a roast chicken, complete with steam effect and smell!

I asked Neil if this dog was rather partial to chicken and he replied,

"Absolutely!" Apparently it was top of his list of favourites! So we knew what he wanted, but how, and in what way? Well, very simply, when Neil picks him up if he could have some roast chicken ready for him, that would make all the difference.

I wished Neil's girlfriend all the best for the rest of her birthday and left. A couple of weeks later I saw Neil and he gave me a big hug and said I'd never guess what had happened. He told me he drove down the kennel lane and parked up. When he opened the back passenger door the dog actually jumped out, and proceeded to run up to the kennel maid, wagging his tail at her.

Neil admitted that he didn't know who was more shocked, him or the kennel maid. For the past five years or so, he had been literally prising the dog off the back seat and dragging him through their gates.

Neil said that they had a great weekend and everything had gone to plan, apart from the detour driving round and round trying to find a supermarket that sold ready cooked roast chickens!

A Jigsaw at Christmas

As a general rule I only ever do animals that belong to the person asking for a communication or, at least, are in their fulltime care. The reason being, that if there are problems, the owner/carer is in a position to change things, and if possible help and, hopefully, solve the problem.

Henry, a large black and white Collie was a different story, but with some soul-searching, I decided to take it on. It was being asked with the best possible intent by a lady who regularly walked him and had him habitually to stay in her house. Penny explained to me that she lived opposite Henry's owner; she knew the owner had rescued him but was struggling with his various problems, due to the owner's lack of time.

Penny came to my house on a cold winter's day, produced a photograph and soon Henry was 'chatting' away. This was much to our relief, there really was a good connection between him and this considerate lady, and he was very forthcoming.

Very early on, we learned he was older than anyone realised, and his eyesight was as poor as Penny thought. I asked him to let me look through his eyes, it was just like looking through a moving haze but outlines could be made out. We asked him how old he was, and he said nine (normally I avoid this question, as some genuinely get it wrong, and others will tell fibs, and not just to me, but to other animals!) but this added up to other attributes so we took it as said. Whilst joining in our three-way conversation, he obviously noted that the age was different from previously thought. He volunteered,

"Maybe I am six... but I do have hearing problems too... so this being a degenerative thing ...I actually do think I am nine!"

Penny had come to me, as she was concerned that he was struggling slightly with life in general, and to see what we could find out and change for him where possible. He was very sweet about his present home, albeit a bit loud with boisterous children, and truly appreciated Penny's efforts taking him out, due to his family's limited spare time. He told us how much he likes her other dog, Otto, who bless him, was letting Henry share his home on occasions when required. Henry inevitably asked the question,

"Can I not just come and live with you?" which I was obliged to pass over to Penny. This she said would be her dream, but he was not hers to have. Suddenly he gave me a picture of a cat; this to me made no sense at all, but Penny knew exactly what it was about. His owners were just about to get a kitten and Henry thought this would be the ideal reason for them maybe deciding he should go. They were fraught at the moment, so surely a kitten and a semi-blind Collie would be all too much. We told him that we would just have to wait and see what happened.

Henry said that even with his poor eyesight, he enjoyed his walks and he showed me a picture of him pulling on his lead; again, this was exactly what he did (something we would work on at a later date). At that point, Penny said she would love to take him further afield but there was a problem about the car journey. I asked him to show me how he reacted towards a car, and to be honest, I couldn't get a picture of him in one - just a frantic dog, desperately pulling away from the open door.

This all rang true, but suddenly left me with a feeling of true sadness and despair, coupled with the words, 'That was when my life went downhill.' I gently asked him to explain, and then the full account of his fear was shown. He had been in a car crash; a vehicle had crashed into the right hand side of the car he was travelling in, very much like a car coming out of a junction without looking. This memory was very frightening and very upsetting due to its consequences. I didn't push for further detail, but reading between the lines; his owner/s either lost their lives or were so badly injured that it was thought to be kinder for him to go to a re-homing centre and, oh, how this broke his heart.

I explained that this was one very unfortunate life incident and that it is very, very rare. If he could travel, even a few miles, he could get to beautiful woods and have even better walks with Otto. This he did take on board and said he would have to really summon up strength to be able to do that.

I thanked him for talking to us, and he told us not to worry, this situation was all like a jigsaw, and the pieces would all fall into place. Penny left and said she would keep in touch and let me know of any changes.

Animal Insight

Within ten days, I got an email to say that he had pulled so hard on the lead (again) that his owner had fallen over, and had now decided she couldn't cope. She had asked if Penny would be prepared to have him! Penny was panicking as she was going away for the Christmas holidays; she decided to get a house/dog sitter but wanted me to let him know that he was now going to be hers. I also explained about her pre-arranged holiday, and that she would be home in two weeks. She also wanted to check how he was feeling, now knowing that he was getting what he had craved for.

"Elated," was his word, but that was a total understatement compared to the emotions he gave to me. He was fine about the sitter, I had a quick word about the pulling, and why he shouldn't really do it. He gave me the word 'patience' to be said to him to remind him of the pulling issue conversation. He also said that when Penny came home it would be like the lid being put on the jigsaw box....job done!

Penny came home, slightly sooner than arranged, I don't know who was more excited. Henry was there to enthusiastically greet her and had made himself perfectly at home. He now spent his days lying on a duvet with Otto, doing lots of Heavenly doggie snoozing but waking in time to be fed and doing his local walks.

Some time later, Penny called round with her friend Cybil for me to have a chat to her dog Polly. (Polly being the fashion conscious one in the 'Weighty Issue' story.) I took the opportunity to tune in with Henry to check on him and ask how things were going. He made all three of us blink to hold back the tears... by saying,

"You know how people have all their birthdays come at once; well I have just had all my Christmases in one!" He was so at home, and when asked about Otto, he said, "It was lovely because when Mum goes out, we keep each other company," (again, more quick swallowing and blinking done by us).

He also wanted Penny to know that one of her Christmas cards was 'rather apt'. She looked at me quizzically and said she didn't know what he meant. I asked if she had been sent any that were not general type Christmassy ones. Again, she shook her head saying she didn't think so. Fortunately her friend Kate was on the ball, laughed and said,

"Yes, you did, the same one as me... it has a picture of a dog in a car!"

Very clever you might think of a dog to notice this, but if you remember, this dog is nearly blind, so that insight was totally brilliant. With that, he added that he was still thinking about the car and maybe one day he might manage to get back in one. Henry was right, this situation was just like a jigsaw, the new cat, the blindness, the pulling etc. were all the pieces. As true as my word, within two weeks of our chat, they all fell in place, and guess what? He now doesn't pull on the lead!

I think it will be a long time before we get Henry to travel, but if he does before this goes to print, I will let you know, if not I will surely do so in the next book.

Sally, Our own Little Angel

This is a poem I wrote describing the actual story of how, back in 2005, Sally, our little tri-coloured Collie, came into our lives and our hearts.

Such a worrying time, that's for sure
Wondering if I'd be knocking on Heaven's door
Although my body ill, my mind pushed ahead
Sitting there watching my little dog scratch his head

Bruce resembled Dougal from the Magic Roundabout
Hair here and there, just wherever it wanted to sprout
And on closer inspection, I suddenly did see
What truly looked liked a jumping flea

Straight to the medicine drawer I went
And rummaged through its much collected content
Damn, I was sure there was some unused left in the drawer
Oh well, I will go to the vets and get some more

The vets was local, only a few miles down the lane
I could manage that, I had learnt to live with the pain
I parked up and went to the desk to ask for what was required
And just happened to remark on a little dog that I admired

Animal Insight

"I have rescued her and she needs a home," came the reply
My ears pricked up, had that been why she caught my eye?
I asked her name and age and what they thought was her breed
And for more detail as to why a new home did she need

This hunched up little girl was Sally, thought to be a type of Collie
So quiet and pretty, but with the air of desperation and sorry
Ignoring my own complications, my heart was ruling my head
Off home I went to tell Bob, my husband, what had been said

With flea treatment in hand I pulled open the drawer
And in front of me I was dumbfounded at what I saw
There was the original packet of pipettes as clear as day
Confused, I shut it again and thought of what to Bob I would say

Home from work he came and could see by my face and smile
That I was excited, something he had not seen for a while
I spilled out the details of Sally and how desperately I wanted her
Even with talk of my illness he knew I was going to be hard to deter

It wasn't long before Sally was in our home to share her life with us
Filled with fear and mistrust, but desperate for love and fuss
Previously she had been so abused, that people seemed such a threat
She would curl and slink away from any stranger she met.

My health was deteriorating with frightening speed
It would be Bob now that she would rely on and need
This meant he didn't have the time to sit and brood
She was his distraction, just perfect to lift his mood.

Jackie Weaver

Two months later my cancer battle was seriously on
But this little angel our hearts she had both won
I now know that I was put in the right place at the right time
Going to the vets for no reason, she was destined to be mine.

A Christmas came and passed and I whiled away the time with sleep
As for Bob, Sally was there for his attention to keep
Eventually my body mended and now my strength to gain
She was now my companion to walk through sunshine and rain

This little girl had transformed to now, "Hey, look at me!"
We even did dog training and afternoons of agility
She is so honest and quick to learn and tries from the heart
You would never believe she had such a rocky start

Bruce has since gone to Heaven, but I thank him for getting fleas
Making me go to the vets to see those begging eyes saying, "Please"
Sally came into our lives and is still filling our days with love
I truly believe she was sent for both of us by the Angels from above.

Animal Insight

Nodding Off

For a Charity fundraising event, I was asked to do a demonstration at a pony club camp. This was actually one for adults, designed, I think for the participants to learn something, have a good gossip, and get away from their husbands for five days!

As usual I always ask people to choose animals that are happy/cheeky/sweet etc. as obviously if an animal is having a bit of a difficult time, a public forum is not the place to discuss it. I never like to leave a reading if they are having problems, it would be so wrong.

Imagine yourself just having gained enough strength to tell someone something, then they walk off half way through it! The other reason being that we take talking for granted but people that are psychic and can communicate like me, tend not there every day, so to an animal, that could be a huge opportunity missed. The other important thing is to establish that they choose an animal that the owner has had for at least a few years as they have an established relationship and should hopefully recognise things easily.

A lovely horse called Jake was chosen and was an absolute star to talk to. Apart from being very chatty and funny and very accurate with his information, he was what we call a 'nodder'. This is exactly as it sounds; they nod their head when what we say is right.

Now having learnt at the beginning that my work is to the subconscious, for some reason these animals do react when being communicated with, and I really don't know why. This boy had us all in stitches and he loved the attention, but when I asked him what he found difficult, I did get it slightly wrong.

He showed me a pole set up to jump on the angle, so I repeated what I saw to the owner. She said she didn't understand as he was good at diagonal fences.

Rather perplexed I asked him again to show me what he was talking about, and I got nearly the same picture but this time with an explanation. The problem was if he had jumped a pole the first time that was straight that was fine, but then if the same pole was then moved to an angle, that totally confused him. But if it was on the angle in the first place, that wouldn't have been a problem! I passed this back to his owner, fortunately she agreed, and he duly nodded. Thank goodness for that, as that did take some understanding, and even harder explaining!

The riders watching were totally astounded; nodders make it extra special with their added animation. They are not all that common, but I am so pleased when I do get a horse that really does understand the words, 'Let me entertain you!'

Rebel with a Cause

As animal communication is such a personal thing, people quite often give a reading as a present to a friend or a partner.

Helen is the owner of the coloured mare called Smudge from the previous 'Untold Damage' story. She was on her livery yard one day when her young friend, Laura, returned with her horse, Rebel, who had been away for the winter. Rebel is actually a trotter, which is a horse that looks very similar to a thoroughbred racehorse but is bred to compete on tracks and trot at seriously fast speeds.

When racing, the rules state that should they break and go into canter they have to be brought back down to the proper trotting pace required. If you think that sounds difficult, it certainly can be. This is all done by driving them from behind using a cart/trap type vehicle called a sulky, where their jockey will sit to steer and try to control them.

After this winter away, worryingly, Rebel was rather thin and he also seemed quite unsettled. As it had just been Laura's 22nd birthday, Helen offered to buy her a reading, so Laura could see how Rebel felt, and what he wanted to say. Fortunately, apart from talking to Helen's animals, I had also done a reading for horses belonging to a friend of Laura's, so she knew about me and accepted the gift gratefully.

Helen organised with me for that Thursday afternoon at the yard, saying they could sit in the car to keep warm and put me on loudspeaker. Helen volunteered to write the notes for Laura, whilst Laura and I spoke together with Rebel.

I received his photo and yes, he did look rather thin - but quickly and emphatically he told us that he had 'walked his weight off!' This was followed up with the picture and feeling of him never being settled and constantly padding about. Even in his stable he had been agitated, which is the one place they should really be at rest. Laura explained that he had gone to her friend's big yard because he was a horse who loved to work. She thought he would prefer that to a winter of doing nothing with her. This I could totally understand, as he was a very forward-going horse. He proudly explained to me,

Animal Insight

"I could send sparks from my shoes when I trot!"

However, Rebel really didn't like big yards, he found them stressful. Laura knew that her friend had tried moving him to various different parts of the yard to see if he would settle. That was to no avail either; we now know Rebel is very much a one-to-one lad.

He was very relieved to be back with Laura, and wanted assurance that it would stay that way! I explained to him that, yes, he was back with Laura for keeps, and he told me, twice, to make sure I understood, that he was 'cock-a-hoop!' It tickled us that a horse would use a chicken expression, but he got his point across very clearly. So any feelings of stress and anticipation evaporated in that instant. Rebel was also quick to tell us not to worry about his weight; in four weeks time he would look the same as he always had.

I do try and follow some structure when I do a reading, but Rebel decided to keep volunteering information, in whatever order he wanted. This is sometimes the way with some animals, so I just go along with them. He amazed Laura by telling her that he was really looking forward to doing 'the fun rides'. I laughed as she exclaimed,

"But we only just talked about that this morning while riding along!" I told her that by the end of this conversation, she would realise that animals can speak and that they do listen too.

Helen (Smudge's owner) who had been scribbling down furiously for Laura, interrupted to say that she thought Rebel had been ever so patient considering how fast he is in comparison to her little mare. Could we ask if he understood that she would struggle to keep up with him? I took this opportunity, which I love doing, to ask him to give me his opinion about the other horse, Smudge. Taking this chance he said,

"She puts her ears back but laughs at the same time!" Laura and Helen chortled and explained to me that because she kept getting left behind, she would put her ears flat back, then tank along to catch up - which seemed to be an amusing game. Obviously, they couldn't hear Smudge laughing, but evidently Rebel could.

Many horses love being mollycoddled and Rebel was no exception, he told Laura that he loved it when she hugged him and kissed his cheek,

"It's very girlie, but I do love it!" This was spot on as he had given him one of her girlie kisses just before our chat.

After a truly inspiring chat for Laura, who had not experienced anything quite like it before, I decided to ask if he had any helpful advice that he could offer her. He gave me information about her car being unreliable:

"Are you having problems with your car?" I asked slightly carefully.

"No," came Laura's decisive reply. "Oh, that's strange," I responded, "are you sure?"

"Well, I have had a few problems, but nothing more than any other car!"

"She doesn't like to be told," Rebel whispered.

"If you don't mind, can I tell you what Rebel has just said?"

She agreed, and light-heartedly, I repeated Rebel's whisper. Helen, a mother of two, quickly, but tactfully asked Laura if she could be stubborn, Laura agreed that she could be a bit, so I just said,

"Well then, I will tell you exactly what he says and leave it with you for you to decide." So, straight from the horse's mouth was,

"I think it will let you down, you will be throwing good money after bad!"

I thanked Rebel for talking to me and he said that Laura was not to feel bad about sending him away; she had done it thinking it would make him happy. I told her that I felt that as long as you do things with good intent, and if things go wrong, then it is just a lesson learnt. He also said he was so glad to be home, and now knew for sure he was staying with her for good.

That was a lovely communication for me to do, it allayed fears on both sides and gave us all a good laugh too, and I do think Rebel will be getting even more 'girlie' treatment in the future.

On Friday morning my mobile beeped, a text from Helen had arrived. I opened it and read, 'Just thought I'd make you smile. Do you remember Rebel telling Laura that her car was unreliable and she disagreed? Well it broke down last night, she is limping it to the garage this morning! He's a clever horse, isn't he?!'

She was right, it did make me smile not to mention laugh out loud, now you can probably see why I spend my life saying, 'You just couldn't make it up!'

Animal Insight

Buzz Off

Danny, a seventeen-year-old black and white cat, was an absolute hoot to talk to. His owner, Susan, actually had two cats but chose him to be chatted to, which in time, he took full advantage of. This was great fun as it was done in the presence of the owners, as they had come to my table at a holistic fair; it's such a joy to see people's reactions of amazement and disbelief!

Susan was astounded at his sheer intent of doing things, like standing beside various kitchen unit doors, just so she would have to pay attention to him by asking him to move. He went out of his way to make his presence felt, by generally just getting in her way.

He had fine-tuned that look of, 'Oh I'm so hungry', followed with his vocal repertoire. Susan would obligingly go to fill his biscuit bowl, only to find there were still plenty in there. Thoroughly pleased with himself, Danny would then swan off glancing back to give her that look of, 'Got ya!'

We chatted away and he just had us falling about with laughter, he really was a feline comedian, and one of those that left me chortling to myself for days.

Further on he gave me a picture of the other cat and then showed me a picture of a pair of curtains. These were looking rather claw damaged and frayed at the bottom, and coupled with the statement,

"It wasn't me!" Susan didn't recognise them and looked to her daughter who was sitting beside her, who then admitted that they were her bedroom curtains. True! It was the other cat that was guilty. In fact, he positively swung on them.

Not content with that, Danny then had to inform them that his mate had also peed on the carpet; well the look on Susan's face was a picture. She admitted that she just presumed it was Danny as he was old and was more likely to have 'accidents'. She then realised that the other cat, who refuses point blank to go out when it's raining would, logically, be the guilty party.

On asking Danny for advice for them, he gave me the repetitive sound of someone trying to light a gas cooker. Susan chuckled and said her gas cooker had seen better days, she had to keep pressing the button to get it to light. Danny had described this as 'rather annoying and perhaps time for a new one?' With that, she suddenly came up with the idea, if he really will not move out of her way, she could just press the ignition button!

Danny just laughed as only Danny would, but then realised that, actually, by raising this point, he had probably said a little too much!

TV Debut

Further to my TV debut, on Nick Ashron's Lightworker's Guide to the Galaxy... His show has a diverse selection of guests on, but the one thing they have in common is that they are striving to make a difference in this world. They are often known as 'Lightworkers' and I thought you might like to read a couple of things that kind viewers emailed in, regarding feedback of the show.

"I have just watched the animal communication broadcast with Nick Ashron, and I must say I found it extremely enlightening. Jackie Weaver was such a wonderfully articulate, sensitive and humorous guest, it was the best show that I have seen for a long time. May I wish her all the very best for the future - long may the fantastic work continue and spread throughout the world. I am so very envious of her ability to communicate with animals as that has been a wish of mine for the past 40 odd years. My friends have often thought me insane for chatting away to cats and dogs as I would do a human. It was a brilliant experience for me to listen and hear you give confirmation that it really can be done. So, thank you very much once again." Jan

"This was the first show I have seen, and it was about animal communication with Jackie Weaver. I must say I found it very interesting and straight away made contact with Jackie, as I was having a problem with my dog recently. Jackie has helped immensely and found the underlying problem by talking to my dog. My dog has an inner ear problem that the vet and I had no idea about. However, the vet and I are working to fix this, and it would not have happened, had I not watched Nick's brilliant show. As Jackie says, Nick goes to great lengths to get genuine people on the show, and Jackie certainly is this. It was also nice to find out about my dog's previous life before we got her from the rescue home. It made a lot of sense, and I was sure it was coming from my dog! I wish Nick all the best with his show, it is really nice to see something on TV that is not too commercial and is of interest to myself and others like me." Neshla

I thank them for their kind words, and most of all I thank Nick for giving me the opportunity. In the world we live in, sometimes things do sound impossible, but fortunately with programmes such as his, sometimes they will strike a chord with you and send you down a path you never knew existed.

My guide, Rolf, gave me a very good saying, just to give people a little food for thought:

Scepticism, comes with the thirst for knowledge,

Scathing, leaves you in a sea of ignorance.

A little something for you, from me and him...

A dream comes right from the heart

but sometimes we don't know where to start.

Let the hand of love guide and take you

knowing that the ones you love are right beside you.

For all the loved ones that have gone before,

they *do* live on and will show you more.

By Coincidence?

Once again, I wish to say a huge thank you to all those that helped me to get this book completed, so people like yourself, were able to share in my experiences. The circumstance of how it all came together was nothing short of incredible. So, I leave the choice with you. Was this just a set of coincidences, or maybe something else?

Coincidence, is there really such a thing?
You think of someone, and then they just ring
'I was just thinking of you the other day'
These are the words, so many often will say.

Our thought process is way stronger than we realise
Like déjà vu, we just can't believe our eyes!
You come up with a plan you want to put in action
And someone appears for your idea to sanction.

Take me for example, and this is so true
I was chatting with a lady, "Hello and how are you?"
I was saying how the cancer, my energy it took
She simply suggested that I write a book!

I smiled sweetly, but dismissed this thought
How could I write a book, I haven't been taught!
I have life experience, but only the norm,
On what subject could I write, to which people will warm?

A year rolled on, and I was doing just fine
Simply living, and passing the time
Fate then dealt me a wonderful hand
An animal communicator in front of me did stand

Animal Insight

"Jackie, you can do this, I can tell you know,"
Again I just smiled, and just went with the flow.
But standing in awe, hearing words from my horse
And again to be told, 'It was only a matter of course'.

I didn't believe that I could have this amazing way
That, I could talk to animals every day,
But this was no coincidence, this was certainly meant
For years I told of another lady, to whom animals were sent

Soon I was taken down the spiritual path and shown,
I could now talk to animals, my mind was totally blown
As work flooded in, and the more challenges I took
There was that awakening moment, I could write a book!

Having no experience, I literally wrote like I spoke
But with as much thought and feeling as I could invoke
And soon I had sentences that were never ending
With grammar that really did need attending!

Oh my poor brain, what am I going to do?
Then a lovely girl Sal, said, "Don't worry, I'll help you."
I had spoken to her dog, Sid, who had a problem with his heart
And now here she is for me, with her knowledge to impart.

"You write like you talk; at such a rapid speed,
What you think you write, is maybe not what they read!"
So a change of grammar, and some full stops we'll put
Turning this into a delightful and readable book.

Jackie Weaver

So with words done, I was all up and fired
Some pictures to go with it, I suddenly desired.
Then it happened, and not one person but two
"It's okay Jackie, we draw, we'll do them for you!"

So here we are, back down that 'coincidence' road,
One was a client, whose horse was refusing to load,
And the other, had two horses I'd once been to see
Who met my husband, and sent a 'Hi' to me.

So the story is done and pictures as well
Now, who about this book could I tell?
So what step do I take for little old me?
A huge stride, straight onto TV!!

"On TV... TV!" I hear you cry
"How did you manage that, and why?"
The work of 'coincidence' you might say
Being in the right place, on the right day?

Working at a fair with other spiritual people too
Nick was opposite me, with my work to view
He said my work was different, and more he'd like to know
'In fact, why don't you come on my television show?'

To spread the word for animals was my intention
And if by chance, my book he would mention
During the show, he did his best to try and promote it
What I had written, and why I had wrote it.

Animal Insight

Viewers contacted me, as most intrigued
One with a dog needing help indeed,
The other, a lady wrote to just simply say
She had enjoyed the show; it had made her day!

This lady emailed me, many a time
And I noticed, "You write mighty fine!"
With my book still rough and needing refined
I just wondered if this lady was spiritually divined

As swift as you like, it all clicked into place
She corrected it, sorting out my lack of upper case,
Putting in double quotes and even the odd dash
Amazing, the whole lot done, quick as a flash

She taught me lessons with so much sense
Teaching about trying to stay in the same tense
I now have lists of grammar rules to keep
And this was all done and dusted in one week!!

So back at the same fair, with familiar faces to see
Working with people who are just like family to me
A publisher appeared, as if out of thin air
Following the words, "You need to see that lady over there."

So this is how my book and these words got on the page
With all the people to help me at each and every stage,
And I was right, the publisher excelled herself
By Christmas it was printed, and up on the bookshelf!

Jackie Weaver

The book is filled with laughter, but parts may make you cry
But hopefully gives you a sense of wonder and why.
Why do things happen and sometimes are so immense
Let me tell you, this is not by sheer 'coincidence'.

Although much has happened since writing this book in 2009 and it is now on to its third reprint, albeit not with the original publisher. That publisher, like many others, closed due to the economic climate and the fast onset of digital books. I have now taken it upon myself to get this book back out into the world of literature along with my other titles too.

As I say, a lot of things have taken place over the last few years, but I have decided to leave the postscript as originally written in 2009 and hope you will see how my journey has progressed. When you read it, I think you will be amazed to hear that I ended up chatting to celebrities' pets which you can find out about in my latest book, *Celebrity Pet Talking*.

A big thank you to all those celebrities, and especially to, William Roache MBE, Jacky Newcomb and Jenny Smedley who have been so very kind, and of great help to me. Also to all the people who have trusted me and helped spread the word like, Hollywood actor Matthew Rhys, the world renowned hypnotist Paul McKenna, the gorgeous Stephanie Beacham and so many more – without you, the celebrity book would not have been possible. It has been an uphill task, although a great journey, and I know that if more people experience and talk about animal communication, the better the world will become for the animals themselves.

Postscript

May I take this opportunity to thank you for reading my book and I hope you enjoyed it. I may have made you laugh, and maybe made you cry, but most of all, I hope I have given you a true insight enabling you to have an even deeper relationship and understanding with your own animal.

For anybody that has not had experience of the spirit world, I did mention at the very beginning about Guides that watch over us. I hope they have become clearer to you and the work that they do. Rolf, my amazing guide cat, whom I never met (he died in 1939) came to me after my illness to help me to work with Earth's animals. He is there for every animal I talk to, so had it not been for him, these cases would never come to me, and this book would never have been written. If you thought the titles were imaginative, I have to confess I asked Rolf for help with them too!

My work is an animal lover's dream. How many times has it been said, "I wish they could talk!" Now you know they can, and I am so fortunate to be living the dream. Believe you me, I never take it for granted, I wake up every day so glad to be alive and enjoying the work I have been saved to do.

Other books by the same author:

For the cover, a big thanks to Jane's wonderful horse Sam. He is now in his senior years and is a 'been there, done it' horse and was, I know, very proud to be asked to do this. He has a huge heart and when asked if he was happy with his life, his beautiful reply was, 'I love my surroundings and the people who surround me'.

Thanks also to Rosemary's two Jack Russells, Trumble and Biddy, for their wonderful inquisitive look.

I hope you enjoyed the intricate sketches that were drawn and given to me by my wonderful, and very talented friend, Jackie Fennell.

JacksArt
www.jacksart.co.uk

Jackie Weaver
'The Animal Psychic'
www.animalpsychic.co.uk

Printed in Great Britain
by Amazon.co.uk, Ltd.,
Marston Gate.